24/7

24/7

♣ ♦ ♥ ♠

LIVING IT UP AND DOUBLING DOWN IN THE NEW LAS VEGAS

Andrés Martinez

Villard / New York

All rights reserved under International and Pan-American Copyright Conventions.
Published in the United States by Villard Books, a division of Random House, Inc., New
York, and simultaneously in Canada by Random House of Canada Limited, Toronto.

VILLARD BOOKS and colophon are registered trademarks of Random House, Inc.

Grateful acknowledgment is made to Princeton University Press for permission to
reprint brief excerpts from Fyodor Dostoevsky's correspondence and from the diary
of his wife, Anna Dostoevsky, that appear in *Dostoevsky: The Miraculous Years,
1865–1871*, by Joseph Frank. Copyright © 1995 by Princeton University Press.
Reprinted by permission of Princeton University Press.

Library of Congress Cataloging-in-Publication Data
Martinez, Andrés.
24/7: living it up and doubling down in the new Las Vegas / Andrés Martinez.
p. cm.
ISBN 0-375-50181-9 (acid-free paper)
1. Las Vegas (Nev.)—Social life and customs. 2. Las Vegas (Nev.)—Description and
travel. 3. Martinez, Andrés. 4. Gambling—Social aspects—Nevada—Las Vegas. I.
Title.
F849.L35M366 1999
979.3′033—dc21   99-29309

Random House website address: www.atrandom.com

Printed in the United States of America on acid-free paper

24689753

First Edition

Book design by Mercedes Everett

To Trotsky

*I knew for certain, and had made up my mind long before,
that I should not leave Roulettenburg unchanged,
that some radical and fundamental change would
take place in my destiny.*

—Alexey Ivanovitch
Fyodor Dostoevsky, *The Gambler*

CONTENTS

AUTHOR'S NOTE

◆

This book describes the author's experiences in Las Vegas and reflects his personal reaction to, and impression of, those experiences. In some instances, names and identifying characteristics of individuals mentioned in the book have been changed to protect their privacy.

PROLOGUE

♦

April Fool's Day, 1998

♣ ♦ ♥ ♠ "The computer is down," the teller said nonchalantly, "so the most we can give you is five hundred dollars." Unbelievable. This was to have been my finest hour as a Chase customer, the first time (and the last, it's safe to assume) I would withdraw $50,000 from my account, an amount that dwarfed my average balance by $49,600, give or take a few hundred. You'd think the branch manager would have whisked me to some back office and served me champagne while minions scraped together such a tidy sum. That's how I'd pictured it, anyway. Instead, I was rebuffed by a bored teller after waiting in line behind a gaggle of British tourists seeking to change their pounds sterling.

"You don't understand—I leave for Las Vegas tomorrow, and I need the money," I moaned. This got me a raised eyebrow and a suppressed grin. "Sir, you can check back in a couple of hours, but right now our systems are down," she said, unmoved by the nobility of my cause.

I walked back out to Park Avenue, only to be drenched by a spring shower. New York rain has a cleansing, pleasing quality to it, unless you are stuck in midtown without an umbrella. I darted across Park and into the Waldorf-Astoria, settling down to a beer and the *Financial Times*.

It then occurred to me that this might all be a sham. Perhaps

Chase Manhattan's formidable computer was doing just fine, thank you, but was the scapegoat of choice when the bank deemed it prudent to delay. I hadn't seen others muttering to themselves on the way out, and Chase had every reason to be suspicious.

For one thing, most customers looking to withdraw fifty grand don't wait in line with the masses to see a teller. They presumably have someone they call, someone who sends them a Christmas card and knows the names of their kids. Private banking, I believe it's called, as opposed to my all-too-public imploring. I had tried hard not to say "Fifty thousand" too loudly, lest the people in line behind me think I was bragging, or, worse, get any ideas.

The other interesting factor, at least from Chase's perspective, was that I had never even shown my face at this particular location before. There were probably a dozen branches between it and my apartment. I'd gone to the Park Avenue branch because I was told it was the only one to stock $1,000 traveler's checks. I hadn't been too keen on signing five hundred of the things, if you know what I mean.

Still, some problems are worth having, and this was definitely one of them. I had to laugh at my "predicament," ensconced in a bar in the middle of a weekday, waiting to get at the $50,000 that had been parked in my account for less than a week. Then another suspicion arose in me: Was it possible that my loving wife, Kathy, had phoned Chase and prevailed upon the bank to give me no more than $500— a more than suitable gambling allowance, to her mind?

Kat had lobbied for keeping the money where it was. "Why don't you just write your book about Vegas, but keep the advance?" she had asked that morning, not for the first time, as I'd struggled to keep Trotsky, our neurotic cat, out of the suitcase while I started packing. *What do high rollers wear these days, anyway?*

"I've told you, Kat, the publisher gave me the fifty grand to chronicle a gambling spree; no gambling, no advance," I'd finally responded, for my own benefit as much as hers. It was a lot of money to blow. "It's a chicken-and-egg thing," I added.

"It also would have made a nice nest egg," Kathy said, playfully alluding to Albert Brooks's hilarious movie *Lost in America,* which we'd recently seen as part of my crash course on all things Vegas.

When I returned to Chase a couple of hours later, the computer was still down. Once again I was offered $500 on my word of honor; anything more would have to be vouched for electronically. This despite the fact that I look like a boyish (though now out-of-school and out-of-shape) Richie Cunningham. I've always envied people whose features suggest mischief.

It was a good thing my flight wasn't until the next evening. If the computer was still down then, I'd be forced to call my editor from the airport and tell him there had been a slight change in the terms of our deal. "Hi, Bruce, Martinez here at Kennedy just to let you know that I'll only be risking five hundred bucks instead of the full fifty grand, which my bank won't let me get at—same difference, really." Kat would love that.

The next morning I did get my money, fifty crisp $1,000 traveler's checks. But even with the computer working, the teller and her nervous supervisor had remained suspicious. First, they grilled me. Social Security number? Mother's maiden name? Super Bowls won by the Steelers? Teacher you had a crush on in the fifth grade? That sort of thing. Then they did a lot of staring—at their computer screens, at the stack of checks, at all my forms of identification, and at me. Finally, they surrendered, realizing they had no valid excuse to continue depriving me of my money, no matter how fishy it seemed to them that this Martinez character, with his pathetic paycheck-to-paycheck history, had somehow stumbled across fifty grand. They didn't even wish me good luck.

♣ ♦ ♥ ♠ Because life is nothing if not a series of gambles, colorful gambling terms have long found their way into mainstream slang.

We wear poker faces before passing the buck, determined never to cash in our chips, always looking for where the action is. We ante up for blue-chip investments, trying to stay out of the hole while remaining aboveboard. Sometimes we even lay all our cards on the table.

The blackjack term "doubling down" is on the verge of spilling over into popular culture, following many hallowed poker terms. It has an immediacy and power lacking in the more common but passive expression "double or nothing." In blackjack, to double down is to double your bet before taking a third card, preferably from an 11, hoping to reach the desired 21. In life, to double down is also to raise the stakes when the going seems good.

This is the chronicle of two frantic double downs. The personal one is obvious: I took my advance from my publisher to Las Vegas for a month, enduring ten three-night stints at different hotels and gambling each and every day. The deal: What I win is mine; what I lose never will be. Who knows? I might learn a thing or two about human nature along the way.

On a grander scale, "doubling down" is a fitting description for what the city of Las Vegas is presently doing. This improbable tourist mecca—home to more hotel rooms than any other city on earth and visited by more than thirty million people each year—is not resting on its laurels. Instead, it is spending a staggering $7 billion in the millennium's final two years to build a spectacular new generation of resorts, adding 21,000 rooms to its current total of 106,000. Not for the first time in its history, naysayers are out in force, saying that even Las Vegas cannot fulfill Las Vegas's outlandish ambitions.

Me, I'm hoping both our double downs pay off.

The story of Las Vegas is less about hotel rooms and gambling than it is about American mythology. Las Vegas is our mirror out in the desert, all shiny like a mirage should be, reflecting our basest urges. What type of city did we build in the middle of a desert, a metropolis with no reason, beyond our willpower and playful imagination, to exist? And what does it say about us that this monument to American optimism and technological arrogance in the Mojave Desert has become the largest American city born in the twentieth century and its fastest-growing one going into the twenty-first?

Part One

1

LUXOR

People should not get overly excited over the effects of the new gambling bill—conditions will be little different than they are at the present time, except that some things will be done openly that have previously been done in secret.
—*Las Vegas Review-Journal* editorial, 1931

Thursday, April 2

♣ ♦ ♥ ♠ All things being equal, I noted to the middle-aged woman sitting next to me on the plane before takeoff at Kennedy, people are in a better mood flying west. It must be some sort of primordial thing: the yearning for space, the call of the frontier. It's like we all have a Manifest Destiny gene within us, I added, warming up. I hadn't even gotten to the whole beating-the-clock issue. You know, fly for five hours, get three back upon arrival.

Not that all things were equal. There is something euphoric about sitting on a plane with fifty grand in your coat pocket. It was still there. I'd checked in the bathroom before boarding. But I didn't want to get into that with Ms. 31B, who wore a nylon warm-up jacket from an Atlantic City casino and one of those "it's going to be a long flight" looks. She didn't buy my fanciful theories: "You ask me, I'd say people are just excited by the thought of all those free drinks awaiting them in Vegas."

An hour into the flight, I pulled out my edifying reading: *The*

Complete Idiot's Guide to Gambling like a Pro. I'd been shocked to find so many books at the Barnes & Noble down the street aimed at helping ordinary blokes like me make a killing in a casino. I hadn't expected such specialization. Was I really supposed to buy separate guides to craps, blackjack, and roulette? This was a bad sign. Unless successful gamblers are an unusually literary and missionary bunch, the voluminous you-too-can-get-rich literature suggested that it must be easier to write about it than to do it. Down other aisles, scores of investment guides and peppy write-for-a-living books attested to the same principle.

Confronted by the befuddling array of choices, it was with some relief that I had reached for the gambling installment in the ubiquitous *Idiot's Guide* series of orange manuals on life. A single tome would empower me to play any casino game: This appealed to the generalist in me. I didn't see the point of reading more than a chapter on, say, craps. And while most gambling books claimed that their insights would help you win thousands every time you visited a casino, the claim on the *Idiot's Guide*'s back cover—"a casino trip doesn't have to make you feel like you're completely luckless"— seemed disarmingly modest. Here was something you could read and remain partially luckless.

Ms. 31B didn't read a thing during the entire flight. She didn't sleep, either. Nor did she listen to music or watch the movie. She didn't even get up to go to the bathroom. She just sat there, like the Rock of Gibraltar, looking rather content, neither bored nor tired. As you can imagine, this was driving me crazy. It was unnerving and inconsiderate, not to mention un-American. She sat there for five hours, one of thirty million people making the pilgrimage to the nation's amusement capital this year, without making any effort to entertain herself. She wouldn't even read the airline's catalog, magazine, or safety card, the literature of the truly desperate. Other passengers nervously peered over at her as well. We all wondered: What was inside this woman that allowed her to forsake all external stimulation? A formidable inner tranquillity, or a vast emptiness?

I felt a surge of adrenaline as the 757 touched down at McCarran International Airport just past one o'clock in the morning, four A.M. my time. It's always a thrill to arrive someplace exotic in the middle of the night, and under the circumstances this was an occasion befitting Churchillian melodrama. "I will grow this nest egg with blood, toil, tears, and sweat," I would have growled to the assembled throng of dignitaries and media, had they shown up, as they had in the grainy newsreel of my imagination.

What did greet me upon stepping off the plane was a tinny, digital music—the sound of slot machines. Like the 24/7 metropolis it serves, the nation's twelfth-busiest airport is a night owl, with more flights arriving and departing around midnight than at any other time of day. Slot machines and a barrage of loud plugs for sensual shows and bountiful buffets, which after a while were hard to tell apart, tantalized us incoming dreamers.

Tourism is a cruel mistress, forcing its new conquests and deposed lovers to cross paths at airports, train stations, and resorts the world over. Everywhere it's the same. The excited new arrivals to paradise avoid looking those leaving in the eye. And Las Vegas's frenetic brand of tourism is a particularly harsh mistress, to judge by the looks of McCarran's departing wounded, worn out well before boarding their red-eye flights back to reality. A far greater number of people were crashed on benches, totally spent, than you'd find at the airport in, say, Cleveland. The very sight of them made me feel like a reinforcement arriving at the front.

I took one of the world's shortest $8 cab rides to my first stop, the Luxor Hotel, which sits practically at the end of the runway, at the southern end of the fabled Las Vegas Strip. "In town for business, sir?" the driver inquired politely. "Well, yes," I replied with a grin after what must have seemed a suspicious pause. "As a matter of fact I am." As we pulled into the hotel's driveway, past the columns covered with hieroglyphics, the driver said I should remember one thing, and one thing only, if I found myself with some time to kill in the casino:

"Endeavor to be as crazy on the upside as you are on the down-side."

That turned out to be the most prescient advice I was offered in Las Vegas by anyone. But at the time, untested in battle and exhausted from the long trip, I merely shrugged it off.

The entrance to Luxor is breathtaking, especially when you're pulling in from the airport and have not yet had a chance to adjust to the town's outrageous scale. We pulled up to the porte cochere underneath the sphinx's belly, and I entered the cavernous atrium to see a life-sized replica of the temple of Ramses II, with the casino beyond. To the immediate right is a massive marble counter with thirty-three check-in stations, backed by bucolic murals of Egyptians in funky hairdos frolicking on the Nile. An efficient clerk assigned me to room 8029, gave me a safe deposit box for the bulge in my coat pocket, and wished me good luck.

It took me fifteen minutes of wandering around the circular casino to find my "inclinator." The four elevators, tucked in the corners of the massive pyramid, are wonderful techno-kitsch, traveling at a 39-degree angle. "The more you drink, the more lateral the movement seems," a young man slurred knowingly, clutching a bottle of beer. One of the things you quickly become accustomed to in Vegas is the sight of people carrying liquor all over the place. It's a spring break for all ages.

Las Vegas builds in spurts. Along with the MGM Grand and Treasure Island, Luxor was one of three massive resorts to "come on line"—the local tourism-as-industry jargon—in 1993. Its thirty-story black glass pyramid, guarded by a ten-story sphinx and boasting the world's largest atrium, instantly became one of the city's landmarks and was pictured on the cover of *Time* the following January, when America's sober newsweekly of record proclaimed Las Vegas the new "all-American City."

From the pyramid's pinnacle, the world's most powerful light beam—everything in this town is either a superlative or in danger of being blown up—beckons the world's gamblers to come pay homage. Such is the breakneck pace of growth in Las Vegas that a mere three years after it opened, Luxor deemed it necessary to build two additional twenty-two-story towers alongside the pyramid. Evidently 2,900 rooms weren't enough.

In a painful illustration of the airline-like pricing elasticity at Las Vegas hotels, Luxor was charging me a different rate each night, ranging from $59 to $169. The room was surprisingly tasteful. I hadn't expected much from a hotel with 4,476 rooms—a hotel, at that, with a vested interest in keeping guests downstairs, in the casino. But the cherry wardrobe and the bed's headboard were art deco in styling, with Egyptian etchings on them. Then there was the slanting glass wall of the pyramid. All very cool in an Indiana Jones kind of way.

This being Las Vegas, my view was of a construction site: the Mandalay Bay Hotel nearing completion next door, on the site where the Hacienda long stood (until it was brought down during a New Year's Fox TV special) as the southernmost major resort on the Strip. The $950 million South Seas–themed Mandalay Bay—it's considered rude in this land of conspicuous consumption not to mention a hotel's price tag—will be a sister property to Luxor, owned by the same parent, Circus Circus Enterprises. Mandalay is one of four mammoth casinos that will be opening within the next year as part of the city's latest $7 billion investment in pleasure palaces. Mandalay, which will have a wave pool suitable for surfing competitions, is the one that sounds like the most fun, as the other three—Bellagio, Paris, and the Venetian—will all celebrate staid European civilizations, reflecting Las Vegas's ongoing quest for respectability.

Circus Circus generally caters to folks on modest budgets, but in a nod to the gentrification craze sweeping the city, Mandalay Bay will include a posh Four Seasons hotel within the larger hotel. The Red Square vodka palace and the Rumjungle bar will appeal to Vegas's changing demographics. And—this too is a growing trend—Mandalay Bay is turning to famous eateries from elsewhere to provide the eats: among them, New York's snooty Aureole and China Grill, plus the trendy House of Blues chain. Another sign of the times: Circus Circus ditched its goofy name to become the Mandalay Resort Group after the new hotel opened.

All trendiness aside, the current building binge has given rise to quite a bit of angst. Construction workers had barely started on the foundation for the Venetian Hotel in 1997, in the largest continuous concrete pour in U.S. history, when the economy of East Asia, home to the world's highest rollers, began free-falling into its own deep hole. Having put their borrowed money on the table, Las Vegas's casino moguls are haunted by a single question, which hovers over this desert oasis like the film of dust that makes its air the third dirtiest of any city in the country: This time, have we gone too far?

Glenn Schaeffer, Mandalay's president and chief financial officer, doesn't think so; he remains one of the new Las Vegas's more convincing boosters. He calls Las Vegas an "entertainment megastore," a place where people come to see what's new, and where visitors will explore the "most talked-about buildings in America at the start of the new millennium." This vision of Las Vegas as something more than a mere gambling town, as an all-around "gratifier central," is taking shape. This year, for the first time ever, market research showed visitors picking "entertainment" over "gambling" as the city's main draw.

♣ ♦ ♥ ♠ Before turning in for the night, I took a quick shower. I had a good laugh as I picked up Luxor's plastic shampoo bottle—shaped like an obelisk. I'm easy.

Nest egg: $50,000

Friday, April 3

I ventured down to the Pyramid Café (entered from the casino, of course) for a late breakfast of huevos rancheros, eggs with beans and Mexican sausage. Being in the Southwest has its culinary privileges. While waiting, I read over the day's *Las Vegas Review-Journal.* Writing a book entails heavy research, and every foreign correspondent worth his salt knows that "heavy research" involves reading the local press and repackaging it for the folks back home, who picture their intrepid foreign correspondents wading through jungles, instead of crowded cafés, to get the scoop.

Two stories immediately caught my eye. First, a small electrical fire had caused about $1 million in damage at the Las Vegas Hilton, Elvis's old stomping grounds, and a familiar locale to anyone who suffered through *Indecent Proposal* with Robert Redford and Demi Moore earlier this decade. Come to think of it, that's the amount Redford offered Woody Harrelson to spend the night with Demi, and what should have been offered audiences to sit through the movie. What makes the *Review-Journal* story intriguing is this: The fire was started by an overflowing toilet.

I realize an overflowing toilet can be unpleasant, but a fire hazard? A fine liberal arts education topped off with a law degree has left me completely incapable of comprehending how this could be, and the article was no help.

The second piece was what editors call a trend story. In this case, a bad trend: "LV Boom Causes Suicides," read the headline. Actually, minus the suicides, the boom would be a good trend. The Clark County coroner, Ron Flud, reported that 272 people had killed themselves in 1997, which was 19 more than in 1996. More people, more suicides; makes sense. But, at 22.2 per 100,000 people, Nevada's suicide rate is almost double the national average.

But *it's not what you're thinking,* the story admonished. Gambling rarely plays a role in southern Nevada suicides, according to Flud. And to counter recent studies showing a disturbing correlation between the spread of gambling and a rise in suicide rates, Frank Fahrenkopf, president of the American Gaming Association, the casino industry's chief lobbyist in Washington, trotted out the Wyoming defense. "You can take Nevada and Wyoming and both have suicide numbers that are high, yet Wyoming doesn't have any gaming," he told the *Review-Journal*. And thank God for that. In other words, it's more of a gun-lovin'-desolate-West kinda thing. (But if the critics persist, I'd advise the AGA to adopt the following slogan: "Slots don't kill people, guns kill people.")

After breakfast, I made my way up to the Luxor's sprawling attractions level, ground floor to the world's largest atrium, one floor up from the three-acre casino. According to my informative "Luxor passport," you could stack nine Boeing 747s in the pyramid's atrium. There's enough here to make the most jaded of kids go nuts: an IMAX theater, a VirtuaLand Sega games arcade, and one of those rattle-in-place rides with computer animation that are all the rage, "In Search of the Obelisk," which I don't advise taking within twenty-four hours of eating huevos rancheros.

I enjoyed King Tut's Tomb & Museum next door, a replica of Howard Carter's astounding 1922 archaeological discovery. "Isn't Caesars Palace also Egyptian, Mom?" a young boy ahead of me on the Walkman-guided tour asked his mother. "Only Cleopatra's Barge," Mom answered without missing a beat, referring to that hotel's nightclub. Who says a trip to Las Vegas can't be educational? For how many of its more than 27,000 monthly visitors is this museum-within-a-casino the improbable spark of an avid interest in antiquity? Picture an eminent Egyptologist decades from now telling his grandchildren, "I was just another aimless high school student interested in nothing but football and chasing girls when one summer my family—Dad had this thing for video poker—took a road trip to Las Vegas, and . . ."

Tut was buried with an amazing number of toys, in the belief he could continue enjoying them in the afterlife. The chamber looked like a basement in need of serious spring cleaning—here a wooden boat, there a throne, all exactly where Mr. Carter had stumbled across them. A gilded shrine contained some of the king's embalmed organs, minus the brains, which were pulled out through the corpse's nose and discarded before mummification, as Egyptians believed the heart dictated one's thinking. This gory nugget was much appreciated by the boy ahead of me. This being Las Vegas, I'd expected to be attacked on the hour by either mummies or Islamic fundamentalist terrorists wielding machine guns, but no such luck.

Naturally, we exited the museum via a gift shop offering not only Vegas souvenirs, but a selection of books and videos on ancient Egypt. I resisted buying a book on Carter's work, vowing instead to acquire a cheesy souvenir at every hotel along the way. And with that, I set off to walk the Strip.

♣ ♦ ♥ ♠ On my way out of the hotel, I dodged dozens of camera-crazed tourists, all trying to capture each and every five-year-old Luxor hieroglyphic on film. I am not usually one to bash tourists (I'd be one full-time, if I could get away with it), but there was something pathetic about this scene. At one point I saw a mother snap at her posing child, who couldn't have been four: "We can't take your picture there, honey, there's nothing behind you." The girl cried.

Americans, it was readily apparent, do Vegas the way they do Europe, armed with film and a checklist of sights. The only difference is that here the sights are megaresorts, instead of megachurches. In time, that difference may be academic. A few centuries from now, archaeologists studying the ruins of our civilization will no doubt determine that Las Vegas was an important religious center, boasting dozens of massive temples to which pilgrims from afar brought bountiful offerings.

♣ ♦ ♥ ♠ The Strip, or Las Vegas Boulevard, is what you picture when you think of Las Vegas, with its massive, gaudy casino hotels lined up, each new one trying to outdo the others in size, design, and crowd-attracting gimmickry. Excalibur, another Circus Circus creation, is Luxor's neighbor on the intersection of the Strip and Tropicana. It would be a masterful rendition of a medieval castle if the only building materials on hand were Lego blocks. From afar, it looks great; up close, it looks like "the granddaddy of all miniature golf castles," as architectural critic Alan Hess described it in his wonderful 1993 book, *Viva Las Vegas: After-Hours Architecture.* Inside, the Camelot theme is well executed. A fair rich in Merlins and roving storytellers makes this a favorite with families, and a particularly pernicious place to critics like Ralph Nader who suppose only Satan would want to make Las Vegas appealing to kids.

I lingered on one of the pedestrian bridges—accessible from the sidewalk by escalators—that link the intersection's four gigantic hotels, Excalibur, New York–New York, Tropicana, and the MGM Grand. This one intersection, locals will tell you with perverse pride, offers more rooms than does the entire city of San Francisco. The festive throngs of people crossing the bridges, gawking at New York–New York's roller coaster overhead or at the MGM's bronze lion, reminded me of Fifth Avenue Christmastime crowds in the real New York. But this crowd, surprisingly, might have been more diverse. Midwestern families showed off their matching Hard Rock T-shirts; Japanese tourists their white polos; L.A. surfers their tans; trophy wives their Prada, Versace, and silicone. Washed-up gamblers just squinted in the bright sunlight.

As much as their diversity, what was striking about all these people was that they were, well, walking. After all, the Strip, the old Los Angeles Highway, had developed in the postwar era as the automobile age's answer to the compact, pedestrian-friendly downtown casino area. It was here that the noted Yale architect Robert Venturi came in the late 1960s to study what he called the "archetype of the commercial strip, the phenomenon at its purest and most intense," whose study was "as important to architects and urbanists today as were the studies of medieval Europe and ancient Rome and earlier Greece to earlier generations."

In his 1972 book, *Learning from Las Vegas,* Venturi earnestly described the low-lying casino hotels and oversized neon signage along the Strip, set back from the gas stations and tacky commerce. Venturi noted that the more densely built and pedestrian-dominated downtown area was more photogenic, whereas visitors on the Strip drove between neighboring casinos, the distance between them being so great and unremarkable.

In the past quarter-century, Venturi's Strip has disappeared. The poster child of commercial drags transformed itself into one of the nation's most vibrant pedestrian venues, presided over by theatrical, ever-closer skyscrapers. To the millions of visiting suburbanites, the theme of a dense urban environment where one can walk between destinations (lugging buckets of quarters, no less) proves as exhilarating and exotic as the wonders of ancient Egypt. You see the same rush—"Look, Ma, I'm walking ten blocks"—among tourists in New York.

Unlike Excalibur, the New York–New York hotel, a whimsical rendition of my hometown's skyline that opened in early 1997, is endearing up close. Past the Statue of Liberty and a tugboat shooting water into the air (Vegas's zoning laws must require casinos to at least appear to be wasting water), the façade becomes an intricate streetscape as you walk north along the Strip. Running parallel to this walkway is a replica of the Brooklyn Bridge. It's one-fifth the original's size, but is walked across by 4.8 million more pedestrians a year. A far cry from the casinos Professor Venturi described as mere "decorated sheds," New York–New York is a grand pavilion in what's become a 24/7 World's Fair.

Across the Strip and next to the radioactive-green MGM Grand Hotel, the largest anywhere, the world's most recognizable trademark—a gigantic Coke bottle leading into the World of Coca-Cola museum—speaks volumes about Sin City's transformation into a mainstream, corporate showcase. So does the neighboring M&M's store, where kids can bag the candy in psychedelic colors that have been rejected for mass consumption. Then you've got your All Star

Café, owned by local wonder André Agassi and some other jocks, which shouldn't be confused with the Harley-Davidson, Motown, and Rainforest cafés, all within a two-block radius. Whatever happened to restaurants where food is the main attraction?

"Voilà, ça c'est l'Amérique," I overheard a backpack-toting Tocqueville tell his girlfriend, pointing at the jarring juxtaposition of retail and gambling monuments across the Strip. Michel and Céline, from Paris, had arrived in town that same morning from the Grand Canyon. "Isn't that national park, too, the essence of America?" I asked them hopefully. "No, that was a geological accident," Michel replied.

♣ ♦ ♥ ♠ Back at Luxor, after relaxing a bit in the room, I ran into Bob from Montana on my way down to dinner. "You winning?" he asked, the way strangers inquire about the weather in other cities. "I'm doing real good," he told me with a thumbs-up as we inclinated downward. "Roulette," he added, as if suggesting a fine restaurant. I had always thought of roulette as a dainty game, but Bob looked like a tough guy. "You know, it's really not that hard to win," he told me as we parted ways.

After dinner at the Dead Sea Room restaurant overlooking the casino, it was time to do battle. But first, I obtained my all-important Gold Chamber card at the casino's promotions booth. This is Luxor's equivalent of a frequent-flyer card. Computers track how much you gamble, and on that basis you accrue freebies—"comps," in the local patois. My pale blue plastic Gold Chamber card has a magnetic strip for slot machines to read and an account number under my name, making it look ominously like a credit card.

Inspired by Montana Bob's infectious optimism, not to mention the size of my bankroll, I determined to dive in headfirst instead of first sticking my toe in the shallow end of the pool. I walked over to my safe deposit box—I had one key and the management the other, as in the movies—and grabbed five of my checks. I cashed three at the casino "cage" and was set to go. Tightly clutching my impressive wad of C-notes, I headed straight for the "High Limit Gaming" temple in the middle of the circular casino, past rows of slot machines, an escalator down to the all-you-can-eat buffet, cash machines that screamed "NOW EXCEED YOUR ATM LIMIT!" and a ring of $5 blackjack tables.

At the entrance to the temple stands a faux limestone wall with carvings that depict a fellow walking like an Egyptian, birds, serpents balancing circus balls on their heads, what looked like cross-country skis, and the ankh, or key of life. In other words, it was Joseph's interpretation of Pharaoh's dream—you know, the one that made his career: Stay away from blackjack for seven years.

It was fitting to begin my quest for unspeakable gambling riches surrounded by these motifs from an ancient civilization, for gambling has been a constant human obsession since time immemorial. From their respective soapboxes, morality-peddling conservatives and elitist liberals, eager to protect "ordinary" people from themselves, bemoan the fact that we Americans wager more in a year— upwards of a half trillion dollars—than we spend on movies, baseball, and apple pie. But don't let them scare you into thinking America's current love affair with Lady Luck is something alarmingly new.

Hadn't Zeus, Poseidon, and Hades rolled dice for shares in the universe (Zeus won, getting the heavens) in the ultimate high-roller showdown? Didn't the Roman soldiers cast lots for Christ's robe? Historians have traced the symbols on playing cards back to the eighth-century Chinese T'ang dynasty; in ancient Egypt, where archaeologists have found loaded dice among certain pharaohs' buried treasures, compulsive gamblers were forced to hone stones for the pyramids; the Pilgrims financed their journey to America with a lottery. Pascal and Fermat advanced our understanding of math because they were avid gamblers, not because they were seeking tenure somewhere. And let us not forget the sandwich, invented by an earl of that name who was too engrossed in his gambling to leave a game to eat properly.

Blackjack, the most popular of table games in American casinos, is derived from the venerable French game of vingt-et-un. According to my Compass guidebook to Las Vegas, the American version of the game got its name early this century in the backroom gaming dens of Evansville, Indiana, where dealers paid a $5 bonus for a two-card hand of 21 when one card was either the black jack of spades or clubs (the other card, of course, being an ace). Today, any 10-value card plus an ace makes that sweetest of hands, a blackjack, paying out one and a half times your bet.

Backed by all this history, I proceeded into the temple where few dare enter, despite the knot I felt developing in my stomach. It was refreshingly uncrowded; the $100 minimum bet tends to thin the crowds. *Relax,* I told myself in an effort to breathe normally, *this isn't really your money.* But then why were the bills damp when I handed them over to the dealer, auspiciously named Kathy?

Casinos are all about rituals. First, you don't hand dealers anything. Bills must be placed on the green felt table, Kathy explained. She counted the money, laying out the bills in neat rows of five, while her supervisor, the pit boss, hovered behind her. "It's all for the eye in the sky," she said, motioning to the black bubbles in the ceiling, which concealed security cameras. She then prepared six stacks of black chips (which Nevada's exacting gaming regulations stipulate must be .130 inches thick and 1.55 inches in diameter), chirped, "Three thousand," over her shoulder, and awaited the green light from her supervisor, colorfully called the "pit boss." The bills were stashed into the locked "drop box" attached to the table, which is taken after each shift to the infamous "count room."

"Good luck," Kathy said, pursuant to corporate policy, when shoving over the stacks of plastic chips picturing obelisks, pyramids, and the beautiful Queen Nefertiti. The colorful chips, so playful and smooth to the touch, were most welcome after all that scary cash. I began to relax.

Initiating my quest for fame and fortune, I placed a chip in the betting circle. It was 7:28, Pacific Time. Kathy dealt me a 10 and an 8 from the plastic "shoe" containing six decks of cards. Not bad. But her "upcard" was a king, which in this game counts as a 10. I had to pass on taking another card, or stay, but with a sinking feeling. You are always to assume the dealer's hole card, the one dealt facedown, is a 10, though the reasoning behind this escapes me, given that only sixteen cards are worth 10 in blackjack, out of a deck of fifty-two.

The good news: Kathy's other card wasn't a 10. The bad news: It was a 9. Kathy swooped up my chip and placed it in the neat rows before her. It was all over in a matter of seconds. Then the pit boss, the only guy in the place wearing a suit, walked over. Now what? "Would you care to be rated, sir?" he asked. I hesitated, picturing an electronic scoreboard somewhere flashing the word "mediocre" next to my name, until he made clear he was asking for my Gold Chamber card to track my betting.

Then a blonde wearing a Cleopatra-esque skirt straight out of a ninth-grader's fantasy paraded about, making the sweetest casino sound known to man. "Cock*tailzzz*?" By the time she came back with my Heineken, I was up $1,600. Alone at the table, I'd found the pace of the game dizzying. I'd get 20, the dealer would get 19. The dealer would show a 10, I'd bust. I'd alternate between betting $100 and $200. We were playing two or three hands a minute. That means I was betting at a rate of some $18,000 an hour. It didn't really feel like it, of course, given the game's affinity to trench warfare—advance, retreat, advance. At times I even played two spots, because I saw a serious high roller at the table next to mine do it.

My big break came when Kathy dealt me two 8s and showed a 7. I obediently "split" my 8s—always split 8s, I'd read on the plane—into two separate $200 hands. This is what gets the adrenaline flowing in blackjack. Kathy then dealt my first 8 a 3, which was beautiful. Now, from an 11, I could double down, which meant coughing up an additional $200 for a single card, preferably a "monkey," which is what veterans call any face card. Not even close; it was a 2. My other hand drew an additional 8, which I again split. Would you believe I got yet another 8? So again I split. At this point the wary pit boss was looking at me and what were now my four hands with a pitying eye, as if he knew, from experience, that this could not end well. Then again, pit bosses, immunized from tips and concerned with the house's bottom line, don't exactly root for the player.

From an initial $200 bet, this had escalated into a $1,000 confrontation. My first hand, the one I'd doubled down on, was ugly. My next two 8s were topped off by a 10 and a 9. Groovy. On my last 8, I was dealt a 4, for a 12, which I "hit"—always with a hand signal for the camera—and got a 5, for a total of 17. If things went by the book and Kathy had a 10 under her 7, this would all be much ado about nothing. I'd win two hands, lose the double down, and tie, or "push," the last one. But this hand didn't have a by-the-book feel to it; the pit boss's eyebrows were fully arched, and I was feeling pretty numb.

Kathy sighed deeply, saying something nice about "our" needing some help, and unveiled a 9 from under her 7. Yes! The dealer must take a card at 16—it said so right there on the felt—and Kathy busted with an 8.

That's when my Heineken arrived. I tipped the waitress a couple of bucks for my "free" drink and massaged my impressive stack of chips while Kathy shuffled. Only twenty-six minutes had gone by since I first sat down, and I'd already made more money than I'd ever been paid for a week of honest work. And at none of my previous workplaces did scantily clad women make rounds offering cock*tailzzz*. This would be a sweet month, I decided, trying not to break into a stupid grin.

As if on cue, Sam sat down to my left. He was old, sunburned, and in a wicked mood. "I'm getting my ass kicked," he told no one in particular. There's a lot of mumbling in casinos. You'll walk by a guy murmuring about "those $&%#*! bastards getting a %$&* twenty-one after showing a six," and you'd never guess that one hand was played out days ago.

Sam brought no cash to the table, but asked for a $2,500 "marker." More cool rituals ensued. The pit boss took the gentleman's Gold Chamber card, studied the computer screen, and printed out what looked like a check. Sam signed it, the dealer signed some form, chips were lined up in plain view of the gods in the sky, and all the paperwork was stashed in the drop box.

A marker is essentially an IOU that a player with an established line of credit signs over to a casino. Patrons have a month to pay it off at no interest, though their aspiration is to win enough to buy back their marker with chips at the cage, rip it up (this is a very public, very satisfying ritual to a gambler), and walk away with their profit. Markers are how high rollers avoid carrying a lot of cash. Only someone (that is, yours truly) gambling way over his credit-worthiness, or someone needing to do some serious laundry, would carry fifty grand into a Las Vegas casino.

Kathy shuffled up and was relieved by another dealer. I came to love this changing of the guard, the peculiar way the departing dealer claps, raises her hands, and twists them, magicianlike, to show the eye in the sky that she has nothing up her sleeves. Later, back in New York, one sign that I'd spent way too much time in casinos was that I was mimicking this ritual to Trotsky, our cat, whenever I wanted to let him know I was done bugging him and he could now sleep in peace.

No need to read the new dealer's name tag. R-A-M-O-N, his bracelet spelled out. "I am Cuban," he told me, and we broke into Spanish. I figured I'd appeal to his sense of Latin solidarity. Ramon is a handsome guy, probably in his late twenties, all slick jet-black hair. He fled Cuba on—get this—a makeshift raft in 1991. Incredibly, he was picked up by a Carnival cruise ship. I presume Kathie Lee wasn't on board, because Ramon didn't swim back to Havana.

Chatting with Ramon was expensive. He hit a hot streak, but tried to pretend nothing untoward was happening. Only sulking Sam remained fixated on the game. "Dammit, that's the fourth seventeen I get in a row. It's the mother-in-law of all hands—you want to hit it but you can't," he slurred. He was downing Jack Daniel's.

I focused on my own dwindling stack of chips. It was a sign of Ramon's luck that 17s were giving my playmate ulcers; against a dealer who doesn't bust, that's not going to be a winning hand. I raised my bet to $300 for the first time and got a blackjack, which was electrifying, until I realized Ramon had done the same. What should I have expected from a guy who managed to escape Fidel Castro's regime and take his first luxury cruise in the same week? "It would appear that I am lucky," Ramon told me in Spanish. I caught his drift, and decided to go for a walk.

It was still only 8:45 and I was down to nine chips—down $2,100 from my original buy-in and down a gut-wrenching $3,900, about what I used to earn in a month, from my high. Stunned, I paid a visit to the temple's marble bathroom—I'd earned the use of real towels—and stocked up on fruit from the adjacent high-roller lounge. Then I set off for the crowded general casino area.

I cashed the other two $1,000 traveler's checks in my pocket, vowing to make the money last. I then wandered through the Giza Galleries, a shopping promenade off the casino. The store peddling casino wear seemed to be doing brisk business. A group of Japanese tourists were taking pictures inside the store. More intriguing was the Treasure Chamber, which was near the furry talking camels and sold genuine Egyptian antiquities. For those wondering, a sign on the wall disclosed that every item in the store was lawfully obtained outside of Egypt. My favorite trinket was a 2,300-year-old piece of limestone with lion-worship hieroglyphics (and "later Greek graffiti" from around the time of Christ) for $9,500. Too bad I'd already bought my Luxor souvenir, a deck of "used in actual casino play" cards.

I next chose a $25 blackjack table in the main casino area. The guys already there all seemed to be in a lousy mood—few people betting more than $5 a hand ever look as if they're on vacation—as did the French dealer who grimaced every time the player farthest to her left, sitting in what's termed the first-base position, puffed on his cigar. After a few hands I realized what the jerk (a surgeon from Texas, he volunteered, more than once, as if trying to drum up business) was doing. The better the dealer's hand, the more blatantly he blew smoke in her face. Piss off the dealer: Now, *there*'s a strategy.

She consistently came up with 20s and 21s, the hard way. She'd be showing a 5 or 6 at the outset, presumably her weakest cards, then draw four or five more small cards and inform us her hand was a 20 or 21 before we could add it up—it can get pretty hard with an ace thrown in the mix, not to mention all the Heinekens. We all just stared, as if witnessing a magic trick.

Dr. Texas ran out of money. Flat out. Five times I saw him throw "one last" $300 on the table, which he'd peel off a rubber band in his shirt pocket. I thought this a bit uncouth; only later would I learn that serious gamblers call such rubber bands Vegas money clips. Thus reinforced, he would stack four of his green $25 chips, grumbling "This'll change now," watch the dealer do her magic, and then lean forward to exhale. She checked her watch every time he fumbled for money; she was bored silly. The routine came to an abrupt end when he went to his pocket the sixth time and came up empty-handed. "Shit, I'm out," he said in a heavy drawl. He then asked the pit boss to direct him to the credit office. As he left, the dealer tersely wished him better luck next time. Corporate policy.

"How fascinating this work must be," I said to the dealer, wearing my most earnest smile, "to have a front seat at fortune's amphitheater, to see human nature in its rawest form, stripped of all pretense, to witness the ultimate agony and the ecstasy."

"Yeah, it's not so bad," she replied, glancing once more at her watch with the ennui of the salaried. "We get a break every hour."

Certain lessons were beginning to gel in my impressionable mind. For a game in which the house should beat you fifty-two times out of a hundred (if you know what you're doing), blackjack seemed awfully streaky. The dealer had been on a serious roll for almost an hour, and we just sat there, as if we had no choice. A casino is no place for defiance. It's best to identify who's got the momentum, and act accordingly. Increase your bet or take a walk. It's not as if you're ever forced to make a bet.

So much wisdom, so little money. By 10:30 I was down to a mere $350. Somehow, in three hours I'd gone through almost 10 percent of the nest egg. I walked back in a huff to the high-stakes temple. Incidentally, by then I'd consumed five beers, my average monthly consumption. Guess what happened?

Fifteen minutes later I asked the pit boss for a pass to Ra, the new nightclub off the casino that's taken the town by storm. This, too, was imitative behavior; I'd seen someone else ask him for one. "My pleasure, Mr. Martinez," came the response, and he handed me a slip of paper to wave to the goons manning the door, holding back what must have been seventy-five people in line to get in. Amazingly, the velvet cordon bouncers are so fond of was lowered and I was in. I didn't even have to pay the $10 cover.

I'd never accomplished such a feat at haughty clubs back in New York, which is one of the reasons I stopped going to them during the Bush administration. Standing in the cold forever until someone in a purple jacket and a black mock turtleneck decided I looked presentable enough to be ripped off was never my idea of a good time. But for a mere $5,000, Luxor was revealing to me how gratifying it is to be among the chosen.

Ra, named after the canine-looking sun god, is wild, with a futuristic, industrial décor. An imposing eagle towers over the dance floor. It looked especially creepy when enveloped by the disco fog discharged on the dance floor. Scantily clad women danced in cages along the side, though it was unclear whether they did so for business or pleasure.

I lit up a Baron de Rothschild—this is a cigar town, to be sure— by the bar and nursed a scotch. I was standing next to seven collegiate types from Kansas City. It was a bachelor party; the wedding would take place the next day at one of the kitschy chapels at the northern end of the Strip. "Stan is so lucky," one of the guys told me, "she's gorgeous and she cooks." Utter bliss. I bought Stan a drink, wished him eternal happiness, and headed for the exit. Ra, I'd quickly determined, was no place to be alone—or over thirty, for that matter. I was starting to feel like a lecherous old conventioneer.

I was shocked by how much I'd already gambled—mainly because I'd lost. I'd been psyching myself up for this for weeks, talking myself into the fact that I would be gambling heady sums of money and should do so from the outset of my odyssey. But no pep talk could have prepared me for the crushing reality that I had lost $5,000 in the time it takes to have dinner and see a movie. Winning it back seemed like the only way to alleviate the guilt. It was only midnight, after all, which in a crowded Vegas casino feels like six in the evening. So I signed back into my safe deposit box to retrieve ammo: five more $1,000 checks.

The next four hours were a blur. A triumphal, drunken blur. I was doubling down, splitting cards left and right, doing God knows what, tipping the cocktail waitresses liberally and generally kicking ass. The pit bosses were learning my name. By four I had dug myself out of the hole. I made my way over to Nefertiti's Lounge with roughly $3,000 in cash and ten yellow $1,000 chips in my pocket, and there I chatted with a gay Spanish couple while downing a Bailey's. The bar was still busy at this hour, which I found intoxicating (not that I needed any help). I've long relished the anonymous romance of a grand hotel, the electrifying bustle produced by so many people on the make, freed from the burdens of their everyday lives. Inspired, travelers yearn to tell one another why theirs is a particularly noteworthy journey but usually succumb to modern notions of privacy. It is this palpable but unshared excitement that make hotel bars—not to mention casinos—fantastic people-watching venues.

This would have been a good time to go to bed, admittedly, but instead I pressed my luck. The consequences were unpleasant. In three hours, I gave back $6,200. A casino turns ugly in the wee small hours of the morning, after the band has packed up and the casual gamblers have gone to bed, and I don't say that merely on account of my losses. It's called the graveyard shift, after all, when these 24/7 establishments do most of their maintenance. People desperate enough to be gambling at five in the morning do not need to be coddled. They do not mind the vacuum cleaners at their feet, nor the spooky money trains with their armed guards that go from table to table collecting the house's bulging drop boxes.

I called it quits at eight, when I realized that a lot of the people filing by me were no longer coming back from a night on the town, but heading for breakfast or the pool after a good night's sleep. I wandered around hopelessly looking for that elusive inclinator number 2, serenaded by Celine Dion's theme song from *Titanic,* which was playing in the casino for about the fortieth time since I'd started gambling, some twelve hours earlier.

Nest egg: $46,800

Saturday, April 4

Five hours later I was inclinating down to the casino level again. In Kingsley Amis's hilarious *Lucky Jim,* the hero awakens from a night of drinking feeling as if he's been "expertly beaten up by secret police." My sentiments exactly. In my case, a secret police rather fond of mixing Heineken, scotch, and Irish liqueurs.

I walked around the hotel, allowing blood to irrigate my parched extremities. Kids were having a ball at the pools, running around the various Egyptian-themes statues and swimming under the waterfalls. Beyond, next to the hotel's parking garage, an office marked "Employment Center" caught my eye. This being a Saturday, it didn't appear open, but a group of people huddled by a bulletin board taking notes.

The job listings made for fascinating reading. Luxor was looking for the usual assortment of employees you'd find at a resort anywhere—busboy, spa coordinator, accountant, bartender, security guard, and so on. But you could also apply for such exotic occupations as "cage pit clerk." Probably the most enticing listing was for a "poker proposition player," preferably with a year's experience. Where else can you be hired to play poker all day, even if it's as the casino's shill? The most demanding qualifications, oddly enough, appeared to be those for "coin wrapper," for which applicants must have experience with both "numbers" and "heavy physical activity."

I attempted to strike up a conversation with a kid studying the list. I formulated the words with care, but the previous night's goons had pressed the mute button and all I could muster was a windy raspiness. My voice was shot. It hadn't mattered; Alejandro didn't speak English. It turned out he was from Chihuahua, in northern Mexico, where I grew up, so I switched to raspy Spanish and we talked about our old hometown. All conversations among Chihuahua exiles invariably start with the wistful observation that what makes the dusty place so darned special is, well, the people. With that out of the way, I asked, Why come to Vegas?

Alejandro's uncle had been coming for about eight months out of the year for over a decade, he explained, and always returned home with a decent wad of cash. "He's a roofero," Alejandro explained, using a marvelous borderism, "and in good times in the construction business, well, they don't always check papers."

Alejandro had come up last winter with his uncle. But the work was grueling, and he fantasized about getting a job in one of the glittering casinos. "To work in a casino is very good, very elegant work, but I'm afraid they check papers," he said sadly. They also check your blood, the board advised; drug tests are mandatory.

While elegance may be in the eye of the beholder, Alejandro was right about the money. The more than 170,000 jobs at Las Vegas hotels and casinos pay relatively well. The housekeeper who had come to clean my room earlier—painfully, I'd forgotten to hang the "Do Not Disturb" sign—told me she made in the neighborhood of $10 an hour at Luxor, twice what she'd made in Los Angeles, where the cost of living was a lot higher. When I asked her, as New Yorkers are prone to do, in which part of town she rented, she answered, rather indignantly, "I don't; I own a home." Must be nice.

Historian Hal Rothman of the University of Nevada, Las Vegas, calls Las Vegas, among other things, America's last Detroit, the last place where an unskilled worker can make a middle-class wage. Unions naturally get a lot of the credit. In a boomtown where most hotels have opted not to resist unionization, the Hotel Employees and Restaurant Employees Union local membership has soared to some forty thousand from eighteen thousand in the late 1980s. AFL–CIO president John J. Sweeney has taken to calling Las Vegas "the hottest union city in America," and last month the union held its first executive council meeting in Las Vegas. President Clinton, Vice President Gore, and House Minority Leader Richard Gephardt all flew in to address the meeting and fawn over local culinary union members who'd staged a six-year strike at the Frontier Hotel on the Strip.

At a news conference during his stay, Vice President Gore, acknowledging that Las Vegas is now the fastest-growing major city in the country, told the union members: "The atmosphere of hope and opportunity brings people here searching for a better life, and they've got the gumption to say, 'I'm not going to work for dirt wages. I want something that gives me dignity and the ability to raise my family and have a middle-class lifestyle.' "

That Las Vegas has become an exemplary union town is apt, given that before most commercial banks or Wall Street would have anything to do with Sin City, it was Teamsters money, often controlled by the Mob, that built the resort's first generation of postwar casinos.

♣ ♦ ♥ ♠ Seeking to improve my own family's lifestyle, I wandered back into the casino and parked myself at a $5 blackjack table. I bought in $200, asked for some coffee, and resolved to take it easy. I started playing $10 a hand, but soon eased my way up the color ladder as momentum swung my way, moving from red to green and finally venturing back into black territory. By the time I "colored in" and got up to leave the table, I was ahead $1,865 for the session.

I was quite pleased with myself. Without being able to point to any one spectacular moment, I'd walked away from the table with nine times more dough than I'd bought in for. But of course there's no such thing as a perfectly satisfying gambling session. As I went up to my room, a small voice within me nagged: Couldn't we (in my experience, pernicious thoughts invariably present themselves in first-person plural) just as easily have sat down with $20,000, instead of $200, played our sensible game for an hour and a half, and walked away with $180,000 instead of $1,800?

At five, eight on the East Coast, I went up to the room to call Kat. She was at her parents' place in Connecticut. Unfortunately, she didn't pick up. Judy did. I love my mother-in-law dearly, but I really didn't want to talk to her just then. Maybe I was feeling a little ashamed. She's no fan of gambling, to put it mildly, and probably couldn't have thought of a less worthy subject for her son-in-law's first book. I wasn't keen to tell her that I'd spent my whole first evening (and dawn) in town boozing and losing dough in the casino. So I latched on to poor old King Tut the way President Clinton latched on to "the people's work" whenever asked about his personal life.

"You know, ancient Egypt was a fascinating place," I said, going on about the tomb for what must have been a half-hour. The fact that Judy has been to the real thing helped my cause. "Now, did you get to see the jars with Tut's actual organs?" I asked. By the time she handed Kat the phone any worries she'd had about my becoming a gambling addict must have been supplanted by a more pressing concern—that her son-in-law might be a total nerd. Who goes to Vegas to get into archaeology?

Afterward I bought the *Review-Journal* and headed for the All Star Cafe, where tourists don't think twice about paying André Agassi, Joe Montana, and the other jock restaurateurs $7.50 for a cheeseburger and $18 for a T-shirt. Blame it on the booming stock market.

"Megabucks Slots Bursting at Seams as Record Jackpot Continues to Grow," read the only headline in the paper to catch my eye. This was just what the doctor ordered. "For the uninitiated," the article offered helpfully, "Megabucks is a series of linked, progressive slot machines whose jackpots begin at $5 million." Statewide, 129 casinos each have a few Megabucks slot machines, provided by a company called International Game Technologies. In the past, the average length of time between jackpots had been roughly six weeks, but now more than eight months had gone by without a winner. The jackpot was approaching $15 million. "It's way overdue," an IGT spokesman enthused to the *Review-Journal*. It was now past seven, which meant this article must have been written at least twenty-four hours ago. Megabucks could be long gone by now.

My editor would never forgive me. "Martinez, you're telling me you could have won fifteen million—you know how many books that triumph alone would sell?—but instead were eating some over-priced burger cooked up by a bunch of jocks?" I shuddered. That could torpedo my plans for a sequel: a lavish around-the-world cruise.

♣ ♦ ♥ ♠ Back at Luxor I found a row of the pregnant Megabucks machines. To my immense relief, a digital ticker, of the kind concerned citizens put up to keep tabs on the mounting national debt, showed the jackpot closing in on the $15 million mark. To win the jackpot, I knew from the article, you had to play $3 a pull. If you played only $2 and the three Megabucks eagles popped up, you'd win only $10,000 instead of the $15 million. And you'd probably need more than that to cover the ensuing therapy bills.

I fed the machine a crisp $100 bill, which, considering how hard it is to force a single buck down most vending machines' throats, it digested with frightening ease. I then inserted my Gold Chamber card, and a "Good luck, Andrés" message scrawled across the machine's readout. This, too, was frightening. On my first "pull"—you can actually just press a button these days—I hit some cherries, which meant I'd doubled my three bucks. Only 6 cents of each dollar played goes to the progressive jackpot. About 86 cents goes to these smaller payouts.

It was all downhill from there. Eyes glazing over, I kept pressing the $3 bet button. Every so often an eagle would land teasingly close to the winning line, but the most I ever won was $15 a pop. I was disappointed when the tokens didn't cascade onto the metal tray. No, in this electronic age, your winnings are added to your credits, so you can keep playing them without ever seeing them. To get paid you have to take the additional step of pressing another button. Then, of course, you'd have to take the tokens to a change booth. You may efficiently feed money into these machines, but, as far as I can tell, odds and logistics conspire to keep you from ever seeing any of it again. Signs everywhere bragged that Luxor machines pay back 98.4 percent of all monies put in, but I quickly lost 100 percent of my $100. I hate slots, I muttered, regardless of the payoff. There is no human factor involved.

Ten minutes later I sat down at a blackjack table, only to realize that I'd left my card in the Megabucks machine. This is why a lot of older folks around town carry their frequent-gambler cards on plastic leashes. Walk around any casino and you see presumably serious folks back in Ohio attached to machines by a plastic umbilical cord.

I found a bride playing "my" machine, racking up points on my card. Talk about a sight. She wore an extravagant white dress with all the bells and whistles, a long train even, and a glum expression. She looked absolutely ridiculous, dressed for a fairy tale but engaged in battle with the faceless International Game Technologies company. She seemed to be alone. The smoke enveloping her from a neighboring gambler's cigar made her look even more pathetic, and her headpiece was beginning to tilt alarmingly to the right. Most worrisome, she was only feeding the machine $1 at a time.

"You know," I said in my raspy casino voice, "you won't get the millions by playing a single dollar at a time." She turned to look at me, her big brown eyes swollen from crying. "I just got married less than two hours ago, and you expect me to give a flying fuck about winning or losing at this machine?" she asked me, in a surprisingly sweet southern accent. I'd never before heard a woman from the South—Texas yes, but not the Deep South—say "flying fuck." It was kind of sexy.

She said her new husband—in fact, the entire wedding party—was "way too into craps," and gestured toward a game of that charming name, where four young guys in tuxedoes and three women in slinky bridesmaid dresses did indeed seem to be having a blast. They all had the healthy glow and good looks of a Ralph Lauren ad. I couldn't tell which gentleman was the groom, but none of them seemed troubled by the lack of a bride.

"It's not like we didn't gamble all day *before* the wedding," the lonely bride wailed. "I just came over to pout, but it doesn't seem to be working," she added, a tear streaming down her rosy cheek. I then graciously offered to take her and some of her friends to Ra later if her husband was still gambling. "I can cut the line," I told her after a dramatic pause. But I don't think she knew what the hell Ra was, because she looked at me like I was some kind of pervert and beat a hasty retreat.

♣ ♦ ♥ ♠   What most surprised me about blackjack, by far the most popular table game in American casinos, is the ease with which it brings players into the fold. The game has a well-developed liturgy to it, built around Basic Strategy, a road map developed by a generation of the nation's most brilliant mathematicians indicating the "correct" decision for all scenarios. Have a 13 and the dealer shows a 4? B.S. tells you to stay. A 13 and the dealer shows a 7? Hit! You can buy a laminated B.S. chart at any casino gift shop. I know this because two women from Chicago at the table actually consulted their cards before making their decisions. They kept giggling about it, as if they were getting away with something. But the casino doesn't care, so long as you aren't counting cards. B.S. does lessen the casino's edge (because you know what you are doing), but it doesn't take it away. In fact, when asked, dealers are always happy to clue patrons in on what "the book" says before they make their decision.

Leave it to Americans to reduce gambling to such a regulated exercise, downplaying the role of guile or intuition. It's amazing how few people who've played for more than an hour dare stray from B.S. And those who dare to disregard the scripture and—gasp—gamble do so at their own peril. Like their Puritan ancestors at Salem, blackjack players are notorious for pouncing on heretics who deviate. Typically this happens when someone takes a card they "shouldn't have" and that card would have busted the dealer. Of course no heretic gets patted on the back when an unscripted move helps rather than hurts the table; it's still messing with fate.

♣ ♦ ♥ ♠ Dozens of brides paraded about the casino, usually with their smiling grooms in tow. Our pit boss tonight was a Sharon Stone look-alike named Juli, from South Dakota, the first in a long procession of Dakotans I'd meet in Las Vegas. (I became convinced that the only flight out of either Dakota is to this desert oasis.) Juli told me that on one incredible Saturday night not long ago she managed to have an all-bride blackjack table. She beamed at the memory, as if recalling a royal flush on a video poker machine. Picture, she said, seven brides in varying degrees of baroque white sitting side by side, their grooms standing attentively behind. Then she broke into a throaty laugh: "I had to walk up to them and ask exactly what part of the whole 'wedding night' concept didn't they understand."

I counted my chips at midnight, and was pleasantly surprised to discover that I was ahead a couple of grand for the session. The nest egg was once again in the black. So I called it a night and dropped off my fistfuls of chips and cash in my safe deposit box.

Twenty minutes later, my sense of triumph at finding my room soon crumbled upon realizing I'd locked myself out. These things happen in Vegas, what with all the sensory overload. Security swung by some twenty minutes later to let me in. On the floor was a friendly letter from the hotel's manager to deprive me of another hour of my life. It was a reminder that tonight the nation sprang forward an hour. Did we really have to do this in Las Vegas?

Nest egg: $50,315

Sunday, April 5

And on the Sabbath I met Bob Miner, casino host. Decked out in a suit, Bob pumped my hand amicably and offered me a seat in his office. I felt as if I were in a small-town bank, seeking a loan. Not sure about the protocol, I handed over my Gold Chamber card and mumbled something about wanting to find out if I was entitled to a break on my bill. With a noncommittal expression, Bob punched in my account number on his keyboard. Then, as I saw the reflection of glowing green figures appear on his eyeglasses, Bob's jaw literally dropped a bit. A tiny bit.

"You've been busy," he said admiringly.

I began to blush, pride rearing its ugly head, and then stammered: "Well, I, um . . ." What was there to say? I'd done good.

Based on the input of all the pit bosses who had "rated" my play, Bob's computer indicated that I'd gambled for 16 hours and 45 minutes, at an average bet of $252.00. *Geez, that's scary,* I thought, but tried my best to look calm and collected.

"How did you set up your visit?"

"Well, I called up the reservation number," I replied, confused.

"Next time call me," he said, offering his card, "and I'll take care of you, send a limo to pick you up at the airport, put you up in a nice suite, and all that." Wow. Too bad a next time wasn't in the cards. This trip, he added, I'd naturally be RFB'ed.

"RFB'ed?"

"That means you'll get your room, food, and beverages comped for your entire stay. You'll just need to pay incidentals: phone calls, tips, that sort of thing."

Comped. It's such a sweet term.

While I wasn't one of the whales—the highest of high rollers, who can lose a million dollars in a night and not break a sweat—it was dawning on me that I *was* something of a barracuda. At the Luxor, Bob explained, players (he would never dream of calling us gamblers) who average $50 a hand for four hours a day get a special "casino rate" on rooms; $100 an average bet will get you a free room, and $150, the coveted RFB status. I'd clearly done good, real good.

I'd always imagined that casinos dole out freebies to big losers as a form of mercy, but that's not the case. Comps depend on what casinos expect gamblers to lose, as a statistical matter, not on actual results. Casinos typically comp people about 30 percent of the amount they "should have" lost.

Roughly speaking, if you bet $250 a hand at blackjack for four hours, the casino figures you are entitled to some $800 worth of goodies. That's assuming that the casino has an edge of 2 percent in the game and that you play two hands a minute. At that rate you'd wager a total of $120,000, of which you should theoretically lose $2,400, a third of which you get comped.

Before sending me back out into the casino, Bob handed me a "line pass" stamped "VIP," good for the rest of my stay. With this I would never have to stand in another line, he promised. Within a half-hour I was using the nifty safe-conduct to cut the long line at the Pyramid Café, but I wasn't too proud of myself. It had felt great, in a revenge-of-the-nerds way, to be waved into Ra on Friday night, ahead of posing couples. Being spirited past families into a coffee shop just made me feel obnoxious.

I had an early dinner at the Coyote Café at the MGM Grand Hotel. The spicy grilled ahi tuna "with green polenta, red pepper, aioli sauce, and blackened tomato-chipotle sauce and cucumber tomato pico" is, in a word, orgasmic. I'd been to the original Coyote

Café in Santa Fe a few years back, and had happily read that proprietor Mark Miller was among the first of a growing number of renowned chefs across the country to open up a restaurant in Las Vegas. The branch grosses three times as much as the original.

Wolfgang Puck has also cloned his trendy L.A. eateries Spago and Chinois in Vegas, at the Forum Shops at Caesars Palace. Back at the MGM, down the hallway from the Coyote Café, TV personality Emeril Lagasse opened another Emeril's New Orleans Fish House. New York's Smith & Wollensky plans to open a huge steakhouse next door to the MGM. Perhaps most shocking to East Coast gourmands was the Rio Hotel's success in luring Washington's reigning chef, Jean-Louis Palladin, to this buffet capital of the world, where he opened the acclaimed restaurant Napa. The Frenchman is reportedly suffering some culture shock. He recently told *The New York Times* that in Las Vegas, "the money's real, but everything else is fake."

♣ ♦ ♥ ♠ Back at Luxor, I went to my safe deposit box, grabbed five grand (by then I had one of those nifty wrapped bricks of C-notes), and wandered over to a roulette table. There is a certain elegance about this game that is absent in the grubby world of blackjack. It requires far less effort, for one thing. You simply plop down chips on your favorite numbers or, less elegantly, on red or black, and watch the tiny silver ball do the work. Depending on the dealer's outlook on life, the ball will spin madly or softly around the rim of the beautiful wooden wheel, before rattling tantalizingly in and out of the numbered grooves and settling down to proclaim a winner.

Over time, you have no realistic hope of winning. That's part of what makes the game elegant. Unlike blackjack, which dares you to win, roulette is about unburdening yourself of insignificant sums in an entertaining and far-fetched attempt to round them up to a figure worth cashing in and carrying out the door. For those who fret about such things, the house edge at roulette is a daunting 5.26 percent. That edge is the difference between the game's true odds and what the casino actually pays out: there are 38 numbers on the wheel, but if yours comes up, you only get paid 35 to 1.

I'd concocted a little experiment, hereafter referred to as the "DE," or Dopey Experiment. Here's what I'd do: Instead of spreading my largesse around the table, I'd pick one number and stick to it. I'd be true to 22, my wife's birthday. For thirty-five spins. So, if it hit once, I'd at least break even. The earlier it hit, the less stressful the exercise. I'd seen numbers repeat or appear three times out of ten. If 22 never showed up, I'd be out $3,500. But this was the perfect table for my DE: number 22 had not hit in more than fifteen spins.

Ludo would be terribly disappointed in me for falling prey to "the gambler's fallacy," the mistaken belief that the law of large numbers applies also to small numbers. I can't remember his last name, but Ludo—an energetic Dutchman who roamed the campus in a motorcycle and strutted into class wearing his leather jacket—taught the probability and statistics course I took in college because my brother, Roberto, assured me it would be an easy way to meet some distribution requirement I needed. It seemed Yale wanted history majors to have a passing acquaintance with numbers. To this day, I still break out in hives upon hearing the term "standard deviation," and have not forgiven Ro, who as a computer science major should have abstained from opining on what I'd find easy. But enough about family love.

Toss a coin ten times and you are more likely to end up with five heads and five tails than you are to end up with ten straight heads. Right? Wrong; that's the gambler's fallacy. Those ten coin flips are independent events, and do not reflect whatever force tends in the very long run to even things out. That's why casinos are glad to post the numbers at roulette tables and provide players with scorecards; the past is irrelevant. On the other hand, try jotting down notes on what's going on at a blackjack table, as I naively did the first night, and you'll be politely asked to stop. Blackjack hands are not independent events. As aspiring card counters the world over will tell you, the past in blackjack does matter. But more on that later.

So I bought my stack of $100 chips and settled down. At a busy table, thirty-five spins can take a while. Juli, the foxy pit boss, came over with a perplexed "What's he up to now?" look on her face. She remembered my name without needing to see my card, which was surprisingly gratifying.

Five spins went by; I'd lost $500, but I wasn't sweating. I had thirty more spins and—sorry, Ludo—22 was bound to come up. The whole process was rather civilized, relaxing even. While the other players at the table shoved stacks of dollar chips every which way, keeping track of all sorts of numbers and corners, I simply plopped down one chip after each spin, and sat back to enjoy my Diet Coke and the scenery. People soon started topping off 22 with chips of their own. This happens a lot in a casino. If you act possessed enough, other gamblers will buy into it and hedge their own bets by piling on. That makes you The Man.

I explained to Juli that I should be rewarded for my selflessness. I was playing my wife's birthday, not my own. But casinos aren't really in the business of rewarding thoughtfulness. The cruel ball graced my birthday, lucky 13, not once, not twice, but three times. On the twelfth, fifteenth, and, ironically, twenty-second spins. That would have meant a $7,000 profit for my narcissistic twin brother.

By the thirtieth spin, I was no longer relaxed. Every number I'd ever fancied had hit but 22. This was beginning to seem like a pretty stupid way of blowing my hard-earned blackjack money. That's about when I christened this whole endeavor "the Dopey Experiment." It seemed hopeless. I started breaking my own rules, plopping the occasional chip on 13. My playmates, seeing me rattled, abandoned 22 in droves. They figured whatever inner voice had urged me on was now saying "Never mind, false alarm."

Then it hit. On the thirty-second spin the wheel slowed down to reveal the ball comfortably nestled in the domicile of gorgeous, graceful, symmetrical 22, black. I would have screamed, but I had no voice. I would have hugged Juli, but I'd probably have been violating some Gaming Commission regulation. So all I could do was sit there and grin stupidly at the kind folks around me who'd all lost faith in the most majestic of numbers. Passersby gawked at my huge win, unaware of the history.

If 22 had hit the last three spins, this tale would soon be coming to a movie theater near you. No such luck. I walked away from the table with a $400 loss (those cowardly bets on 13 toward the end) and a sense of relief. As I left to go up to my room, Juli told me to come back down, if I couldn't sleep. "We'll still be here," she purred. Just what I needed to hear.

Nest egg: $49,365

2

THE DESERT INN

The Strip is supposed to be synonymous with a good looking female all dressed up in a very expensive diamond studded evening gown and driving up to a multi-million dollar hotel in a Rolls-Royce.

—Howard Hughes, memo to an aide

Monday, April 6

♣ ♦ ♥ ♠ In November 1935, Union Pacific ferried five thousand southern California Shriners to Las Vegas. It was the town's first major convention. Local schoolchildren should parade down the Strip and commemorate the occasion each year, the way Soviet youth used to do May Day.

If the United States is truly a shining city on the hill, Las Vegas has become its proverbial town hall. In 1997, 3.5 million conventioneers came through—more than anywhere else—netting the local economy an estimated $4.4 billion. That this pariah in the middle of nowhere has become the nation's prime meeting spot is Las Vegas's most remarkable accomplishment, and its greatest strength going forward. Conventions are the Holy Grail of the tourism industry, unleashing hordes of expense accounts on a city's hotels, restaurants, and topless joints. Speak to friends and neighbors who work in any number of industries—whether they sell consumer electronics, design shopping malls, develop software, or manufacture women's shoes—and they will probably tell you Las Vegas is where their key gatherings take place.

It is Las Vegas's very eccentricity that makes it an ideally neutral meeting place, a sort of Geneva for commerce. If people come together in Los Angeles or New York, it's alien territory to some, home turf to others. But Las Vegas is universally alien in more than geographic ways, and that gives conventions here a special, adventurous flair. That's one reason the National Association of Broadcasters stopped moving its conventions around in the late 1980s and decided to meet here every year. On a more practical note, few cities can handle a convention as large as that of the NAB, which this year brought together 104,805 attendees. Las Vegas has far more hotel rooms than anyplace else, and 4.2 million square feet of convention space.

♣ ♦ ♥ ♠ Even in Las Vegas such massive conventions prove disruptive, as I discovered trying to get a cab on the first morning of the broadcasters' gathering. I'd woken up early, eager to get out and engage in some meaty reporting, to do something besides gamble. I was happy to see, when I checked out, that Bob had indeed picked up my room and meals, even my cigar. I didn't know whether to be amused or irritated at being charged for local and toll-free phone calls. Being required to pay for these is among my biggest travel peeves.

Seeing the endless line for cabs, I panicked back into the VIP lounge, scooped up a chocolate-covered strawberry, and demanded a limo on the spot. Bob had earlier offered to set me up with one to take me to the airport, but I'd declined, not wanting to get into the fact that I'd actually be moving on to another hotel. On second thought, I didn't much care what Bob thought.

There was no limo to be had: the entire fleet was ferrying people about already. But the solicitous woman sitting behind the counter, after checking on the computer to see "what kind of a player" I was, asked if I minded being taken in a "staff car." And so, Abel, a bellhop, drove me to the Desert Inn in one of those nondescript but comfortable institutional cars, a Crown Victoria or something. Abel is a nice kid, working full-time while studying at the university.

He'd lived in Las Vegas his whole life. I asked whether he gambled. "Not so much anymore," he told me. Anymore? He couldn't have been much older than twenty-one. And you must be twenty-one to gamble. Right? Apparently, certain downtown casinos were mellow about such things, and Abel and some buddies from Las Vegas High used to slip in after school. State regulators have been trying to crack down on underage gambling in recent years, particularly after newspaper polls revealed several years ago that 52 percent of local high school students said they had gambled, mostly in casinos. They said it was easier than buying alcohol. In fact, it was the easiest way to get beer. Free beer, no less.

"But I now use direct deposit," Abel told me in a more solemn tone as we headed north on I-15, bypassing the Strip traffic. This was an interesting insight into Abel's banking practices, but I thought it an odd non sequitur. It wasn't. He explained that a lot of his buddies cash their paychecks at casinos. Casinos that cater to locals compete fiercely for this business, with each offering paycheck-cashing prizes and bonuses. The whole thing is kind of scary, and Abel wouldn't be the last resident who'd reverentially bring up direct deposit as some therapeutic watershed in his life.

♣ ♦ ♥ ♠ Walking into the Desert Inn Sheraton, which recently underwent a $200 million renovation, was a soothing experience. The seven-story vaulted lobby was all marble; the casino was nowhere in sight, and the hotel's only theme seemed to be "elegant Mediterranean resort." I think even my Vegas-loathing mother-in-law would like this place. The DI would qualify as a large hotel in most cities, but after the Luxor, which has six times as many rooms, it had the intimate feel of a boutique hotel.

My plush room in the main tower had a view of the pool and golf course. It didn't take long to realize this would be a tough stay, involving tough choices. I had two sinks and three phones at my command. The toiletries, I noticed, were stamped with one of those royal seals that indicate they had been concocted "by appointment" to some majesty, a cool concept I've always fallen for if never quite understood. I made a mental note to swipe them daily for Kat. After all, the room was setting me back $285 a night.

I picked up one of the three phones and called Citibank's toll-free number to report the loss of my credit card (something else I'd accomplished at Luxor). I felt sheepish asking to have a new card sent to me at a Las Vegas hotel, of all places. But instead of forwarding my call to the fraud department, the voice on the other end told me she, too, was in Las Vegas.

Citibank is one of Las Vegas's prized trophies in the uphill battle to diversify the local economy. To lure one of the New York giant's credit card processing centers, which now employs 1,700 people here, Nevada's legislature in 1984 passed a law allowing out-of-state banks to establish a Nevada subsidiary. And because Citibank felt queasy about the notoriety of its new address—would customers appreciate sending their hard-earned money off to what comedians have long called the city of Lost Wages?—the bank was allowed to call its parcel of land The Lakes, Nevada. I wonder if this geographic subterfuge would have been deemed necessary nowadays, Las Vegas having come such a long way in the past dozen years.

Citibank is not alone. Williams Sonoma and other companies also find Las Vegas an ideal location for call centers, and not just because of the low cost of living and welcoming tax climate. What makes this city ideal for an around-the-clock operation is its 24/7 casino-inspired culture. Residents don't think twice about being asked to work night shifts. Go off the Strip and ask a bartender, a grocery store manager, or a fitness club attendant what time their business closes, and they will look offended. "We're here twenty-four-seven," they'll respond—as in twenty-four hours a day, seven days a week. I find this all deeply appealing. I have never shopped for groceries at three in the morning, lifted weights at four, or driven to a friendly neighborhood bar at five, I must confess, but I'd find it comforting to know I could, if I wanted. Even when I was a child, those "Always Open" signs at Denny's invariably made me smile.

This 24/7 world has its own alluring language. People work either daytime, "swing," or "graveyard" shifts. At most casinos, daytime means noon to eight, swing is eight to four, and graveyard is four to noon. The swing shift is a casino's busiest, and the nightly migration of dealers and cocktail waitresses from the Strip back home (or to the neighborhood tavern or health club) makes Las Vegas's roads some of the most congested anywhere at four in the morning.

After being assured by Citibank that a replacement Visa would be overnighted to me at the DI, I dropped off my nest egg—nearly $10,000 in cash and $40,000 in traveler's checks—in a safe deposit box and rushed off to the Mirage, where I would meet my friend Kyle Pope and attend an NBC press conference. Kyle, bright in an endearingly aw-shucks, let's-not-talk-about-it way, covers television for *The Wall Street Journal.* He's a veteran of these broadcasting industry get-togethers, and he'd offered to let me tag along with him as much as I wanted.

The Mirage lobby was a sea of frantic activity; thousands of name tags milled about, doing what conventioneers do—schmoozing, checking schedules, calling the office, plotting their escape to the golf course, wondering if they could still get a dinner reservation at a decent restaurant. But they all looked appropriately earnest, carrying around the official program with its daunting schedule of events and list of 1,300 exhibitors.

It was funny. I'd last seen Kyle on my final day of work at the *Journal,* a little over a month earlier. Back then, I'd been a serious writer, filled with gravitas. But now, when Kyle walked up to me and asked what was new, I wasn't sure what to say. What *was* new? Commenting on the news of the day—my buddies at Citibank announced they were merging with Travelers Group in the largest corporate deal ever—would have been safe. That's what *Journal* types presumably talk about. But what I really wanted to tell him was that that damned 22 had only come up once, that I'd learned never to double down on a 9, and above all, that I'd been RFB'ed.

In the end, I opted for "Nothing much."

Hordes of reporters are sent to these conventions, Kyle told me as we made our way to the ballroom, past the tropical rain forest and casino, but there usually isn't any real news. "Consequently," Kyle continued, as if narrating a *National Geographic* special on an exotic predator of the Serengeti, "the pack runs around in a panic, as it begins to set in that they are going to have a hard time justifying their expense accounts."

NBC announced at its press conference that it remained a true believer in high-definition digital TV, with all the bells and whistles. What the long-hyped transition to the era of digital broadcasting means, in lay terms, is that you will soon be able to count the pores on Jay Leno's nose. The NBC brass present proudly showed a portion of a recent *Tonight Show* monologue on a giant screen. There was Jay, telling us he'd read that Americans have more sex partners than any other nationality, and wondering if we shouldn't change the national emblem from the bald eagle to the spread eagle. Just another night on *The Tonight Show,* powered by Kevin Eubanks's infectious laughter in the background. But things were different, shockingly clearer. It was as if someone had wiped an inch of grime from your old TV set, the picture was that much sharper.

When I mentioned to Neil Braun, president of the NBC television network, that I was writing a book on Las Vegas, he raised his eyebrows and said: "I hope you have plenty of life insurance." That's precisely the sort of remark that must drive local tourism authorities batty, though maybe it shouldn't. The lingering belief that the Mob still rules Las Vegas is one of the city's perverse draws; L.A. types especially seem to revel in the idea that there is something seedy about this oasis. Soon, I'm convinced, Las Vegas will manage in one stroke to parody this fantasy, cater to it, and make peace with its past by building a gangster-themed resort, complete with speakeasies, creepy wharves, annoying Feds snooping about, and fantastic Italian restaurants. Naturally, the place will be so safe, you won't have to lock your room.

Although none of the city's slate of coming resorts has been quite so imaginative, Las Vegans are willing to embrace their town's dubious past. In June 1999, long after my odyssey, the notorious Mob lawyer Oscar Goodman, who played himself in Martin Scorsese's *Casino,* was elected mayor of Las Vegas, much to the horror of the town's establishment. A political novice, Goodman energized voters with his candor and humor. He is bright and was never accused of wrongdoing. Still, civic boosters were not amused. Just as the town had nearly succeeded in rehabilitating Sin City's reputation, its quirky citizens, as if on a lark, turned to Tony "the Ant" Spilotro's attorney to lead them into the next century. I for one think it's a healthy sign. In the old days, a shady industry needed a façade of respectable politicians. Now, a squeaky clean corporate culture requires a façade of colorful politicians. *A hint of spice.*

From the Mirage I walked over to the Sands Convention Center. I was greeted by a phalanx of beauties dressed as gondoliers who walked me through a model suite of the Venetian Hotel, which would become the world's largest when it opened in the spring of 1999, on the site previously occupied by the beloved Sands. Checking out the suite was like watching a three-dimensional movie preview. *And golly, the minibar will be right here!*

The Venetian will be a veritable faux city within a faux city, with its own renditions of the Doges' Palace, the Campanile, the Rialto Bridge, St. Mark's Square and—I kid you not—what its overheated PR engine claims will be "authentic canals." Real Venetian artisans, presumably unemployed since the Renaissance peaked, are involved in the project. Strewn about this scenery will be the requisite mall, an outpost of the posh Canyon Ranch spa, and legions of big-time restaurants, not to mention the Sands Convention Center next door.

The developer of the $1.2 billion resort is Sheldon Adelson, one of Las Vegas's more colorful tycoons. The first thing setting Adelson apart from the town's other hoteliers is that he is not a casino guy. Hence the significance of the minibar. In the traditional "casino-centric" Vegas hotel room, Adelson is fond of saying with a sneer, you don't find minibars because guests who get thirsty in the middle of the night are expected to stagger down to the casino with their bulging money clip.

The Venetian will have its plush casino, to be sure, but Adelson knows that Las Vegas's future as a permanent World's Fair transcends gambling. He should know. Back when Vegas's casino bosses still scoffed at conventioneers as undesirable low rollers, Adelson, son of a Boston cabdriver, realized the valley's full potential as a corporate marketplace. He developed the gigantic Comdex computer convention, which unleashes upwards of 200,000 attendees on an exasperated Vegas each November, then sold the business for $800 million to a Japanese conglomerate a few years ago.

Adelson considers unions another burdensome relic of the old Las Vegas, so the Venetian will not be part of the great Culinary Union family. Not one to mince words, Adelson recently told a group of Wall Street analysts that if Las Vegas doesn't start standing up to the union bosses, "we can kiss all the brand-name restaurants good-bye and I'll meet you at the next $1.99 buffet line." The Culinary Union is retaliating in kind, saying all sorts of mean things about Venice—"Those canals are really a sewer"; "Everyone knows Florence kicked Venice's ass as a cultural center"; that sort of thing. The looming battle between the two sides will be on the sidewalk, or rather *over* the property's sidewalk. The Venetian claims the new walkway it is building on the Strip is not a public sidewalk but rather part of the resort, and, therefore, private property. Nonsense, retorts the union, eager to heckle the union-buster. This is part of a larger battle across town involving the privatization of public space; stay tuned.

♣ ♦ ♥ ♠ After checking out the Venetian model suite, one tangible good I could understand, I walked around the convention center admiring row upon row of mystifying gadgets. You had your seamless switchers; your video kiosks; your frame synchronizers; your median noise reducers; and your MPEG-2 encoders, all claiming to be "mission-critical," though I couldn't tell you for the life of me what any one of them does. Less baffling were the news vans on display in the parking lot. A Des Moines station manager and I checked out what we were told was the "absolute latest in mobile newsgathering technology," a snazzy van already painted with the insignia of some fictitious (I presumed) L.A. station. The earnest man from Iowa asked about the rooftop satellite antenna's specs; I looked for cup holders.

At a symposium of network executives decrying the decline of their industry, Fox TV president Larry Jacobson told me broadcasters convene in Las Vegas because it's a larger-than-life, stimulating setting: "We are an industry that deals in illusions, that tells stories, so it is fitting that we convene in a mythical mirage." Over the years, Jacobson continued, people in the industry have come to associate Las Vegas with breakthroughs, the place where they were first exposed to new technologies, concepts, and people.

♣ ♦ ♥ ♠ Back at the DI, I turned on the TV and watched the casino's instructional video. "Blackjack is as easy as 1-2-3," went one of the jingles. Starring Suzanne Somers wearing a ridiculous skin-tight neon dress likely to prompt lucrative offers of employment from male high rollers, this gem destroyed my illusion that the classy DI was immune to Vegas tackiness.

On the local NBC affiliate, anchorwoman Rikki Cheese put an end to my channel surfing: "Coming up, find out how one family was ruined by video poker; but first, good news for women worried about breast cancer." There followed a commercial—a bit ill-timed—for a local casino's "Paycheck Bonanza" promotion. The video poker tragedy—an infant died when left for hours in a stifling car at a casino parking lot—occurred in Mississippi, one of the states Las Vegas's gambling establishment patronizingly calls "emerging markets." The story would be the focus of that night's *Dateline*.

I tore myself away from the TV and crossed the Strip to the up-scale Fashion Show Mall. Kyle and I had agreed to meet at Dive!, a restaurant with a Jules Verne theme and a celebrity co-owner,

Steven Spielberg. Kyle brought along one of his pals from NBC, who claimed, even after a couple of beers, not to know what would transpire on the final *Seinfeld* episode. Rather than talk programming, Mr. NBC griped about his demanding bosses. Ah, the long-forgotten perils of a real job. I was feeling pretty good about life as I walked back to the DI in the crisp desert evening. The sky was a bewildering collage of reds; the mountains had turned blue. I felt that rare exuberance that comes with total freedom.

♣ ♦ ♥ ♠ The Desert Inn is one of Las Vegas's storied landmarks. It opened in 1950, the brainchild of a Reno craps dealer named Wilbur Clark. Clark envisioned an elegant casino resort modeled after those in Palm Springs—a country club with a casino. But Clark's imagination was more expansive than his pocketbook, so he turned to a group of Midwestern investors to help him build his dream. The Desert Inn ended up costing $4.5 million, with Clark retaining a 25 percent share in the property.

In Las Vegas lore, "Midwestern investors" is code for mobsters. In this case, the kind of mobsters old-timers remember fondly. While Bugsy Siegel was a thug with few redeeming qualities—he was a dapper dresser, by all accounts—Moe Dalitz would become a beloved pillar of the community. Dalitz, the reputed boss of the Cleveland Cosa Nostra, had been a notorious Prohibition bootlegger and casino owner in Kentucky. A close friend of Jimmy Hoffa, Dalitz had a great deal of say in how the Teamsters invested their pension fund around town, an investment that, all told, is estimated to have exceeded $230 million. Among projects credited to Dalitz is the obtaining of union financing for Sunrise Hospital, when such a facility was desperately needed.

On Thanksgiving Day, 1966, the reclusive Howard Hughes checked into the DI, one of the pivotal events in Las Vegas history. Dalitz agreed to rent out the top two floors to the magnate's entourage, assuming he'd be long gone before New Year's, when he'd need those suites for the casino's high rollers. But Hughes, fond of

Vegas since his Hollywood playboy days, was in no rush to leave. He'd already acquired 25,000 barren acres in the northwest corner of the valley and was determined to build a new empire in Las Vegas. And having sold his 78 percent stake in TWA for $546 million earlier that year, Hughes had an enviable—and unfathomable for his day—bankroll.

The more Dalitz pestered Hughes to leave, the more powerful Hughes allies in town pressed Dalitz to desist. Savvy community leaders such as *Las Vegas Sun* editor Bud Greenspun realized that, whatever his personal eccentricities, the legendary aviator, movie producer, and industrialist Howard Hughes was the type of above-board investor Las Vegas needed to overcome its pariah status and become as respectable in corporate circles as it was in union circles.

Tiring of Dalitz's whining that his high-roller suites were being taken up by a nongambler, Hughes offered to buy the damned place. He paid $13.2 million and took possession of the hotel on April Fool's Day, 1967. Reflecting the local establishment's glee at Hughes's arrival, the Nevada Gaming Control Board unanimously voted to grant him a gaming license even before he could submit the necessary paperwork or appear before the board. "Hughes's life and background are well known to this board," said board chairman Alan Abner, explaining the unprecedented haste.

Hughes considered Nevada a backward desert kingdom in need of his enlightened rule. In addition to casinos, he bought a TV station and became a behind-the-scenes political force. He did all this while locked up at the DI, where he would remain ensconced like a hermit through 1970. Because he wouldn't allow maids to clean his suite, it wasn't until after he'd left that sealed jars filled with his urine were found in the closet.

Because he was such a fascinating figure in so many ways, one of the most significant aspects of the Howard Hughes saga in Las Vegas usually goes unmentioned. Like Sheldon Adelson but in contrast to most of Las Vegas's other colorful builders, Hughes was not particularly interested in gambling (which made it easy for wiseguys entrenched in the count room to continue their skimming). The once-dashing Hollywood producer and fearless aviator, who'd traveled so far in life from his father's sober tool company in Texas, was drawn to Las Vegas for reasons that transcended the green felt. Hughes hoped the city would become the West Coast's hub for supersonic jets and the world's capital of aviation. He tried luring Boeing away from Seattle to his vast landholding northwest of the city. (The core of that acreage is now Summerlin, the nation's largest master-planned residential community, named after Howard's grandmother.) The dreamer's most ambitious dreams for the city might not have materialized, but he was alert to Las Vegas's potential in a way that few gambling aficionados could be, and chances are the eccentric billionaire wouldn't be surprised by the city's current transformation into a permanent World's Fair.

The Nevada legislature passed the Corporate Gaming Act while Hughes was still in town, another crucial step in Las Vegas's journey to respectability. The law made it possible for corporations to obtain gaming licenses without having every stockholder's background investigated, as had previously been required. From today's vantage point, it is puzzling that such zealous reformers as Governor Grant Sawyer opposed this legislation throughout much of the 1960s, fearing it would make it easier for undesirable elements to control casinos. What it did, of course, was open the door to the Hiltons and other public corporations to come to town, and build on a scale that would soon dwarf anything "Midwestern investors" could finance. The new law didn't affect Hughes, as he was his company's sole shareholder, but his involvement in Las Vegas did make corporate America more willing to invest in the city.

♣ ♦ ♥ ♠ The DI's intimate, renovated casino exudes country-clubbish elegance. The high domed ceilings, hand-painted in royal blue and gold leaf, charmingly depict stars bursting across a night sky; in the sports book, where you can bet on any horse race or professional sport under the sun, the chairs are of sumptuous leather. Stunning crystal chandeliers hang above. Everything is new, but the musty tone set by the casino staff recalls a grittier time. It didn't take long for a pit boss to call me "Mr. M.," which made me feel pretty cool, like an appreciated fixture. Most of the dealers and cocktail waitresses in the casino looked as though they'd been at it since at least the Hughes era. No nubile waitresses here; these were matronly women who call you "hon." One with classic cone-shaped hair told me she put her two children through college serving drinks at the DI. "It's a nice living, hon."

DI dealers, the best paid in town, have more personality than their counterparts elsewhere; having moved here in the days when Las Vegas was known more for its action than for its jobs, they've been around too long to hide behind a corporate mask. One welcomed me at his table by announcing that "fresh meat" had arrived. He peered at everyone contemptuously through the bifocals perched a good way down his nose. He called my neighbor a wuss for not doubling down on an 11, a comment that undoubtedly would have violated some corporate policy over at Luxor.

The ornery dealer told us he'd moved to Las Vegas with his girlfriend a quarter-century ago, armed with a trust fund. All he did his first couple of years in town was gamble and treat his body in such a way, he boasted, as to prevent old age. Even now, he goes on gambling binges that take days to recover from. Lucky for him, his inheritance was to be paid out in three installments and the third one, "the one I'll keep," is due soon.

By midnight, I had lost $10,000. I can't tell you exactly how it happened; it was a gradual free fall, with nothing spectacular about it. I just kept losing and chasing. Chasing and losing. But I still could laugh. Out of the blue, riding the elevator up to my room, I remembered that it was at the DI where in one night Julie Hagerty lost her and husband Albert Brooks's six-figure "nest egg" in *Lost in America,* the hilarious 1985 movie in which a yuppie couple leaves the rat race of Los Angeles to "touch Indians" and find themselves. (*Easy Rider,* but in a Winnebago.) Brooks, a former advertising executive, then proposes to the casino manager that he return the couple's money—they just made a mistake, after all, they're not really gamblers—and advertise the fact on billboards, in the "boldest experiment in advertising history." Let's face it, he tells the DI man, "Vegas is not associated with feelings," and goes on to sing a jingle for the campaign, along the lines of "The Desert Inn has heart."

"Won't everyone ask for their money back?" asks the casino manager.

"No, we make a clear distinction between the bold—that's us—and all the schmucks who come to watch Wayne Newton," Brooks says.

"But I like Wayne Newton."

Remarkably, they were still RFB'ed.

Nest egg: $39,365

Tuesday, April 7

I woke up mad as hell, and I wasn't going to take it anymore. I'm not proud of it, but I stormed into the empty casino by 8:30, intent on winning my money back. This time, I didn't chat with the dealers or admire the chandeliers. I just ordered a coffee at a blackjack table, bought in $5,000, and started piling up those black chips.

It went badly; we seemed to have picked up where we'd left off the previous night. I was determined to make a press conference at ten, so I played at a furious pace. Before nine, I was down to $600. I boldly put it all out on the table, playing two $300 hands. As luck would have it, I drew a 14—two 7s—and an 11; the dealer showed a 6, the house's weakest card. It would be criminal not to split the first hand and double down on the second, but I had no more money on me. All my funds were across the casino, in my safe deposit box. I couldn't imagine that the pit boss would allow us to freeze the action while I went to get it, the way my family would sometimes leave a Monopoly game out overnight because of bedtime.

The dealer merely grunted at my predicament; I'd already established that I was in no mood to chat, and he was going to humor me until the bitter end. The pit boss walked over and quickly sized up the situation. He saw the cards, the lack of chips before me, and the panic on my face. "We can spot you the split and the double down, if you're good for it," he offered matter-of-factly. I couldn't believe it. I muttered something stupid like "That would be great," all the while wondering if the Church would ever modernize to the point where it might consider canonizing a pit boss.

"Anything goes at the Desert Inn," the saint said, as he stacked an additional $300 on each hand. And so, with no fuss and on the strength of my word, I'd obtained my first loan from a casino. It wasn't the last. Once I split the 7s, I drew a 3 on that first hand: 10. This, too, I had to double. None of us said a word. I raised my eyebrows; the pit boss nodded and the dealer produced three more black chips. Then he dealt me a two. Shit. I drew a 7 on the second 8, for a 14, and a 3 on my initial 11. A good thing had turned terribly wrong, and I suddenly found myself with a $1,500 wager on three very pathetic hands. In theory, there was still a good chance the dealer would bust, but somehow this all seemed like a preordained disaster. How humiliating it would be to have to walk across the casino to cash a traveler's check to pay back the saint.

That didn't happen. Much to my relief, the dealer turned over a 10, then drew another, for a whopping 26. Busted! Instead of being forced to take the shameful walk, I found myself with twenty-one black chips to my name, after the pit boss had deducted his nine. I almost kissed his flashy gold ring in gratitude. I played recklessly for another twenty minutes, feeling no more fear, and my luck held. By 9:20 I was back up to $11,300, which meant I'd won back more than half of what I'd lost the night before.

♣ ♦ ♥ ♠ I walked north on the Strip to the Riviera Hotel, site of a press conference, or "revolt of the revolted," being held by virtue czar William Bennett and U.S. senator Joe Lieberman. They were in town to express their outrage over the *Jerry Springer* show and to call on the NAB to clean up its act. Outside the Riviera, tourists crowded around one of the city's most popular photo ops, a life-sized bronze sculpture of the hotel's *Crazy Girls* dancers, all lined up against a wall in their thong bikinis and high heels, butts to the Strip. A fine venue at which to lament society's moral decay. But hey, all the classier joints had already been grabbed by those Hollywood types.

Lieberman and Bennett, the latter looking as dour as any self-respecting virtue czar should in Sin City, arrived and did their thing. We're not censors, they protested, but *Jerry Springer* is out of hand, it's "must-sleaze TV" in the afternoon, when kids are often home watching TV unattended, and so on. True to form, Bennett then threw something in about this being the greatest country in the history of the world, Mr. Springer and the Crazy Girls notwithstanding.

The dour duo brought clips, which made most of the reporters giggle despite themselves, particularly when the announcer called for future participants in the same eager tone with which game-show announcers tell lucky winners what they'll be taking home. "Have your in-laws moved into your home and destroyed your marriage? Would you like to tell them to move out on our show?" Or, better yet: "Are you pregnant by a man who has another woman pregnant and want him to make a decision?"

"This cannot be good for you to watch, and that can't be a controversial statement," Bennett scolded, reminding me of Señor Valencia, my junior high principal, the way he looked straight at the loudest giggler.

The scolding over, I approached Senator Lieberman, who months later would take a big step toward becoming a household name when he became the first Democrat to denounce President Clinton's behavior surrounding l'affaire Lewinsky. The senator from Connecticut told me that after what he'd seen on his morning jog, he wanted to come back to Vegas with his family. Much to my surprise, he said he'd gambled, too: He budgets $25 per casino visit, and only plays the slots.

Gambling has come a long way. Not long ago a politician seeking to be known as a social conservative wouldn't have dared acknowledge a fondness for casino gambling. Then again, the largest casino on earth, Foxwoods, is located in the senator's home state.

♣ ♦ ♥ ♠ That afternoon I had a tennis lesson. Within ten minutes of hitting from the baseline, Randy Grosso cataloged my game's many ailments, nasty habits that neither frequent lessons in childhood nor tennis camp could vanquish: the lousy footwork, the exaggerated topspin on my forehand, the lateness of my backhand, the inflexibility of my knees. But it didn't matter, it was still exhilarating to be out working up a sweat under the vast blue sky. I was taken aback by the sight of the snowcapped Mount Charleston in the distance. The West is amazing; I hadn't imagined people ski in April within an hour's drive of Las Vegas.

Randy is not like most resort tennis pros, smooth, aloof guys who invariably grew up in southern California and drive convertibles. Even though he's got the tan and the ageless good looks, there is something coarse and genuine about Randy. Maybe it's the way he constantly says that greatness is monotonous, the ability to make the same shot over and over, or the way he talks about Las Vegas being the easiest place to get laid. Or maybe it's his touchingly uncool hero worship. He summons someone from the pantheon of greats, from Jimmy Connors (your serve motion should be all rock and roll) to Martina Hingis (it's not how hard you hit the ball), to support each insight.

Randy's enthusiasm is that of the late convert. He didn't pick up a tennis racket until he was twenty-four, which means I was paying him for a lesson even though I have a twenty-year head start at the game. Randy left his hometown of Green Bay, Wisconsin, in the fall of 1975, upon hearing that his college roommate Gardy T. Weber and his girlfriend were moving out to California. He asked them for a ride to Vegas, and on October 1 they dropped him off at the corner of Maryland and Tropicana. All Randy carried was $400 he'd borrowed from his sister, and his bicycle.

At first, he got by painting houses and doing landscaping. He moved into the Grand Plaza Apartments and roomed with Tony Orlando's drummer, who was involved in a long-distance relationship with Olivia Newton-John, before she was famous. "I used to love taking those phone calls from Australia and listening to that sweet voice and great accent," he reminisced. Especially when he was stoned. The days of disco, before the age of AIDS, were a good time to be young and single in Vegas.

Far more important from Randy's perspective, this was also the golden age of tennis. Diane Smith, a tennis player friend of Randy's from back home, was visiting in the late summer of 1976, and together they watched Jimmy Connors take on Björn Borg at the U.S. Open. A soccer player in school, Randy had always considered tennis a "faggot sport." Sitting in his living room watching Connors's serve, Randy told Smitty that he could do that too, no problem. She dared him to try, and together they went down to the Grand Plaza's tennis courts. Randy's very first serve was in, and he was hooked.

He began taking lessons at the Desert Inn, where he'd hang out, eager to play anyone. Among those he'd beat up on was a boy wonder named André Agassi. Randy had a lot of time on his hands to play tennis because he'd stumbled upon a decent-paying nighttime gig. A couple of guys who lived down the hall from him had signed him up to work backstage at one of the big production shows in town. He got the call, joined the union, and reported for work as a wardrobe boy at the *Hallelujah Hollywood* show at what was then the MGM Grand, now Bally's. The job paid well, entailed a mere three hours of work a night, and allowed Randy to hang out with a hundred gorgeous women in various states of undress. ("How great was that?") By late 1982, Randy was giving tennis lessons.

"But enough about me, what I want to know is how a wife lets her husband take off for a month in Vegas," Randy said after I told him how long I was in town. "This has got to be the world's coolest wife."

◆

♣ ◆ ♥ ♠ After a shower, I ordered pasta from room service. It seemed the height of luxury to be able to sit there in my DI robe and eat while watching *Frasier*. Afterward I called the World's Coolest Wife to tell her I was heading out to a topless joint. Duty called. I would be missing out on the full convention scene if I did not partake.

As an editorial writer at the *Pittsburgh Post-Gazette* a few years ago, I'd pointed to the timeless convention–strip club synergy during a particularly heated discussion on whether the newspaper should support a statewide referendum to shut down topless bars. No goal was more sacred to us than making the city more attractive to conventions. So I told my esteemed colleagues, who up until that moment thought they knew me, that what we really ought to be concerned about wasn't the presence of sleazy topless bars, but the absence of more upscale ones of the kind conventioneers flock to in Orlando, Las Vegas, Atlanta, Dallas, and other major convention cities. Now I could see what I'd been standing up for.

For guidance, I accessed the Web on my laptop computer. "How do I find the best topless joint in Vegas?" I typed in at the askjeeves.com search engine. A few clicks later I was at stripclub-review.com, which, naturally, is about Vegas. It's good to be wired. The site's author is a real connoisseur who takes the art of topless dancing rather seriously. In his—I here make an assumption as to the author's gender—FAQ section, he poses the question: "What clubs are best to go to for taking a dancer home?" He then answers with an indignant How dare you? "First of all, the dancers are at the clubs to work. Yes, work. Believe it or not, they are not there to get picked up. Sure, some may make you feel like you might have a chance, but hey, reality hurts. Get over it."

The earnest reviewer gives clubs a letter grade in five different categories. The best club overall: the Olympic Garden, an appraisal borne out by the market. I later learned that it is the only club in town that does not feel the need to give kickbacks to cab drivers. For those wondering, here's an excerpt from the site's review of the club:

> There are [sic] an incredible amount of gorgeous gals here.
> Mostly in the 7–8 range with 9's and 10's thrown in for good
> measure. There are usually about 40 to 60+ women during the
> night shift during the weeknights and up to 150 to 200+
> women over the weekend nights or during convention season.
> A lot of augmentation, but that's a plus in some books. You get
> a lot of attention when tipping by any of the four stages. Many
> would rub their assets either in your face or squeeze them to-
> gether on your hand/tip.

About half an hour later, at the bar of the cavernous Olympic Garden, April was explaining to me that she flies in from Atlanta for about six of these conventions each year, the money is so phenomenal. This came as a revelation, one of those fascinating nuggets you stumble across but don't know quite where to file in your brain. Who would have guessed that topless dancing, like tennis, has a traveling pro circuit? I ordered myself a Corona, my new friend a Coke.

April—a popular nom de guerre among strippers the world over, was intently playing a video poker machine and chain-smoking Salems while we talked. She wore a lime-green bikini and sarong; her toned and bronzed body, dirty-blond hair, and large green eyes all brought to mind the Dallas Cowboys cheerleaders we used to drool over in junior high, the girls who made so many of my otherwise sensible classmates in Mexico root for Staubach, Jones, and Dorsett over Bradshaw, Lambert, and Harris. Poor souls.

The bar seemed safe, the one place where the women (they call themselves girls, which I guess is part of the thrill) didn't approach patrons to solicit a $20 private "lap dance." Every table and every seat around the four stages was occupied. Near the entrance, between the club's two main rooms, a crowd of nervous conventioneers sipped beers and peered into the dark rooms to admire the per-formers onstage. But here the talk was all tech, all the time.

Girls paraded around in tight-fitting clothes, sidling up to cus-tomers, introducing themselves, and asking if they'd care for a dance. When a customer said yes, the girl would go at it during the next song, stripping down to a G-string and then unveiling her (al-most invariably) artificial breasts. Now the fun started: The formi-dable mounds got knocked about in front of the customer's glazed-over eyes, while his hands lay (house rules) agonizingly idle by his sides. She'd then gyrate, slap her taut buttocks (a compulsory movement), and then sit on his lap for a nanosecond, coaxing an erection and a bigger tip. Two minutes later the song would be over and the girl would purr into her conquest's ear: "Do you want me to go on?" Four songs later she'd have earned a C-note. A particularly stunning girl might be monopolized for hours by a single table, passed around by a group of horny guys like some spicy appetizer. Yet there was something a tad clinical about the whole scene. Look into the girls' eyes and you'd see the same bored expression black-jack dealers wear when "servicing" gamblers.

There's no full nudity at the Olympic Garden. There are all-nude clubs in Las Vegas, but they can't serve alcohol. For full disclosure and a cold Bud, you have to take a $15 cab ride to North Las Vegas.

"What guys like most about a place like this isn't the flesh, but the nice talk," April said in her syrupy southern accent, never averting her eyes from the video poker. "We make them feel like kings at a time when men have been told they can no longer act like men." This was her halftime, a break from the more than fifty dances she'd do that night. The club took its cut, but she'd still clear a grand, on account of tips. One guy had already tipped her $100 that night, be-fore asking if he could "get to know you better" back at his hotel for $10,000. "What a jerk," she muttered at the memory, "not that plenty of girls here wouldn't take him up on his offer." That's my April, good girl.

"Getting so close to these guys and turning them on isn't in itself sort of weird?"

"At first, a couple of years ago when I started, it totally grossed me out, to the point where I quit after two days and went to work at a video store for four-fifty an hour."

Horrors. "Then what happened?"

"I adjusted my attitude. The main thing was to realize that I am in control of the situation, not the other way around. It's really what you make of it."

That's what my father used to say about college.

Another fascinating tidbit I picked up from April is that it takes a sheriff's card to dance in a Vegas strip club. I can see the guy wearing his sunglasses and cowboy hat, boots on his desk, as he greets each new arrival in town. "Well, hello there, purty one, so you think you got what it takes to lap dance in my county . . . ?"

April and I hugged adieu, and I was off to the men's room, never dreaming I'd find the highlight of my field trip there.

There's a camaraderie among guys in a public rest room at a ball game or at a nightclub that is absent in a rest room at, say, the mall. At the first two, strangers will look sideways at each other at a urinal and grunt something about that fourth-down touchdown pass or the chick in purple. But at the mall, look sideways and enthuse to your pissing neighbor about those tremendous markdowns at your own peril. Maybe it's because, unlike at the ballpark or a nightclub, neither of you is carrying a beer.

A topless joint is in some ways a cross between a ballpark and a nightclub. There are pros, and you can sort of pick them up. So the camaraderie in the Olympic Garden's men's room was inspiring. The triumphal "Let's go get 'em" attitude couldn't be dampened by the inconvenient fact that it would cost $20 a song.

When I first saw Joe Alston, I cringed. Hovering bathroom attendants who hand out paper towels and mints have always made me uncomfortable, more than is accounted for by the hassle of suddenly having to fish for spare change simply because nature calls. I think it's an Upstairs-Downstairs thing, a mixture of embarrassment and guilt at being waited on when it's not really necessary.

"You're fucking blowing my mind," a drunken conventioneer to my right yelled at Joe, the poor attendant, as I fished for some change. "You're reading the Bible in a topless club," he continued, drooling on what looked like a Ferragamo tie. Must be with one of the networks.

Sure enough, Joe was reading the Bible. At a topless joint. Gasp. All of us merry conventioneers in the vicinity of Joe's sinks fell suddenly quiet, digesting the presence in a place like this of the well-worn black leather book with the gold lettering on its spine. You'd think Joe had been packing heat.

"I'm a minister," Joe said calmly. He was a soft-spoken black man, with piercing eyes the color of amber. "You're fucking blowing my mind," repeated the one-man chorus to my right, more softly this time.

"This is where the Lord wants me, to talk to people who need it; there's a lot of hurt here," Joe said, answering the obvious yet unspoken question. "Do any of you think I work here because I want to?"

Well, uh, no, not really.

Nest egg: $45,584

Wednesday, April 8

After a hearty Belgian waffle at the hotel's pleasant Terrace Point restaurant, I headed back to the convention center to attend a 10:30 panel on the Federal Communications Commission's notoriously cumbersome political advertising regulations. No, I'm not into self-flagellation. A former boss of mine was one of the panelists, so I figured I'd drop in and say hello.

Michael Berg, who looks like he could be Gary Hart's younger brother, practices communications law at the powerful Washington, D.C., firm—a string of five names in descending order of spelling difficulty—I worked at for a time in 1994, before fleeing to a career in journalism. (The firm has since hired such heavyweights as George Mitchell, Lloyd Bentsen, and Bob Dole to try to compensate for my departure.) Michael seemed surprised to see me when I walked in late, halfway through the panel's cheery "50 Ways to Lose Your License" quiz. Last he'd heard I was writing editorials in Pittsburgh.

After the panel, on the bus back to the DI for lunch, Michael told me he loves the odd juxtapositions of a Las Vegas convention. He still gets a kick out of going downstairs early in the morning, preoccupied with his presentations or stressing about sending out a fax, only to run into haggard souls who've been gambling all night and may still be drinking. "You don't encounter such a scene when you cross the lobby at the Four Seasons in Washington," he said.

It was another perfect day, eighty degrees without a cloud in the sky, so we decided to eat outside, by the DI's magnificent pool. We draped our jackets over the wrought-iron chairs, loosened our ties, and ordered sandwiches from a tanned blonde wearing a bikini top. "Do you ever regret leaving the firm?" Michael asked me as I bit into my swordfish sandwich. I looked at the glistening pool, which took on a greenish hue through my Vuarnets, and grinned.

The firm, contrary to what my hasty departure might suggest, was a pleasant place. But my inability to account for time in six-minute increments and my lack of passion for furniture were immediate tip-offs that, while I'd enjoyed law school, I was not law firm partner material.

Success in law firm life, as in much of corporate America, is measured by the amount of furniture you have crammed in your office. Typically, you start off with a desk and a spare chair or two. Kill yourself for a decade at one of the nation's most grueling white-collar sweatshops and you might have a sofa delivered; conference tables are given to the mightiest of rainmakers. But no matter how much furniture you accumulate, you'll always account for your time in six-minute increments. (Incidentally, that's the cycle on my alarm clock's snooze feature.)

A third tip-off that I was not cut out for law firm life was the terror I felt every time Bridget approached. Bridget was not some tyrannical partner, but my secretary—a sweet and efficient lady who tried hard to make my transition to the real world as smooth as possible. Trouble is, I never had the damnedest idea of what to ask her to do. Having been in school since Richard Nixon was president, being of a generation accustomed to drafting from scratch on a word processor, I was entirely baffled by how people managed to keep their secretaries occupied.

"I think I might have enjoyed being a journalist," Michael said, interrupting my reverie, and for a moment, we both contemplated roads not taken.

♣ ♦ ♥ ♠ After our lunch, I checked out the Las Vegas Hilton's new attraction, Star Trek: The Experience. This is Trekkie heaven, built last year by the somewhat stodgy convention hotel to broaden its appeal. It has another of those rattle-in-place rides, a funky Space Quest casino (complete with windows looking out on to the stars), a café, and the obligatory gift shop. When the Experience first opened, long lines at the entrance would spill out into the casino, upsetting the Nevada Gaming Control Board, headed these days by the aptly named—for an industry eager to cleanse its image— William Bible. State law doesn't bar kids from casinos (at most hotels you can't get nourishment without walking past miles of slots); it bars them from "loitering" in them. The Hilton was forced to pay a hefty $350,000 fine for violating Ben Franklin's admonition to "Keep flax from fire, youth from gaming."

Waiting in line, I fell into conversation with an executive from Spain's television network, in town for the convention, and his daughter. The girl was rather quiet, taking in the impressive exhibit of Star Trek paraphernalia, and the seemingly never-ending, wall-sized twenty-third-century time line with a reverential air. "Soy una Trekkie," she admitted in a hushed tone, as Dad beamed, pleased with himself. She's at an age, no doubt, when Dad's power to get her this excited about anything is quite diminished. Soon, Klingons tried to kidnap us, because one of us was one of Captain Kirk's ancestors, and the *Enterprise* folks were determined to get us back to the late twentieth century. I later read that the show's entire cast is trying to join the Teamsters.

♣ ♦ ♥ ♠ Michael had told me over lunch that the network hospitality suites at the Hilton can be pretty lively in the evenings, so I went up to CBS's. The door was ajar when I arrived, and I let myself in. The two bedrooms plus balcony were stunning, though nothing like the three 13,000-square-foot "villas" the hotel reserves on the top floor for whales willing to risk a million bucks per visit. Not a soul was to be seen, but I knew I was in the right place because plenty of CBS propaganda was lying around. I helped myself to a beer from a refrigerator and took a seat out on the balcony, admiring the sunset.

Next thing I knew I was being shaken by a clean-shaven CBS public relations type, who handed me a pamphlet entitled "CBS at the NAB." I mumbled my thanks and tried to resume my dozing. More shaking. Strange form of hospitality, I thought, getting annoyed. Then I realized Mr. CBS was pointing at something in the pamphlet. I could hardly read, it had gotten so dark. It said one could drop by the hospitality suite any time, through five. Ooops. I looked at my watch; it was after seven. So much for Michael's memories of rockin' nights.

I walked to the door in an awkward silence, desperately trying to think of a CBS show to praise—to make amends. But as hard as I tried, I couldn't think of one. My escort finally broke the silence, offering me a beer "for the road." Did I really look that shabby? Of course the shows only came to me once I was in the elevator: *60 Minutes! David Letterman! Nash Bridges!*

On the twenty-fifth floor a nervous-looking man in a tan polyester leisure suit got on the elevator and asked me if I was in town for the convention. He was the oldest person—thirty-five would be my guess—I'd ever seen wearing braces. Come to think of it, his haircut looked a lot like mine when I wore braces, back in the late 1970s. He had the acne to go with the outfit, too. Looking at this guy I realized why my mother in 1978 fretted about what we'd look like when we grew up.

"Have you ever heard of Ken Uston?" he asked.

"Vaguely." It was an odd thing to be asked in a Las Vegas Hilton elevator.

To any serious blackjack player, Ken Uston is a hero. And unlike poker, games like blackjack, in which you play against the house instead of against other mortals, don't offer up many inspirational figures. A graduate of Yale—Phi Beta Kappa at age twenty—and the Harvard Business School and a senior executive at the Pacific Stock Exchange in San Francisco, the mathematically gifted Uston became a notorious card counter. He joined a team of card counters that would blitz into Vegas for profitable weekends in the 1970s, but despite some elaborate disguises, he was eventually barred from most casinos. He wrote a number of amusing, boastful books about his experiences.

Uston was found dead in a Paris hotel room in 1987 at the age of fifty-two. Though French authorities ruled out foul play, plenty of conspiracy theorists would like to think it was the Mob's last laugh.

Card counting, mind you, is not cheating. A card counter doesn't mess with the cards or with his chips; he simply plays with more information than the rest of us, having kept close track of what cards have already been dealt. With a six-deck shoe, it's arguably not even possible to count effectively. Nonetheless, casinos remain paranoid about counters.

Casinos have the right to show card counters the door. It happens all the time. Last fall, on *48 Hours* (another CBS show I couldn't come up with under pressure), the Tropicana casino asked a well-known counter on camera to take his game elsewhere, or to perhaps try his luck at craps or roulette. "We don't want your action here" is how the pit boss put it. That's the way those guys talk. The show clearly wanted viewers to be outraged at such an un-American injustice. This gambler's being thrown out simply because he's good at the game!

That was Uston's reaction when he was barred, and he sued a number of casinos, the Hilton among them, in both state and federal courts. But he could never sell his extravagant claim that his constitutional rights had been violated by the casinos' actions, much as the rights of African Americans had been violated when they were denied access to public accommodations throughout the South. As a result, casinos, even though licensed by the state, are free to bar card counters.

Incidentally, there is a category of people Nevada casinos *must* bar, and that is anyone listed in the Black Book, or list of excluded persons, compiled by the Nevada Gaming Commission. The list dates back to 1960; it was part of an effort under Governor Grant Sawyer to clean up the industry. There are currently thirty-two names in the Black Book—slot cheats, mobsters, racketeers, and other undesirables. These characters aren't even allowed into a casino's buffets.

Frank Sinatra learned the hard way in the 1960s that Nevada could get serious about its Black Book. The crooner who did his part to put Vegas on the map hosted Sam Giancana at his Cal-Neva Lodge at Lake Tahoe in the summer of 1963. Giancana, whom a prim Governor Sawyer politely called a "hoodlum of national repute" in his memoirs, was on the list, and Sinatra lost his gaming license as a result of his hospitality. He had to relinquish not only his control of the Cal-Neva, but his stake in the Las Vegas Sands, where he'd held his famous Rat Pack Summit. In his memoirs, *Hang Tough,* Governor Sawyer claimed that President Kennedy tried to intervene on behalf of the Chairman of the Board, but that he would have none of it.

♣ ♦ ♥ ♠ Braces and I milled around the elegant Hilton casino together for a bit. He seemed to want company. "Tonight's not the night," he kept mumbling as we watched the action at a $100 blackjack table. "Gotta wait, wait, wait . . ."

For what? A full moon?

I had trouble deciding whether to be fascinated or bored by Braces, who made me promise not to use his name, even after he told me it wasn't his real one. Such was the magnitude of his suspiciousness. But since I'd spent most of the week consorting with people my editor would probably consider far too normal, I stuck with the guy.

I was tiring of the convention scene at the Hilton and wanted to check out a new place. "Let's go hang out at the Rio," I suggested, "if you have nothing better to do." Braces agreed. The Rio is in many ways the hottest hotel in town. About a half-mile off the Strip, it was an unassuming casino when it first opened in 1990, catering mostly to locals on the strength of its buffets. In the last couple of years, though, it has reinvented itself as one of Vegas's flashiest spots, able to accommodate demanding high rollers as well as any other casino in town.

Last year the Rio opened a new tower and casino, which includes Jean-Louis Palladin's Napa restaurant. Underneath the restaurant, master sommelier Barrie Larvin, formerly of the Ritz Hotel in London, presides over a cozy wine cellar that provides a heavenly escape from the madness of the casino. Here one can indulge in some heavy-duty wine tasting. As befits the town's "If we ain't got it, damn it let's buy it" philosophy, the hotel reportedly gave Larvin $6 million to build one of the world's most enviable wine collections.

Braces marched off to the john as soon as we stepped into the two-story Masquerade casino. He didn't come back for what seemed like ages, so I settled down at a blackjack table. That was what I did when no longer distracted; I gambled, and it was starting to feel as if that was what I'd done forever. The dealer was a nice fellow from South Dakota, who told me the wisest thing he and his wife ever did was sell their pig farm and move to Las Vegas. "You know the kind of conversations you carry on when working with pigs?" he asked. The answer, much to my surprise, was "Boring ones." I would have guessed none. Here he gets to talk to interesting people all the time, without even needing to get dirty. "Not long ago I dealt to Tiger Woods himself," he said.

The dealer was entertaining, but the cocktail waitresses were mesmerizing, as our cabdriver had warned us. So this was why the Rio had been the locals' favorite since the day it opened. Buffets, my ass. Being a nonunion property, the Rio is free to employ whatever criteria it desires in hiring its waitresses. And it makes the girls wear a carnival-themed outfit with a thong bikini, a tribute to what Tom Wolfe termed "buttocks décolletage" when he visited Vegas in the late 1960s. If Vegas were a massive, gaudy prom, the Rio girls would be its queens. They pull down close to six figures a year and are free to take off work when they please.

Braces and I rode the elevator to the fifty-first floor to have a drink at the trendy VooDoo Lounge. The Cajun bar and restaurant, one of the few places where conventioneers and locals actually come into contact, has that rarest of Las Vegas assets—an outside. We snatched a table on the terrace, overlooking the Strip. I ordered a cigar and a cosmopolitan; Braces, much to the waiter's dismay, ordered a brandy with milk ("and be sure it's skim").

He still seemed nervous. He wouldn't tell me where he lives or—this would have been interesting—what he does for a living. What he did tell me, in fragmentary bursts, was that in the 1980s his older brother—"My bro was pure money"—put together a team of blackjack card counters which made a killing in Atlantic City. His brother went around calling Uston his high priest.

A successful card counter will dramatically vary the amount of his bets, depending on whether the cards are running favorably or not. In theory, the more high cards are left to be dealt, the better the odds for the player. So a counter wants to increase his bets when the count is low—that is, when a disproportionate number of low cards has already been dealt, and vice versa. Casinos therefore are wary of players who appear too serious, too focused, and too uninterested in free booze, especially if they dramatically alter their wagers at a table. These are the symptoms of card counting.

In order to camouflage their counting, Ustonian teams place

counters who play conservatively at a number of tables. When the count is good, a counter covertly signals the team's "Big Player," who floats between the tables, preferably in an apparent alcoholic stupor. The BP is above suspicion because he always bets high and doesn't follow a table's action all that closely for any significant period of time.

This is easier said than done. Team members must be great actors, ignoring each other for the most part while signaling the BP without arousing the suspicion of vigilant pit bosses and cameras. Braces told me his brother eventually "freaked out," became a crackhead, and committed suicide.

Braces was looking to follow in his brother's pre-crack footsteps. Two of his brother's associates were assembling a team in Las Vegas and had asked Braces to join them. They were planning on starting next week, and had been in training. Braces claimed to be a gifted counter. Yet I had the feeling all might not turn out well for him. Long before doing battle, Braces already appeared to have freaked out. And even under the best of circumstances, he doesn't exactly blend in.

"I'm telling you all this shit because I want to ask you something. After all, since you're writing a book, you know a lot of shit about this place. Right?" Braces haltingly asked, having torn his napkin into sixteen squares.

"Oh, tons," I said, trying to look wise beyond my days in town.

"You don't suppose a casino, you know, a reputable carpet joint, would come after us with fuckin' goons if they catch on to us?"

I couldn't help myself. I was buzzed and having fun with this character, who seemed to have stepped out of some implausible movie script. So instead of shaking him and saying, "Don't be a moron; sophisticated, publicly traded companies like Hilton and Starwood don't go around beating up customers," I didn't say a thing for a minute. I leaned back in my chair, sighed deeply, and puffed on my Dunhill cigar, then looked up at the stars, as if haunted by all the ugly, behind-the-scenes knowledge I carried around.

"No," I finally said in a flat "I don't want to get into it" tone. As I'd expected, this alarmed Braces more than if I'd screamed, "Yes, they'll kill you." He ordered his third brandy and milk and said: "Sweet Jesus, what am I getting myself into?"

After sitting with Braces for another hour or so, I wished him and his team great luck and got him to promise to call me in a week and let me know how it was going. I gave him a C-note to cover our drinks and left him sitting there, staring out at the alluring sea of neon.

It felt good to be back at the DI. Realizing it was my last night in this tranquil oasis, I retrieved a wad of bills from my box and walked over to an empty $100 blackjack table. I got in a groove with a dealer named Bob, and soon I was again feeling that wondrous gambling rush I'd experienced my very first half-hour at Luxor, the one that whispers, *The possibilities are endless.* It was my best session so far. From my first $300 bet, which was a blackjack, I could do no wrong. In forty-five minutes, I was up $10,166. It was three A.M. and I decided to call it a night, exhilarated at again being in the black. I "colored in" for two $5,000 chips and put them in my box. This is what old-timers call winning a lumberyard with a toothpick.

Nest egg: $54,150

3

MIRAGE

It is pretty to see what money will do.

—Samuel Pepys

Thursday, April 9

♣ ♦ ♥ ♠ "There's a Martinez here with eleven thousand two hundred dollars," the casino cashier whispered into the phone, as if sharing a good joke. The thought had actually crossed my mind earlier in the morning while I was walking to the tennis courts: What if they laughed at me when I presented my hard-earned fortune? What if they dismissed my four chips as worthless pieces of flimsy plastic? What the hell would I do then? I'd dismissed this vision with a chuckle and had gone back to fretting about playing Randy with a wicked hangover, but two hours later a balding clerk was hesitating to show me the money.

In fairness, the man had apologized before getting on the phone. The computer was down, preventing him from verifying that I'd won those chips in the middle of the night. Eventually I was paid, but not before the DI made a copy of my driver's license for what's called a Currency Transaction Incidence Report. Since 1985 casinos have been compelled—as are financial institutions—to report a variety of transactions exceeding $10,000 to the state of Nevada and the U.S. Treasury Department. Needless to say, for those who miss the city's more freewheeling days, 1985 was a dark year indeed. No longer can suitcases filled with cash make anonymous appearances, and that's been a blow to Las Vegas's old self-image, for better and worse.

I checked out at the VIP lounge. Once again, my hefty room and board charges were magically wiped off the bill. According to the revived computer, I'd played six hours during my stay, with a stunning average bet of $391 a hand. Mighty impressed with myself, I took the short cab ride over to the Mirage. Things were looking up. My pockets were stuffed; I was ahead after a week of frantic gambling. What was more, the NAB hordes were heading home, the weather was approaching optimal pool conditions, and both Kat and my mother were coming to spend Easter with their favorite high roller.

Las Vegas years are like dog years. Residents who have lived here for three years are old-timers; hotels open more than five are old. But not the Mirage, still fresh and awe-inspiring nine years after its opening. With its outdoor volcano and indoor rain forest, the three-winged, thirty-story tropical resort was the first hotel built on the Strip in fifteen years, and its ensuing success signaled the town's renaissance. The fun begins as you wait in line to check in, staring at the exotic-colored fish and cuddly-sized sharks in the soothing 20,000-gallon saltwater aquarium behind the registration desk.

The Mirage's creator is the irrepressible Steve Wynn (as in "I Wynn, you lose"), the man most closely identified with the "new" Las Vegas. Everyone who has ever come into contact with Wynn calls him a visionary, but I'll restrain myself. In response to my fax requesting an interview with the casino mogul, a Mirage flack left a curt message on my answering machine: "Mr. Wynn will be busy building hotels into the next millennium." Poor guy can't take off his hard hat and put down his shovel, not even for an hour.

The Mirage is a monument to American ingenuity—financial ingenuity, mostly. Wynn may be a true visionary, but it's the cleverness of American capitalism that made his dreams a reality. We think of such imaginative characters—Steven Spielberg, Bill Gates, Walt Disney—as quintessentially American, but that's because their counterparts in other nations usually can't fund their visions. In what other country would a guy babbling about a casino, tropical rain forests, erupting volcanoes, and dolphin habitats gain access to $620 million in easy money to build his exuberant dream? Lucky for him, Wynn was buddies with Michael Milken at the height of the junk-bond craze. He got his money.

Wynn, whose father was a serious gambler and bingo parlor operator, grew up back east and attended the University of Pennsylvania. He came out to Vegas in the late 1960s, invested in land, made valuable connections, bought a small stake in a Strip casino, then started and sold a wholesale liquor business. But his big break came in 1973, when after buying up 5.5 percent of the company's stock, Wynn was elected the downtown Golden Nugget casino's president and chairman. To this day the Golden Nugget is part of the Mirage empire, now a publicly traded company listed on the New York Stock Exchange.

Wynn is driven by the belief that his adopted hometown should think of itself not only as the world's gambling mecca, but as one of its entertainment capitals as well. The Mirage, and most of the other Strip resorts built in its wake, embody this belief. There is much here to entertain the nongambler. Ever the showman, Wynn cannot help but tell you himself about all the fun. He is unusually fond of the sound of his own voice, to judge by its omnipresence. Whether you take the people-mover from the Strip into the casino, watch the Mirage channel on your TV, or listen to the audio tour of Siegfried & Roy's Secret Garden (a family attraction, mind you), Steve Wynn's seductive voice is there, at once gravelly and silky, prodding you to relax. The man could sell Yugos with a voice like that. And all his sentences seem to start with the same phrase: "Whether you're a child of six, sixteen, or sixty-six . . ." This is the key to the Wynn vision: Entertainment is about indulging the child within, so a great resort must be as whimsical as it is plush.

For lack of a better word, Wynn has Disneyfied Las Vegas, and gambling, for adults. He might not have been the first to build a theme park for gamblers, but he was the first perfectionist to do so.

Locals were skeptical back in 1989 when the Mirage opened. It was spectacular, everyone conceded, but the place had just cost too darned much to ever turn a profit. It was widely reported that the resort would have to take in $1 million a day to be profitable. By 1995, daily revenue exceeded $2 million. Most impressive, against the backdrop of a "casino-centric" industry, the company derives almost half its revenue from other sources. Evidently someone was coming for the food and shows, after all. The Mirage paid for itself ahead of schedule, and the company's stock became one of Wall Street's darlings in the early 1990s. By 1997, thanks to Wynn's fanatical attention to detail, Mirage emerged as the second most admired American company, right behind Coca-Cola, in *Fortune*'s annual survey of executives. If he hadn't long ago been executed by fellow mobsters, Bugsy Siegel would have died of envy.

Wynn brings to mind the character of Martin Dressler in Steven Millhauser's 1996 Pulitzer Prize–winning novel by that name. Dressler is a visionary turn-of-the-century New York hotelier who builds a series of ever more outrageous and expensive themed palaces, wildly successful until he finally goes too far, losing all touch with reality.

Will that be Steve Wynn's fate? It's a question skeptics asked once again as he put the finishing touches on Bellagio, his even more grandiose $1.6 billion resort, which would open in October 1998. The visionary fond of upping the ante on his competitors simply says it will be "the most romantic hotel built in the history of the world."

♣ ♦ ♥ ♠ After dropping my things in my room, a tasteful beige affair with plenty of draperies, rattan furniture, and a copy of a lithograph from a Kipling text showing "the Great Pagan Pagoda at Rangoon," I rushed down to the salon to get my hair cut. It's a good thing I did. I can now tell my grandchildren that Dustin Hoffman, Demi Moore, Sylvester Stallone, and I shared hairdressers.

At $25, my time with Anthony Rais was among Las Vegas's best deals. He is as talented a storyteller as he is a hairdresser, and he lacks the haughtiness of most who cut in his circles. He moved to Las Vegas from Boston sixteen years ago to pursue his career on stage. You can cut hair anywhere, as he did in Boston, but if you're eager to live off your skating-magician act, you're destined to move to Las Vegas sooner or later. But a funny thing happened on the way to entertainment stardom: The old hairdressing gig provided Anthony with the greater opportunity in his new hometown. Within a few years, Anthony found himself managing the salon at Caesars Palace, without question the Strip's premier resort before the Mirage opened. Anthony and his staff of nineteen pampered the casino's high rollers, its showroom entertainers, and the never-ending parade of celebrities passing through town.

You can catch a glimpse of Anthony, who looks like Barry Manilow with less accentuated features, in the 1988 film *Rain Man,* grooming Tom Cruise and an Oscar-winning Dustin Hoffman before their night on the town. "You can tell a lot about people the way they treat the backstage help, and I can tell you Dustin is a real class act," Anthony confided. He complained about the behavior of some other household names he'd encountered through the years, but that dirt will cost you $25. It was off the record.

Anthony moved over to the Mirage last year. He and his wife have a sprawling house with a pool and a Japanese garden in one of the city's older, leafy residential neighborhoods east of the Strip. They used to run into Liberace in the grocery store all the time.

For Anthony, much of the city's allure remains its entertainment scene. In his mind, the whole town is in costume, living backstage. The guy in the car next to yours at the red light might be dressed as a pirate headed for work at Treasure Island; the woman sitting next to you in the casino's employee lunchroom might be dressed as Cleopatra. And though no casino boasts a skating magician on its marquee, Anthony is active in the artistic community. He is a movement coach to magicians and other performers. He also works with the Nevada Dance Theater's Future Dance Program for at-risk children, and participates in the Rainbow Show, an annual extrava-

ganza that entertainers from all the big revues in town put on together to benefit AIDS research. In addition to working backstage,
he'll be playing Merlin in this year's show.

"My one regret is that I didn't move here earlier," Anthony said.

Freshly coiffed, I was eager to be a mindless tourist for the rest of
the afternoon. I checked out the two attractions behind the hotel's
tropical swimming pool—the dolphin habitat and The Secret Garden of Siegfried & Roy, where the durable magicians' magnificent
animals are kept. I'd never seen a striped white tiger before, and
he'd never seen a tourist not bearing a video camera.

Then I went down the Strip to the World of Coca-Cola museum,
which you enter by riding up an elevator within the world's tallest
Coke bottle. Instead of elevator music, the soothing sound of a Coke
being poured into a glass filled with ice serenaded us as we rode up.
The fizz at the end, in full stereophonic splendor, was pure seduction. The museum is a shrine to America's flagship consumer product, and I cannot speak with any objectivity of its merits. I drink
more Diet Coke in a day than anyone would deem advisable. Anyone, that is, except the pleasant voice at the toll-free number listed
on the can. Once, when Kat mentioned that I drank too much of the
stuff, I picked up the phone, dialed the 800 number, and asked if
there was such a thing as too much of a good thing. It's the sort of
impulsive gesture I used to make to amuse her during the wooing
stage. Now that we're married, I just go off alone to Vegas for weeks
at a time. "How much do you drink in a day?" the sweet voice had
asked, trying to mask her concern. I told her. Silence. Then I heard
noises in the background at Coke HQ. Was it the sound of a heli-
copter coming to evacuate me, to whisk me down to Atlanta for
some intensive R&D? I could picture them all lining the helipad at
HQ. "Doctor, we're finally going to be able to cut open a twelve-
canner and see what we've wrought," one mad scientist would tell
another, a Strangelovian gleam in his eye. It was just my imagination. Ms. Coke regained her composure and assured me there was
no known limit, adding something about inconclusive caffeine tests
on rats. Everything was going to be okay. I chugged on.

The museum's theater shows Coke commercials going back to the 1950s "Things Go Better with Coke" campaign, including my personal favorite, the Mean Joe Greene one from the Steelers' glory years. But much to my dismay—there were children in the audience, for heaven's sake!—the museum also showed a couple of mid-1980s ads for New Coke. Hadn't anybody in Atlanta edited this stuff? How about some good old-fashioned Stalinist revisionism? So you skip a few years.

Significantly, Coke's year-old shrine in Vegas is its only museum outside its hometown of Atlanta. Along with the nation's top convention planners, chefs, and a growing number of other retailers, Coke's marketing gurus have realized that the Las Vegas Strip has become a national marketplace, where tradespeople come together to meet, frolic, be merry, and see what's new. It's an understatement to call this an improbable transformation for Sin City, where once only the Mob felt comfortable investing. Here you have one of the most mainstream, conservative, and family-oriented companies on earth embracing Las Vegas wholeheartedly.

♣ ♦ ♥ ♠ In the evening I met up with my mother, who'd flown in from Boston. We had a leisurely dinner in a restaurant inside the tropical rain forest, where Wynn's gardeners plant two hundred fresh orchids and a hundred bromeliads a week. We sat next to a waterfall. I told her she should focus on winning the Megabucks jackpot during her stay, to add some spice to my tale. Hunter Thompson's mom never won a jackpot. Afterward we went upstairs to watch *Friends* and *Seinfeld*.

There was something reassuring about watching these shows in Las Vegas, in the same way going to McDonald's in Europe can be. Remarkably, I went to bed by eleven.

Nest egg: $54,150

Friday, April 10

"It was the worst call in the history of baseball," Dick Carson told me over an omelette at the Egg & I, a breakfast joint on Sahara Avenue, a couple of miles west of the Strip. Like most key east-west avenues in Las Vegas, Sahara is named after the Strip casino it emanates from. It's kind of charming.

Dick talked about the Call with great authority and conviction, as if he were not biased by the fact that it cost him $3.1 million. It was October 26, 1985, the ninth inning of the sixth game of the World Series between the St. Louis Cardinals and the Kansas City Royals. The Cardinals, winning 1–0, needed one more out to win the Series. Dick needed that out just as badly. He had bet $2 million on the heavily favored Cardinals, for which he'd get a $1.1 million payoff. Things were looking good. Then first-base umpire Don Denkinger made it—the worst call in history, that is. He called Royals pinch hitter Jorge Orta safe at first, "when he was about as far away from being safe as I am from you," Dick told me, reaching over my Diablo Santa Fe omelette for emphasis. Denkinger later admitted he'd blown the call. But Dick still lost his money. Everyone knows gamblers are the silent victims of bad officiating. The Royals went on to win the game 2–1, and to win the Series in the seventh game. Amazingly, Dick is no fan of bringing instant replay to baseball: "It would kill the human element." What a guy.

I have a hard time watching a blackjack hand unfold when I have more than a few hundred bucks at stake; it's beyond me how anyone could sit through a baseball game on which he's bet $2 million. But Dick is a pro, which he'll tell you requires cold water running through your veins. Stoutly built, with wavy silver hair firmly matted into place, he wore a solid gold ring with a diamond ace of diamonds, and a nylon jacket plugging not a casino, but the International Swimming Hall of Fame in Fort Lauderdale.

Dick had been reluctant to talk, but I was eager to meet him ever since hearing about him from my friend Julie Spellman back in

New York. Julie went to college in California with Carolyn, Dick's oldest daughter, and still recalls with awe the sight of her beautiful Vegas friend arriving on campus in her high school graduation present, a Mercedes convertible. While most Las Vegans away from home spend a great deal of energy convincing people that they do not come from a family of gamblers, the fact that Carolyn's father was indeed a professional gambler proved endlessly fascinating to her classmates. What intrigued me was Julie's description of Dick as a devoted family man; a strict father of six successful, well-adjusted children, and husband of thirty-two years to his high school sweetheart. This did not fit my mental picture of a professional gambler, not that I'd ever met one.

As a kid growing up in west Texas, Dick always managed to have more money in his pocket than the other kids. He was a born hustler. By the time he was in high school, Dick was running a lunchtime craps game under the football stadium. This got him suspended. He began playing poker in earnest in Dallas in 1962 in the back of a bowling alley, where he worked. He and his buddies played deuce-to-seven lowball. "If one of the guys had five bucks in front of him, that was a huge deal," Dick recalled, with the nostalgia with which high rollers recall the days when it didn't take much to get the adrenaline flowing. He also worked as a rack boy at the pool tables, and became a pool hustler.

Dick made money at pool to feed his poker habit. He graduated from high school in 1964 and took on a series of odd jobs, selling magazines and candy door-to-door. On the night he married his high school sweetheart, Matilda, in May 1966, he left for a pool-hustling trip. The judge who married them had thrown him in jail the previous week for hustling an undercover cop.

This was life on the edge, and not just financially. Dick was robbed at gunpoint seven times and knew a pretty rough crowd. Once, he recalled with a chuckle, masked gunmen hit the club where he was playing poker, taking all the players' cash, some five grand total.

"What did you do then," I asked, "call the cops?"

"Hell no, we kept playing for credit."

Dick was always out there, "on his belly," as he puts it. Once he and a buddy were locked in the trunk of their car after hustling a couple of local pool champs in Cheyenne, Wyoming. That was the week *after* his wedding.

"I wasn't one of these guys who was ever going to have a shot at owning a casino," he explained, as if in life one must be on either side of the table, so long as there is action. "That's why I had to live through these things."

Doesn't Matilda object to the lifestyle? "She knew what I was all about when we got married," Dick said. When they dated in high school he could never take her to school dances, because he was too busy hustling on weekend nights. Sometimes she'd go anyway, and dance with other guys, trying to make Dick jealous, but to no avail.

Matilda gave him the ace-of-diamonds ring, which she had custom-made for $4,000 when times were good. Now, she is considering taking an office job for the first time to help pay the bills. But throughout their marriage, she has never suggested that Dick give up gambling. And my tennis buddy Randy thinks Kat is a saintly wife!

By the early 1970s Dick was playing poker with some of the best players in the world in Dallas—Johnny Moss, among them—and doing some sports betting. He became a bookmaker, setting odds and taking bets from clients. This got him arrested, although the charges were eventually dropped. But the authorities did take away his bankroll, which kind of soured him on Texas.

"I wanted to go somewhere where people don't look down on gamblers, where my kids could tell their friends at school that their father was a professional gambler and it wouldn't be a big deal," he told me. So he took his family on the well-beaten road from Dallas to Las Vegas in 1975. He'd already spent some time in the tolerant oasis and knew this was the place to pursue his own peculiar version of the American dream. He was so broke at the time that when his car died en route, in Deming, New Mexico, Dick had to call a friend to send him $100 to get it fixed before proceeding on.

Dallas had proven an excellent training ground in the fine art of no-limit hold 'em, and Dick made a killing in the city's poker rooms, which he frequented most nights. He then parlayed his initial poker winnings into a thriving sports betting operation. By the late 1970s he'd become one of the more respected baseball oddsmakers in town, providing action to bettors across the country.

Incidentally, this was illegal. "It's all relative, you know," he said when I raised that prickly issue. "Who would have thought the day would come when you'd have a state lottery in Texas, that bastion of Baptists?" And, in case that didn't settle the matter, Dick added that he paid taxes on all his earnings, which in his mind conferred upon them eternal legitimacy.

The early 1980s were good. Dick was a man about town, friends with Benny Binion, Frank "Lefty" Rosenthal, and a lot of other fixtures of the old Vegas. Not even a 1983 conviction for bookmaking, the result of the FBI's clampdown on a Shreveport gambler who happened to be one of Dick's customers, clouds his memories of the time. He got probation when he pled guilty, he was such a respected member of the community.

By the time Ronald Reagan's reelection juggernaut was proclaiming it "morning in America," a decade after Dick had moved his family to Shangri-La, he was worth "about seven or eight million dollars." That's right, *millions*. He rented Learjets to take the family on ski trips, built himself a million-dollar basement, and basked in the gratitude of the many who benefited from his largesse.

His bookmaking operation was so successful it attracted the attention of Tony "the Ant" Spilotro, the mobster immortalized by Joe Pesci in Martin Scorsese's *Casino* (from the Nicholas Pileggi book), who came calling for a piece of the action. Dick demurred, opting to run his business out of Dallas for a time—"You know: Out of sight, out of mind"—until things quieted down. In those days Dick had bodyguards covertly trail his kids. Though no fan of the new "Disneyfied" Vegas, Dick admits it's nice not to have thugs breathing down his neck anymore. "Of course, I'd be off the hook now, anyway, being broke and all," he added, chuckling bitterly. It's funny to lose $7 million, really, it is.

"Dick is a decent family-oriented man who defies most people's image of us gamblers sitting by a pool, drinking champagne all day, with a couple of showgirls as bookends," the well-known sports gambler Lem Banker told me. The two gamblers have been friends for two decades. Lem, who resembles a muscular version of British actor David Niven, himself defies the stereotype. He is happily married, a natty dresser, and an exercise aficionado. And he doesn't play any casino games, he told me, because he can't stand all that smoke at the tables.

Lem calls Dick the most generous of friends, who threw the most sumptuous parties imaginable back in his glory days. "Dick would serve bottles of Château Lafitte-Rothschild 1945 at these parties as if it were grape juice, not that most of the bums there would have known the difference."

Dick's longtime passion was the Las Vegas Gold swim team, which he presided over. He incessantly lobbied the city to build a decent pool, but with no success. "This is not a community-minded place where people look after each other, it's too money-orinated," Dick said bitterly, molding the language as he often does to fit the gap between his wisdom and his lack of education. So he spent $200,000 of his own money to provide his team with a decent facility. He also covered the travel expenses for team members who couldn't afford them, and still treasures letters from the grateful kids he mentored. In one of his more grandiose gestures, in 1985 Dick hired Rowdy Gaines, winner of three gold medals at the 1984 Los Angeles Olympics, to coach the team. This, too, he paid for out of his own pocket.

"I can't tell you how influential Dick has been in my life, having taught me so much about what's important in life, about putting one's work in perspective and valuing family and friends above all else," Rowdy told me when I later reached him at his home in Birmingham, Alabama. He recalled having had qualms at first about moving to Vegas, but then was struck by Dick's commitment to the sport and by the opportunity to promote swimming among the city's youth.

"Dick would blow me away, the way he could set aside his stressful business for his family," Rowdy said. He was amazed, for instance, that Dick could spend a key game of the 1986 World Series between the Mets and the Red Sox—"on which I don't know how many kazillions he had riding"—timing an under-twelve swim meet, as if he had not a care in the world. Although, when Rowdy mentioned in passing that day that he was a longtime Red Sox fan, Dick did tense up and say, "Rowdy, believe you me, we want the Mets to win this World Series."

A few years after Rowdy moved away from Las Vegas, Dick learned, while changing planes in Dallas en route to his daughter's swim meet, that Rowdy had been struck by the rare neurological illness Guillain-Barré syndrome and was hospitalized. Dick got on the next plane to Hawaii, where Rowdy then lived, and stayed for two weeks, helping Rowdy's wife and offering (though it wasn't necessary) to cover all the medical bills. Once Rowdy was out of the woods, Dick threw him a huge "This Is Your Life, Rowdy" surprise party, complete with a filmed tribute, in Las Vegas. He had flown Rowdy into town on some swimming pretext, and then flew in about twenty-five of his family members from across the country behind his back.

Sometimes he wishes he could have back all the money he spread around, Dick conceded, but it's a fleeting urge. "If a man goes through life only affecting his own life, what has he really accomplished?" He considers his family his greatest accomplishment: "Whether I die broke or not, I've been a success in life." There aren't too many gamblers around—there aren't too many people, period—who can say they've been married to the same woman for thirty-two years, he added.

Dick's luck started changing with that infamous 1985 World Series. Though he should have won the bet, Dick insisted somewhat stubbornly, he added that it was greed that put him in a position he shouldn't have been in. "It was a mistake, poor money management, to have bet such a large portion of my bankroll on one event." In other words, he endeavored to go crazy on the upside.

Dick made a comeback in the early 1990s, which Brett Favre put a dramatic end to with a last-minute, fourth-down, forty-five-yard touchdown pass to Sterling Sharpe in the 1993 divisional playoff game against the Detroit Lions. "I've had luck so bad in recent years, you couldn't begin to comprehend it," he said. Dick had about $900,000 riding on that game, a game he pointed to as Exhibit B in the case of how greed can be a gambler's downfall. "Greed is a sin, you know," Dick added thoughtfully.

The notion that greed has little to do with "well-managed" gambling would have struck me as odd a mere month ago. "Isn't greed the essence of all gambling?" I might have responded then. But sitting at the Egg & I with this old-timer, having myself been tested in battle, I nodded knowingly. Damned greed. But not to fret. As we parted, Dick assured me he had one more comeback in him.

♣ ♦ ♥ ♠ Back at the Mirage, I found Mom dutifully plugging away at Megabucks. She'd already made friends with a couple of the change girls and seemed very entertained, so I decided to hit the pool. The Mirage has the best pool in Las Vegas; interconnected lagoons, waterfalls, slides, saronged waitresses bearing piña coladas: You get the picture. Was this too hedonistic a way to spend Good Friday?

Just in case, I brought down some sober reading from my traveling library. It's true: I'm an aspirational packer. I'm not sure when I started viewing travel as the ultimate self-improvement opportunity, but I do. Back in New York I'd resolved to set aside a daily "reading hour" while in Las Vegas, which now seemed pretty funny. Here's another good one: I'd also resolved to exercise every day. My running shoes have seen the world, mostly from the inside of a suitcase.

I found a chaise near one of the waterfalls, ordered a raspberry daiquiri, and settled down to read Eugene P. Moehring's *Resort City in the Sunbelt*. Moehring teaches at the University of Nevada, Las Vegas, and his work is widely hailed as the seminal text on Las

Vegas's history. My sleep was interrupted by the daiquiri's arrival. I dismissed the waitress with a signature, "room charge" being one of modern civilization's greatest accomplishments, and turned over to toast my back and to be able to access the daiquiri's straw without having to raise the glass.

The couple next to me was Russian: a young, heavily bejeweled beauty and her older, heavily tattooed sugar daddy. Russian Mafia, I hopefully assumed. I didn't want to think of the Mirage as just another resort whose guests all belong to the polite, refined society that inhabits the world's peripatetic first-class bubble. For all its Disneyfication, thugs will always be attracted to Vegas, and there is something comforting about that.

I turned my attention back to Professor Moehring. Instead of another tale of gangsters and showgirls, his is a serious attempt to place the city's development in a greater context, drawing parallels between the development of seemingly unique Las Vegas and other major cities of the desert Southwest—Phoenix, Albuquerque, Tucson, and El Paso. Moehring contends that the common denominator in these cities' development was the "federal trigger." And therein lies an irony. In no region of the country is self-reliance more highly valued and disdain for Washington and its ways more loudly proclaimed. Yet the Southwest owes its development, in a way no other region does, to Uncle Sam. In the case of Las Vegas, the "federal trigger" consisted in the construction of Hoover Dam in the early 1930s and in a series of World War II–related projects. Las Vegas thrived during the war. Cheap dam-generated electricity led the federal government to build a massive magnesium plant, crucial to the war effort, in the town of Henderson, now a suburb of Las Vegas.

Nellis Air Force Base came into being thanks to the city's optimal flying weather, and its presumed invulnerability to German bombers. When it opened, this million-acre shooting range prepared pilots and gunners for airborne combat. Within a year of America's entry into the war, the base was graduating four thousand gunners every six weeks. All these youngsters passing through town en route to war's vagaries were a godsend to the city's fledgling casinos. After a twenty-year hiatus, the state of Nevada had legalized gambling again in 1931.

The Nevada Nuclear Test Site was by far the most controversial element of the federal trigger. The town was gripped by fear in anticipation of the first nuclear test in 1951, as Daniel Lang wrote in *The New Yorker* the following year:

> "It got to be pretty grim," a salesman at the local Sears, Roebuck store said to me. "One morning during those last days of waiting, an elderly lady from Los Angeles came in and told me to hurry up and sell her two shirts, that her husband was waiting outside in the car with the motor running. She said she wanted to hand them down to her grandsons, as heirlooms that had come from Las Vegas just before it was wiped off the face of the earth."

Once the city got over its initial nuclear jitters, and before the explosions went underground in the early 1960s, the bright dawn flashes and ensuing shock waves were incorporated into the overall Vegas spectacle. The DI hosted atomic parties, most of the hotels offered "atomic cocktails," and the chamber of commerce printed up advertisements showing a showgirl bearing a Geiger counter. Leave it to Vegas to turn nuclear tests into kitsch.

Some sixty-five miles north of town, the test site and other secretive military installations, including the notorious Area 51, comprise a vast no-fly zone the size of Connecticut, which pilots refer to as Dreamland. Built in 1951, the test site in its heyday was Nevada's largest employer, with twelve thousand people. But the operation was mostly dismantled in the aftermath of the 1992 moratorium on nuclear testing, and Nevada officials are seeking to lure whatever industrial concerns might be attracted to a barren landscape in the middle of nowhere that has withstood 928 nuclear explosions over four decades. One company, Du Pont, puts on a bit of a show every other year for clients at the site, showing them how to handle pesky sulfuric acid spills. Sounds like great fun, but there isn't enough of this sort of business to make up for the nuclear withdrawal.

Locals don't find anything kitschy or heroic about plans to entomb the nation's nuclear waste in the site's Yucca Mountain, a hundred miles northwest of Las Vegas. This proposal has reawakened Nevadans' resentment of their state's image in Washington, as a barren place where undesirable crap can be safely dumped. Fighting the Yucca Mountain Project is severely testing Nevada's formidable lobbying power in the nation's capital.

♣ ♦ ♥ ♠ I met my mother after a quick shower and we took the short tram ride to the Mirage's neighboring sister property, Treasure Island, to see Cirque du Soleil's *Mystère* show. Treasure Island's colorful Strip façade is reminiscent of Disney's classic "Pirates of the Caribbean" ride. The hotel has swallowed the sidewalk, so that pedestrians enter the set, walking along a wooden boardwalk, overlooking Buccaneer Bay, on the other side of which plundered loot lies in plain, tantalizing view. The whole scene is lit at night by swaying lanterns. A wooden walkway that branches off the boardwalk takes you over the water into the casino, where you pull open the resort's doors by grabbing skull-shaped handles. It's an eight-year-old's dream come true.

We stood in a sea of humanity to watch one of the town's biggest shows, the battle between the pirate ship *Hispaniola* and the H.M.S. *Britannia,* which "sails" on to the scene from around the corner. An actor playing a stuffy British naval captain calls on the pirates to surrender their vessel and loot. They refuse, cannon shots are exchanged, most of the cast ends up in the water, and, this being Las Vegas, the pirates ultimately prevail. For the third of six times that evening, the British captain sank with his ship and the pirates invited the crowd into their hideaway—the casino. The pirate battle is an improvement over the Mirage's erupting volcano, further bolstering the Las Vegas ideal of scripted space, where buildings themselves perform.

Along with impersonator Danny Gans over at the Rio, the Cirque du Soleil show gets the most buzz in town. *Mystère* tickets cost a Broadwayesque $75, but are well worth it. More than a circus, *Mystère* is a surreal, acrobatic opera of haunting music, inspired choreography, and extraordinary physical feats. Treasure Island built a splendid permanent home for the French Canadian circus, which also has other troupes on tour.

I was transfixed throughout, but Cirque du Soleil may not be for everyone. My neighbor seemed a bit disappointed. During one of the more impressive numbers, involving only two male gymnasts, he grunted to his wife: "Those two seem to know each other a little too well, if you know what I mean." I think he might have been happier with a more traditional revue of topless showgirls.

Mom and I had dinner at Moongate, the Mirage's Chinese restaurant, a wise choice at a hotel that caters to Asian high rollers. After ordering some standard Hunanese dishes, I regretted not ordering the $47 shark fin on the menu. I'd never had this Chinese delicacy, and wasn't the purpose of this odyssey to take such risks, whatever the price? I called the waiter over and asked if we could change our order, substituting the shark fin for one of our chicken dishes. "But that's a soup," he replied matter-of-factly. I tried keeping my cool. *Forty-seven dollars for a freakin' soup!* "Oh, in that case, please substitute it for the wonton," I replied, before Mom could say anything sensible. For the record, shark fin broth is delicious. It tastes kind of like chicken broth. Only later would I learn that the fins are cut off the living shark, which is then thrown back because it's not profitable enough to keep. Yuck.

After dinner I signed up for the Mirage's frequent-gambling card, withdrew a conservative amount from my safe deposit box, and headed for a row of intriguing *Wheel of Fortune* slot machines. Gimmick slots are all the rage; you could also play Monopoly and *Jeopardy!* machines, and Elvis-themed ones are in the pipeline. Shareholders love slots, because of their relatively stable, predictable results. You never read of a casino reporting an unexpected plunge in quarterly earnings on account of lucky slot players, the way you do for some of the table games. As a result, all casinos have been pushing the one-armed bandits in the past twenty years. In 1983, slot revenue surpassed table-game revenue for the first time in Nevada, and that trend is expected to continue. Still, I hate the machines, and was underwhelmed by all their new bells and whistles. A slot is a slot is a slot.

In places, the vast Mirage manages to convey an intimate feel. The ceiling comes down low over some of the tables, with a thatched-hut motif. I settled down to a $25 blackjack game near the edge of the casino. Nearby a Brazilian band jammed away at the bar inside the tropical rain forest; I ordered a Singapore sling from a Thai waitress. I was back.

The strange thing is, my heart wasn't in it. I'd grown conservative in my affluence. I lost $200 before my drink arrived and it hurt more than it should have. Two yuppie Mexican couples at my table, in town for Holy Week, were telling me how they'd bought scalped tickets earlier that evening to a Luis Miguel concert over at Caesars. Luis Miguel, a young Tony Bennett, is Mexico's hottest singer these days. "We paid fifteen hundred dollars, and it was worth it," said the gentleman to my left, the one who kept taking cards when he shouldn't. I found this obscene: Has money no value? I was shocked, shocked. . . .

After an hour or so of inconclusive WWI-style trench warfare, I made a break into positive territory. In one particularly sweet spot, out of five hands, I was dealt three 20s and two blackjacks. When I was $300 ahead for the evening, I cashed in and headed for the elevators. Walking across the casino, I thought I saw Braces over by the poker room, but he was gone as I approached. It could have well been my imagination; earlier, I'd been wondering about him and his so-called team. I wanted to see my nervous friend in action.

Nest egg: $54,450

Saturday, April 11

Before Kat's eagerly anticipated arrival, I was inspired to break away from the touristy world of the Strip and do some good. You know—give something back to the community that, knock on wood, would end up giving me so much. In its weekend section, amid all the ads for headliners and buffets, the *Review-Journal* had plugged a Saturday morning "Desert Clean-Up" meeting at a local high school. What could be more rewarding than helping the natives clean up their beautiful desert?

Isaac Sweet, from New Delhi via Syracuse and Iraq, didn't have a clue where Cimarron-Memorial High was. He seemed amused that somebody staying at the Mirage would want to take a cab to a local school bright and early on a Saturday morning, though he was thrilled when he found out the school was far out, in one of Las Vegas's newer northwest residential neighborhoods. "It will cost you a good amount, sir, is that okay?" he said in his melodic Indian accent. "Yes, of course," I replied, feeling very much the imperialist, which I always do when someone speaks to me in than Indian accent, punctuating the conversation with a string of "sirs."

"How is it going, sir?" Isaac asked, once we were on I-15. I'd been in enough taxis in town to know that Vegas cabdrivers do not ask this to make polite conversation; they really want to know whether you are winning or losing. I'd wrongly assumed that gambling would be viewed as a tourist trap by cabdrivers; actually, many of the ones I met were heavy gamblers, or had been at some time. And, like cabdrivers everywhere, they have strong opinions. But here their opinions aren't just about where to get a decent meal or a stunning broad; they're about which casinos in town have the loosest slots and whether you should split 8s.

Isaac was one of the few nongambling cabbies I came across. He'd moved to Las Vegas in 1984, after skidding into an eighteen-wheeler during a snowstorm in Syracuse. "I was tired of winters, sir, if you know what I mean." That he never became enthralled with the action made Las Vegas a very affordable place to live. The work was good: more than one driver told me it's easy to clear $40,000 in a year, if you hustle.

But no, Isaac wasn't a gambler: "I can't be, sir, not with what I see." And he ran down his list of woeful tales. "Just the other week, sir, I picked up a man at the MGM Grand who was so distraught I thought he might kill himself in my cab." He told Isaac he'd lost $27,000 while on a business trip by maxing out on credit cards, and was afraid to go home and tell his family. Earlier in the year he'd taken a sobbing woman to a Western Union office to pick up some money to go home with, after she'd lost $24,000. "It's a terrible thing to see, sir.

"Do you do much gambling, sir?"

"Not much," I replied, feeling vaguely ashamed.

We pulled up to the high school as the meter closed in on $30, and Isaac commended me on my environmental activism. I may have been hesitant to 'fess up about my gambling, but I was more than happy to brag about my good deed. Yup, going to clean up the desert. Or so I thought.

Desert Clean-Up was a major disappointment. I had imagined the school would merely be a staging ground, whence we hardy volunteers would be bused into the wild and let loose, equipped with nothing but our wits, a compass, a canteen, and a garbage bag. Instead, "the desert" in need of cleaning was a vacant lot next to the school, off Lake Mead Boulevard, a major commercial road. It was past eleven, and most of the volunteers were heading home. The paper had said this would go on until two, but the lot was cleared. I did manage to grab a "Desert Clean-up" T-shirt—the kind you get at races, with all the sponsors' names—before they were packed up. The affair's main sponsor was Associated General Contractors, which was slightly unsettling (only slightly, given that I had done no work). Had these good citizens been duped, the phrase "Skill, Responsibility and Integrity" in the AGC's logo notwithstanding, into volunteering not for the environment, but for some developer's planned strip mall? I asked one of the organizers who was leaving if that was what was going on, and he laughed. "These here people are just trying to keep their city clean, that's all," he told me, before shepherding his three young kids into a white minivan. So now it was the city, not the desert, that needed cleaning?

Disheartened, I walked along Lake Mead Boulevard, wondering if I'd ever find a cab in this suburban sprawl. I walked past a Taco Bell and some other nondescript commerce before reaching Beano's, which a banner proclaimed the *Review-Journal*'s pick for best neighborhood bar. Cool. It took a minute to adjust to the darkness as I stepped in. I picked a table with a view of a women's tennis match on the large-screen TV set and ordered a beer and a burger. Beano's, "where everyone is a winner," typifies Las Vegas's 24/7 neighborhood joint. A waitress told me the place is crowded at five in the morning with casino workers grabbing a beer after work.

After finishing my burger I went over to the bar to play some video poker. Most bar surface areas in Las Vegas are taken up by these games. You don't have to play when drinking, but it's awfully convenient. Sit on the stool, set your beer on the glass top, and stare down at the cards being dealt. It wasn't even noon, and there were already (still?) nine people playing. I put in a $20 bill and joined the fun. I hardly knew what I was doing. The last time I'd played poker was with my grandmother, when I was about six. Was I supposed to cling to pairs and get rid of everything else, or was I supposed to aspire to fancier hands?

An elderly couple next to me seemed amused at my amateurish exuberance. "Come here often?" I asked the gentleman. "We used to be here all the time, but now I really don't play anymore, it's too dangerous," he replied, feeding his machine another bill. "I see," I said, trying not to sound ironic.

Later in the year I heard Robert Hunter, a clinical psychologist who works with addicted gamblers, call video poker the "crack cocaine" of gambling. Most of the people he treats were brought down by this increasingly popular game, which is also notorious for causing pathological gamblers to "hit bottom" a lot quicker than other games. Like slot machines, video poker offers players a form of escapism not associated with table games. It's just you, the machine, and its mesmerizing sounds and graphics. You need not interact with other people. But unlike slots, video poker machines offer the illusion—mistaken, it turns out—that skill makes a difference, as it does in table games.

Researchers have long differentiated between gamblers who are drawn to machines and those drawn to table games. Roughly speaking, blackjack and craps players want action; the thrill of battle. What's more, they want to win. I know, I've been there. You muster your courage, intelligence, and guile to drain the casino of those damned chips. Action gamblers are disproportionately male.

Escapist gamblers are drawn to the more solitary, less confrontational world of slot machines. Winning is less important to these addicts. Gambling is just about getting away from the tedium of everyday life, much as playing Nintendo games might be for a twelve-year-old boy. Escapist gamblers are disproportionately female.

Escapist or not, I was on a roll. After getting four of a kind, I was up to four hundred quarters. I cashed out and had the bartender/cashier call me a cab. "This is easy," I told him, loud enough to goad my neighbors. "You'd better be careful," the man said, before sending the *ingénu* back to the Strip.

I knew Kat must have been waiting for me in the room for an hour already, and an hour is a long time for a new arrival in Vegas to waste in a hotel room. Nevertheless, I was distracted crossing the Mirage casino toward the elevators by a great commotion at one of the $1 slot machines nearest the walkway. Bells were going off and a crowd was forming around a nervous woman and her slot machine, on which three 7s were lined up. A middle-aged Catherine from New Jersey had won $25,000.

"I wanted to show my mother where the tigers are," she kept saying, looking around. "Have you seen her? I lost her for a moment, and decided to play this machine. I figured she went to the bathroom, but I can't see her anywhere." The mob was too transfixed by the three 7s to focus on something as mundane as a missing mother.

"How many coins had you fed the machine?"

"I'd only played twelve dollars. I told you, I was waiting for my mother—have you seen her?"

"What, only twelve dollars! I'm telling you, Stan, these machines hit quick, or they don't hit at all," one woman exclaimed. Poor Stan sheepishly looked down at his white shoes; he must be the persevering type.

Catherine said the family had checked into the hotel less than an hour earlier. No longer the *ingénu,* I groaned—this unearned luck was insulting to a hardened pro like myself. "Less than an hour ago," I repeated stupidly.

"Yes, we just flew in from Newark this morning."

"On Continental?"

"Yes, why?"

"My wife was on your flight," I said sadly, as if the victim of some bureaucratic snafu. Katherine on the Continental flight had been fated to win upon arrival, but my tardiness had kept her in the room, allowing this false pretender, who spelled her name with a C, to waltz in and take what was rightfully ours. No doubt everyone around me was consumed by equally self-centered thoughts. "I played that machine for hours yesterday," Stan muttered.

Just then a phalanx of Mirage employees descended upon Catherine. They took charge of the situation the way cops take over a crime scene, imposing a sense of ordered calm. Their mission was to capture a smiling winner on film for future propaganda, smother her with congratulations and freebies (as if it's the $25,000 winners who need the comped buffets), fill out the IRS paperwork required for any slot payout above $1,200, cut a check, and, in this case, find Mom. Catherine looked scared and lonely as I walked away.

Upstairs, I found Kat napping. I was thrilled to see her, but I felt compelled to chastise her for following my instructions and waiting in the room, instead of being downstairs playing the slots, particularly the one on the edge of the walkway, about six down as you turn to go toward the lobby.

We spent a good part of the afternoon in the Mirage's luxuriant spa. Kat had a facial and a massage, after which she was ready to proclaim Las Vegas a worthy vacation destination (she'd been skeptical). I did a very proper posh-spa workout. That is, I spent twelve minutes on a treadmill and two hours consuming a variety of juices, watching ESPN on a leather couch, and wallowing in a procession of hot tubs and steam rooms, all the while doing my best to go through as many towels as some small nations do in a month.

Later, wandering around the casino, we came upon a mirrored, guarded door across the way from the high-stakes baccarat pit. This was the Mirage's *salon privé,* where players willing to bet $10,000 or so a hand are invited to do so in splendid isolation. Somewhere I'd read that Wynn had decorated the place with some of his impressive art collection, but I wasn't about to blow my nest egg in ten minutes to check it out. I could go to the Met back home for $7.50 and see better stuff.

The burly guard allowed Mom to coax him into letting us go inside ("just for a peek," she said), because it wasn't very busy. In fact, it was totally empty. Bored tuxedoed croupiers looked up expectantly as we walked in, only to be disappointed. The mix of awe and envy with which I eyed the private dining room in the back let them know right away that I didn't belong. The two clubby rooms seemed almost too plush for a blackjack table, but there was one, awkwardly thrown in with the lower, more graceful baccarat tables and the gleaming roulette wheels. These were the first tables I'd seen in town without the minimum and maximum bets posted. You know what they say: If you have to ask . . .

The salon was surreal. It seemed too genteel a setting in which to lose a million dollars—or win it, for that matter. But Wynn was aiming for the serenity of Europe's old betting palaces in Monte Carlo and Baden-Baden. Most surreal, of course, was the art. In the last few years, Steve Wynn and the Mirage have joined the ranks of the world's most serious art collectors, embarking on a $300 million shopping spree that would have made the likes of J. P. Morgan proud. Wynn has become knowledgeable and passionate about art under the tutelage of a New York art dealer and the former director of the Kimbell Art Museum in Fort Worth. Later in the year, after I left town, Wynn would tell a *Vanity Fair* writer previewing the new Bellagio resort that nothing had brought him more pleasure in his entire life than his art collecting. What makes this poignant, it's fashionable to point out, is that Wynn was diagnosed with the degenerative eye disease retinitis pigmentosa when he was twenty-nine, and is gradually going blind.

Pending the Bellagio's opening, some of Wynn's famous buys—*recognizable* paintings—were here, surrounding the bored croupiers, hidden from the throngs of people on the other side of the mirrored doors. Okay, so a guy like me couldn't name them, but they were all vaguely familiar: Edgar Degas's *Dancer Taking a Bow;* Paul Gauguin's *Tahitian Family;* Vincent van Gogh's *Entrance to a Quarry;* Edouard Manet's *Portrait of Mademoiselle Suzette Lemaire;* Miró's *Dialogue of Insects;* Henri Matisse's *Pineapple and Anemones;* Pierre-Auguste Renoir's *Young Women at the Water's Edge* . . . The three of us, veterans of plenty of venerable museums, were speechless, the way people are awestruck when they go on safaris and see majestic animals in the wild. We were seeing these masterpieces in the wild, outside a museum, decorating a space whose primary purpose was not to show art.

I tried picturing the room crowded and smoky, whales going at it in the middle of the night, praying in front of Degas's delicate dancer for the right numbers to come up. "Do you think the players appreciate the art?" I asked one of the baccarat dealers. "You'd be surprised," she replied without missing a beat, a wonderfully enigmatic and diplomatic answer. Like a good banker, a good dealer should be discreet.

Some elitists from afar cannot fathom the notion that Las Vegas might embrace anything tasteful. They question the sincerity of Wynn's new hobby, as if it's all an act that's good for business. Perhaps they imagine that when the lights go down, the showman sneers in disgust at the Picassos in his midst. I haven't had the privilege of meeting Wynn (not that I'm bitter or anything), but my suspicion is altogether different. Might Wynn's obsession be harmful to his business? Presumably that question was raised by the Mirage's board of directors, which usually gives Wynn, who controls 14 percent of the company stock, free rein. According to news accounts, the Mirage board balked at acquiring more art after spending $162 million on masterpieces, and Wynn has since sold stock to continue the buying spree on his own.

Meanwhile, instead of plugging showgirls, slots, and buffets, the marquee of the rising Bellagio playfully reads: "Coming Soon: Van Gogh, Monet, Renoir & Cezanne," with "special guests Pablo Picasso and Henri Matisse."

Why are Wynn and some of Las Vegas's other casino moguls spending a fortune to attract genuine art to a city famous for mocking good taste? A discriminating gambler might appreciate the new highbrow amenities, but he'd come regardless, for the action. For their part, nongamblers who value such fine things—my mother-in-law comes to mind—are precisely the people who make it a point to steer clear of Las Vegas.

Las Vegas's wild success lies in its ability to draw gamblers, revelers, families, and conventioneers. Wynn wants more. He desperately wants Las Vegas to evolve into a destination for America's most sophisticated and pampered travelers, the kind of people who use time spans as verbs—those who "summer" in Maine, "winter" in Vail, "weekend" at La Jolla. Generally, this crowd considers gambling uncouth, and it hates, well, crowds. In catering to them, is Wynn trying to make of Las Vegas the one thing it cannot be?

A man who thinks, dreams, speaks, and lives superlatives, Wynn is betting that by plopping down the greatest hotel ever built in the middle of the Strip, one packed with prestigious restaurants, luxury retailers, and the most spectacular live show anywhere, he can pull this crowd away from Palm Springs, Scottsdale, and Aspen. He's throwing in a world-class art gallery to make it worth their while. And that is what's most telling about the transformation of Steve Wynn: The paintings at Bellagio will hang in a gallery instead of behind baccarat tables in the high-roller joint. This casino owner and—don't tell Judy this—trustee of the Bush Presidential Library desperately wants to earn the respect and admiration of those who are not necessarily seeking to get comped.

It's quite a gamble. Entertainment and corporate chieftains will no doubt appreciate the Bellagio when they pass through town to attend some convention, but whether they would ever opt to vacation on the Las Vegas Strip is another matter. No matter how much money Wynn spends to make Bellagio a must-see fin-de-siècle monument, it's hard to imagine the wealthiest among us thinking of a 3,005-room hotel as an exclusive hideaway. But I wouldn't bet against Steve Wynn's imagination.

Nest egg: $55,295

4

HARD ROCK

*What non-gamblers do not know is the feeling of virtue
(there is no other word to describe it) when the dice roll as
one commands. . . . It is as close as I have ever come in my
life to a religious feeling. Or to being a
wonder-struck child again.*
                                —Mario Puzo, *Inside Las Vegas*

Sunday, April 12

♣ ♦ ♥ ♠ My poor mother. At about the time the majestic Easter Sunday service would have been reaching its crescendo back at her beloved Trinity Church in Boston, one of the nation's nineteenth-century architectural gems, we found ourselves standing by the shark tank in the Mirage lobby, wondering where the nearest church might be. Sacrifice is what families are all about.

We were worn out from another raucous night in Vegas. I'd surprised Mom with tickets to see impersonator Rich Little, who still does a wicked Richard Nixon, at a casino off the Strip. From wherever he's taping these days, Tricky Dick must be stunned to find we're *still* kicking him around, though he's got to be pleased it's not in one of the town's premier showrooms.

The Mirage concierge informed us that the nearest church, a Roman Catholic cathedral no less, was on the Strip, just north of the

DI. We're not quite Catholic, but close enough. We hopped in a cab for the short ride.

The modern Guardian Angel Cathedral was overflowing with Canadians, unless my sampling techniques are faulty. Of the eight thousand worshipers who attend services in a given week, four out of five are tourists, and you have to wonder about the fifth. The cathedral in the world's fastest-growing Catholic archdiocese plays up the fact that this is no ordinary neighborhood congregation. Instead of focusing on upcoming bake sales and the like, the Guardian Angel's bulletin informs curious visitors that casino chips make up about 10 percent of the weekly collection, necessitating a priestly "casino chip run" on Mondays.

Much like watching *Friends* and *Seinfeld* on Thursday, sitting through the mass's familiar rituals was a therapeutic escape from Las Vegas's escapism. And the bishop was so welcoming I thought he might look out at us and ask, "Anyone from Ohio with us in the audience today?"

The cathedral's artwork is mostly the product of two sisters, Isabel and Edith Piczek, Hungarian émigrées who were the first women allowed to work in the Vatican's Pontifical Biblical Institute. Their stained-glass windows depicting the Stations of the Cross are exquisite, and the last window to the right of the altar, depicting various human activities, includes a refreshingly unpontifical collage of famous Las Vegas casinos from the 1970s. The bulletin's back-cover advertisements—all laid out under a "Please support these advertisers" supplication—were another amusing novelty to those of us hailing from stodgier congregations. The most prominent ad was for a casino. Show this bulletin and get a free pull at the slots?

♣ ♦ ♥ ♠ After a leisurely Easter brunch at the DI, Kat and I gathered our things and checked out of the Mirage. My gambling had become so halfhearted that for once I had to pay my bill. Then we were off to the Hard Rock Hotel. I wasn't going to let a conjugal visit throw me off schedule.

Kat couldn't have been thrilled about moving on her second day in town—leaving behind the splendor of the Mirage's spa and pool, no less—but she showed her usual unflappable good cheer in the face of adversity. In fact, I had a bit of a surprise in store for her. The $250-a-night suite I'd booked at the Hard Rock was considerably larger than our apartment back in New York.

It is a tribute to Las Vegas's allure that Peter Morton, father of all themed eateries and mastermind behind the century's greatest T-shirt craze, is now wholeheartedly devoted to the hip gambling joint that was to be my fourth home away from home. In 1971, Morton opened his first T-shirt outlet disguised as a restaurant, in London. A quarter-century later, he sold the Hard Rock Cafe chain for close to half a billion dollars, to focus on his Las Vegas hotel, which opened in 1995.

The graceful white, curvy eleven-story hotel, on Paradise Road east of the Strip, is bathed in purple light at night, looking very much as if it belongs on Miami Beach. Tiny by Las Vegas standards, with only 339 rooms, the Hard Rock, having operated at 100 percent occupancy, had recently announced plans to expand.

As soon as Kat and I swung open the Flying V guitar-handled doors, we felt we'd left Vegas for an Ian Schrager hotel in New York or Miami, where staff members are uniformly good-looking and slightly condescending to nonceleb guests. I don't know what Ian's plans are, but I did read somewhere that Virgin's Richard Branson is interested in building a Las Vegas hotel, which would touch off a major hipness duel in the desert. Until then, the Hard Rock rules.

A beautiful hardwood floor ringed the entire casino, where no one looked older than thirty-five. We walked past Elton John's jewel-covered piano, Elvis's gold lamé jacket, and a Springsteen guitar on the way to check in. The hotel claims its collection of rare rock-and-roll memorabilia is worth $2 million.

Our two-room, two-bathroom suite had a retro feel and a view of the pool and the Strip beyond, through French doors. The living room stereo was wired to speakers in the bathroom so you could jam while showering. Our biggest regret after settling in was that it was too chilly, unseasonably so, to go to the pool, which featured a sandy beach and, rumor has it, piped-in underwater music. Only a few hardy Canadians—I recognized them from church—splashed about.

My mother, who was going home the following day and had stayed behind at the Mirage, came over in the evening to check out our cool digs. I ordered up a bottle of Santa Margherita Pinot Grigio and we enjoyed a glorious desert sunset. I treated her (for once!) to dinner downstairs at Mortoni's, which Mom said was the best Italian meal she'd ever been served at a restaurant. I felt a high roller's ultimate satisfaction. George Washington called gambling the child of avarice, but most of the gamblers I came across, particularly those who couldn't stop themselves, were motivated to some extent by a desire to spoil their loved ones.

After dinner we went back to the Mirage to catch Siegfried & Roy. More people have watched this show than any other in Vegas history. What's scandalous is that we paid $89.50 a head to join their ranks. The show is an exhausting, overwhelming assault on the senses, with statuesque dancers, fire-spitting steel monsters, the two aging German magicians, and some of the most majestic animals you've ever seen (and now you don't), all in search of a story. "Simply know we love you," the performers assure audiences in the glossy program, and, at these prices, they should. They also ask to be called not just magicians, but storytellers, which is pushing it. The magic is awesome, the story a mess. But then what do I know? The Mirage has built a shrine to these guys on the Strip and paid them $33 million last year.

I've never been a big magic aficionado, but this is as impressive as it gets. A white tiger disappears from one cage, Roy from another, and they both reappear in a third. The cages are suspended in midair, mind you. In one of the more garish scenes leading up to the grand finale, Roy appears on a gigantic reflecting disco ball with one of the endangered white lions he and his partner are raising. The feline looked positively mortified.

The onstage flying sequences in the Siegfried & Roy show were designed by Flying by Foy, a family enterprise housed in an industrial space near the airport that specializes in, you got it, airlifting people during live performances. While we tend to think of showgirls as the ultimate symbols of the Las Vegas entertainment scene, I was rather taken by the flying Foys when I later visited them. "*Peter Pan* continues to be our best moneymaker," company founder Peter Foy told me with a grin as he showed off his latest harnesses and pulleys. The Foys work with more than two hundred ongoing theatrical productions around the world. Recent special projects recently included lifting Garth Brooks eighty feet in the air at a concert in Houston's Astrodome and helping plan Britain's Millennium extravaganza. The Foys not only help choreograph a show's flying sequences, they also build the equipment.

Peter Foy is an affable seventy-three-year-old Englishman whose half-century obsession with onstage flight was triggered serendipitously when as a young actor he floated about in a 1940 London production of *Where the Rainbow Ends*. He moved his family to Las Vegas in the mid-1960s. Walking me through his bustling enterprise (there's a mock stage in the back with fifty-foot ceilings to try stuff out on) that employs some twenty people and last year cleared more than $1 million in profit, Foy still seems a bit dazed at his own success. "Johnny Carson used to ask me if there was enough of this around to make a living," Foy said, a twinkle in his eye, clearly sharing Johnny's astonishment.

♣ ♦ ♥ ♠ The Hard Rock casino is dominated by a raised circular bar. This is the epicenter of Vegas hipdom, a great place for gamblers and nongamblers alike to have a drink and people-watch. Overhead, a string of saxophones forms a chandelier. Cocktail waitresses wear leather vests and caps and tight leopard-patterned shorts. The dealers, too, wear vests, and black jeans, and sway to the blaring tunes. Late Sunday nights are usually a sobering time in the

Martinez household, but with Kat on vacation this week, we had to revel in our freedom. We decided to hit the blackjack tables.

The emphasis here is less on gambling than on being cool. It didn't take long at Teri's blackjack table to realize that players here are less versed in basic strategy than those elsewhere. Scary, that I should realize this. The Hard Rock caters to a lot of college kids celebrating their twenty-first birthdays and youthful baby boomers in for the tunes. Blackjack purists stay away from the place because of its unusual rule that dealers must hit—take a card, that is—on a "soft" 17. In a soft hand, one of the cards is an ace, which in blackjack can be either a 1 or an 11. In most casinos, a dealer must stay on a soft 17 (an ace and a 6, for example). The Hard Rock rule, according to mathematicians, dramatically nudges the odds further in the house's favor, but then so does an ignorance of basic strategy, and the Hard Rock's clientele doesn't want to be bored by such details.

Despite its unfriendly blackjack rules, the house itself tries not to seem too eager to win. This is, after all, the casino that seeks to "Save the Planet." And so it has "Save the Rainforest" slot machines, whose profits are donated to the National Resources Defense Council and Conservation International. No word on whether contributions to these charitable machines are tax-deductible or if, like some politically correct mutual funds, investors' returns on these machines lag the overall market.

Even the Hard Rock currency defies conventionality. I'd assumed that $25 chips must be green by law in all Nevada casinos, so that gamblers, even if sloshed, can walk into an unfamiliar establishment, throw down a bunch of C-notes and ask for "some green." Well, the Hard Rock's $25 chips are purple—Jimi Hendrix "Purple Haze," to be precise. His picture is on the chip, and he looks angry, as if he's just found out the dealer must hit a soft 17. At a roulette table we saw a young woman, confusing pink with purple, mistakenly lay down a $500 chip, thinking it was a $25 one, on black. She won.

The casino's $5 chips, many of them Red Hot Chili Peppers commemoratives, come in a confusing array of shades of red, and the $100 chips are mostly Tom Petty "You Got Lucky" chips. Amazingly, I saw one young kid, moments after he was carded, "buy" two $100 chips and four $25 chips to take home, "as an investment." He claimed they'd be worth a lot some day, and though I scoffed, he might be on to something. A rare $100 Flamingo chip from Bugsy Siegel's day recently fetched $5,445 at auction.

Other chips commemorate big-time concerts held at the hotel. The Stones played the Hard Rock in February, and dealers here are still drunk with the memory. Where else could you have seen the Stones on tour (with Sheryl Crow thrown in as an opener) in a 1,400-seat showroom? The opportunity lured a mob of Hollywood types out to the Hard Rock—everyone from Brad Pitt and Leonardo Di Caprio to Eddie Murphy—along with invited high rollers and a few other lucky fans who will reminisce about that night years from now the way old-timers look back on their night at the Sands' Copa Room during the so-called Summit, when Frank, Dino, and Sammy partied onstage.

Kat and I alternated between blackjack and roulette for a couple of hours. On this, her second night of gambling, she began to lose some of her initial sticker shock. At first, she'd broken out into a sweat every time she relinquished a $5 chip, but I was corrupting her with admirable dispatch. I don't think she bought my old "This isn't really our money" reasoning, but I do think it helped matters that I was ahead for the trip. After an hour of darting about the casino and a couple of drinks, Kat was confidently betting $50 and $75 a hand at Teri's table. We christened Teri, a dealer who could sing along to Aerosmith as well as to Sheryl Crow and could be as engaging one moment as she was moody the next, the Coolest Dealer in Vegas. She even had me thinking that my earlier concerns about fraternizing with dealers had been silly. And so, bolstered by Kat's presence, I was once again a charming and friendly gambler.

And still a lucky one. By 3:45 A.M., when we decided to bid Teri a good night, we were ahead $2,025. We'd been up even more, close to three grand, but had pressed our luck. Upstairs, I opened up our french doors to let in the unseasonably chilly April breeze, and danced with my bride. Life was good.

Nest egg: $57,300

Monday, April 13

Nevadans are convicted of dodging taxes more than residents of any other state and are among the most likely to be audited, according to the day's *Review-Journal*. This is due not only to the number of resident gamblers, but also to the disproportionate number of workers making a decent living on gratuities. The article was cheerful tax-week reading, though no mention was made of a possible link between these findings and the state's previously reported above-average suicide rate.

I shudder at the thought of what my own 1040 for 1998 will look like, chronicling this month-long showdown in the desert. I might as well take the train down to Washington next year and beg for an audit. Worst of all, gambling foes in Congress are fighting to deprive gamblers of their right to deduct losses from winnings. This would be a monstrous injustice, to put it mildly, and I wish the casino's mighty Washington lobby every success in opposing such un-American nonsense.

Imagine you come to Las Vegas for four days and win $250 over the first two, but then lose it back, plus another $250, on your last two days. As things now stand, you'd be even, tax-wise: You can deduct losses from winnings, but you can't deduct further losses. But if Congress eliminates this deduction, your trip to Vegas would be treated as having netted $250 in taxable income, never mind that you lost it all back and then some. Forget about hypotheticals; just think what would happen to a barracuda like yours truly. Say I continued on my seesaw for the rest of my odyssey—up a few thousand one day, down the next—and then lost the whole nest egg on the last day. The loss of that deduction would mean that in addition to going home broke, I'd also be going home to a tax bill that could easily surpass the amount of my original nest egg. This in turn would prompt one of the most pathetic phone calls an author has ever had to make to his editor. "Bruce, Martinez here. We really need to talk . . ."

In the afternoon I took a cab over to the Sporting House, a 24/7 health club where celebrities, dancers, and casino employees come to sweat. You can pay per visit; this town is far too transient to insist on any long-term commitment. Unlike the Mirage's spa, this club definitely emphasizes exercising, not posturing, at least until you hit the snack bar where, much to my astonishment, I saw some video poker machines. They're everywhere.

What had attracted me to the Sporting House was its squash courts. Squash, a frustrating game played with a long racquet and a ball far too reluctant to bounce, is not easily found outside the Northeast. But ever since I'd first caught sight of the Coke bottle on the Strip, Las Vegas had been confounding my expectations. So I was joyously chasing the ball in what was indeed a squash court with a retiree who'd moved to Las Vegas not long ago from the Pacific Northwest. How surreal to be playing him in the shadow of the Stardust and Circus Circus casinos, like a dream in which two irreconcilably estranged parts of your life come together.

I returned to the Hard Rock—"Honey, I'm home," I could have yelled, our suite was so large—to find Kat immersed in some work-related crisis, busily editing something she needed to send overnight back to her office. We went downstairs to ask the attractive female concierge when the FedEx deadline might be and she looked at us as if we were from Mars. This was clearly not a hotel accustomed to catering to working stiffs, unless they happened to be the Rolling Stones.

Eager not to distract Kathy, I nobly offered to kill a few hours playing blackjack until dinnertime, when she'd be done with her work and we could go out on the town. I sat down at a double-deck $25 table, bought in $500, and ordered a Corona. I felt very deserving; my butt was sore from the squash.

Double-deck blackjack is taken more seriously by true gamblers than the six-deck game dealt out of the plastic shoe. Here the cards are dealt facedown, the theory being that seeing all the cards on the table makes it easier to count cards. So you get to handle the cards, which you never do at six-deck tables, where cards are dealt faceup.

Nobody sat down at my table for a while, which can be good or bad, depending on who's got the big mo. It can be frightfully lonely at a table when the dealer is on a roll. You practically beg for reinforcements. But when you are pouncing all alone at a table and someone comes along, you feel as if the casino, or the gods, have sent this person to rattle your karma. The worst is when the newcomer takes a place to your right and starts taking what should have been your winning cards. Of course, if someone sits to your right and gets horrible cards, that's his problem.

My luck hadn't been too hot, so when a fellow New Yorker joined in to my left, saying he was only looking to play for a few minutes until the craps tables heated up, I welcomed him heartily. Joe was about my age, and I guessed he was an investment banker. Most loaded New Yorkers I stumble across I figure—with a bit of class envy, I suppose—to be investment bankers. But then, what did this character figure me to be?

We both got into a good groove. Our double downs were paying off and the dealer was busting far more than the 27 percent of hands he theoretically should. By 7:30 I was ahead $900. I was considering raising my bet to $200 a hand when the game came to a sudden halt.

It seemed Joe and the dealer were having, in the timeless words of the captain in *Cool Hand Luke,* "a failure to communicate." The dealer had already told Joe that when playing two spots he should look at his second hand only after he had finished playing the first, and that he should be clearer about conveying his decisions. You're supposed to tuck the cards under your bet to signal "stay," or scrape the green velvet with them to request another card. Joe had apologized, saying he'd never played the two-deck game and was unfamiliar with its etiquette.

But moments later Joe was crying foul. The dealer had just

shown a 19, revealing a face card under his 9, after we had both stayed on each of our two hands. Joe claimed the dealer hadn't given him a chance to ask for a card, while the dealer pointed out that Joe had tucked his cards under his chips. I believed that this was an honest misunderstanding, that Joe had taken the dealer's admonition not to check one hand before he played the other to mean he shouldn't even look at his first hand until I was done with mine. So he had left them facedown, which the dealer interpreted as a decision to stay. Bolstering this interpretation of events was the fact that Joe's untouched hands were a 13 and a 5, which weren't even close calls. You never stay on a 5, given that no card can bust you. It's only when you get to 12 that you have to start thinking.

But I didn't have the benefit of the tape, and the casino did. The pit boss froze the game where it was until the "eye in the sky" could be checked, and we all fell into an awkward silence, sporadically interrupted by Joe's angry mutterings, of which all I could make out was the word "unbelievable." This was getting unpleasant, and I had been in far too good a mood to be dragged down, so I moved over to the neighboring roulette table, shaped like a grand piano, where people were still laughing, and gambling was still about having fun. From here I could also see how the dispute between the house and Joe was resolved.

I owe Joe big-time. I squeezed into a corner of the crowded roulette table and started liberally spreading my $5 chips around. No dopey experiments for me this time. I would focus on my entire lineup of favorites—2, 7, 12, 13, 22, 27, and 34. Red 27 hit the very first spin I was at the table, and I'd plopped down six chips on it, for a $1,050 payoff. I tipped the croupier $10 and we agreed to keep it up. The guy to my left wisely started topping off my towers of chips with one of his own. Over my shoulder, I could see Joe still muttering to himself at the blackjack table.

Two spins later, 7 hit, followed by, again, 27. That time I had $50 on it. "You can feel 'em, can't you?" an awestruck waitress purred. A cousin of hers could, too, she said. "If I could feel them I wouldn't be playing six numbers, I'd play only the one," I replied defensively.

The last thing wise gamblers on a tear want to do is brag, or have others point to their success. That is to invite fate's wrath. Plus, I couldn't feel a damned thing. All I'd realized was that roulette, too, is a streaky enterprise, and when your numbers are hot, they're all hot.

As if to prove my point, the ball nestled into 13 on the next spin, to a hearty, celebratory yelp. We had all bet on my birthday, and high-fives all around were in order. "This wheel's on fire, rollin' down the road," read an inscription on the purple felt, and it wasn't kidding. Red 27 came next, for the third time, and I had the maximum inside bet of $100 on it. Pity Kat couldn't be here to witness my hour of glory. As the dealer counted out my $3,500 win I saw the pit boss and another suit—actually, at the Hard Rock the powers that be wear colored T-shirts under their sports coats, all very Hollywood—approach my friend Joe, whom I'd abandoned at blackjack so many thousands of dollars ago.

"Sir, we're going to let you keep your bets [his two $50 bets were still there, lamely backing his 5 and 13 against the dealer's 19], but we're going to ask that you take your action to another casino," the new suit was saying. Wow. Joe had been expelled, yanked out of the game, given the red card. Adios.

He was lucky the Mob isn't in charge anymore. In *Casino,* there's a gruesome scene in which De Niro nods to casino security to drag a cheating blackjack player to a back room, where the goons proceed to beat his hand to a pulp with a hammer. Now, in this kinder, gentler corporate era, you get to keep your money when you get kicked out. Of course the comparison isn't entirely fair; Joe may have been clueless, but I don't think he was cheating.

The decent thing would have been to chase after Joe to thank him for causing me to move over to roulette, maybe even slip him a few hundred. The journalist within me also felt an impulse to chase after him as he stormed out of the casino, to record his feelings for posterity. But then, the journalist within me had never seen this kind of money before, or felt this kind of power. I wouldn't have left that roulette table immediately after a 27 for an earthquake.

24 . . . 12! . . . 27! . . . 7! . . . 19 . . . 16 . . .

A new pair of croupiers came on board after the 16 and our im-mortal heroes went on break. How could anyone go on a twenty-minute break at a time like this? To Peter Morton's delight, no doubt, the new crew started off with two insignificant numbers. I knew with an uncanny certainty that my streak was over, and so I calmly asked to have my mountain of chips "colored in." A casino host came over and handed me his card with a clipped "Anything at all, let me know," as I stuffed pink $500 chips into my pockets. It was just after 8:30.

This really was the most sensible way to make a living, I thought on the elevator ride up, chuckling at the Aerosmith quote on the railing: "Love in an elevator—living it up when I'm going down." Kat was finishing up her work as I walked into the suite. She im-mediately knew from my mischievous grin that something was up, but instead of saying anything, I casually strolled over to the coffee table and emptied my pockets. Kat counted the pinks. "Oh, my God!" she exclaimed, having counted out seventeen. I'd made more than $8,000 in less than an hour of roulette.

I dropped my loot in the safe deposit box downstairs, which was by now a veritable treasure trove of cash, chips, and traveler's checks, and we went over to the New York–New York hotel to ride the roller coaster. The Manhattan Express is the world's first coaster to feature a "heartline" twist-and-dive maneuver, which is as nause-ating as it sounds, allowing "riders to experience the thrilling force of 'negative G's' like never before," as the hotel propaganda puts it. We then calmed down at Hamilton's, the hotel's cozy cigar bar, owned by bon vivant actor George Hamilton. I was in a celebratory mood, having taken my nest egg into the sixties. We talked about maybe seeing India next year; anything seemed possible. Hamilton's could almost have been the Rainbow Room back home, so convinc-ing were the art deco touches, the wall-size photo of the Manhattan skyline opposite the terrace overlooking the casino floor, and the as-tronomical prices. But then what's twenty bucks when you can make eight grand in an hour? One of life's most effortless yet satisfying transitions is that from thinking of money as a problem to thinking of it as the solution.

We crossed over the Strip into the MGM Grand, where we had a late dinner at the Coyote Café. This time I had a steak. I felt so much more alive that night than I had on my previous visit, when I had been lonely, poorer, and hungover. Past midnight, back at the Hard Rock, we drank Irish coffees while playing some more blackjack. We lost a couple of thousand, but I hardly cared. For once, I was in no mood to chase. I was in a generous mood, willing to share my riches. This had been about the most perfect Monday I could recall.

I felt like the prosperous King Croesus of Lydia. As the first great historian, Herodotus, recounts, Croesus was on such a roll he summoned the wise Athenian statesman Solon and asked him: "Who is the happiest man you have ever seen?" It was meant as one of those "Mirror, Mirror on the wall" inquiries, but Solon went with some dead Athenian. "Often enough God gives a man a glimpse of happiness, and then utterly ruins him," Solon explained to the mighty—and doubtless annoyed—king.

Nest egg: $63,781

Tuesday, April 14

"We made such a killing at the Dunes," the cabdriver told me when I asked her to drive me to the condemned Aladdin. "We practically furnished my daughter's entire new home for a hundred dollars at that one, and she blew up real nice." The Dunes hotel, that is, not the daughter.

Las Vegas's penchant for blowing up hotels is what makes it the quintessential American city of the late twentieth century. Other cities bring down older buildings, too, but nowhere else is it done so often, with so much glee, or, from the buildings' perspective, so soon. When I lived in Pittsburgh, an old downtown bank high-rise was imploded, but it was treated as a sobering inconvenience, done on a Saturday morning so as to minimize the fuss.

Here, implosions are highlights on the year's crowded calendar, up there with the latest NASCAR race, Super Bowl, or championship fight. Locals are discerning critics by now, having seen the Landmark, the Dunes (to make room for the Bellagio), the Sands (the Venetian), and the Hacienda (the Mandalay Bay) brought down in the last few years. The Dunes and Sands blasts got high marks all around.

Las Vegas has even managed to package some of these implosions for national consumption. Steve Wynn wove the Dunes implosion into the plot of a TV movie he paid to air on NBC when Treasure Island opened. In a merging of illusion and reality of the sort this town is so enamored of, the Dunes fell prey to cannon fire from one of the ships in Buccaneer Bay. More recently, the Hacienda was imploded as the nation welcomed in 1997 (precisely at midnight on the East Coast, in deference to the ratings deity), and Fox carried the demolition live in its New Year's show hosted from the Rio.

The Aladdin's time had come. Luckily for me, its implosion was scheduled for two weeks later, when I would still be in town. But before the big bang, as my cabdriver well knew, comes the big sale. Scheduled implosions prompt the ultimate going-out-of-business markdowns.

The Aladdin's casino was gloomy as it awaited execution. The electricity was long gone, and there was exposed wire everywhere, not to mention gaping holes in the walls. Overhead, there was a lot of heavy pounding and drilling going on, as if the contractors had decided to dismantle the place bit by bit instead of going for the big bang. Really, what was the point, except to make families ordering bedroom sets fret that they were hunting for bargains in a structurally unsound building? The place was literally shaking.

Few casino goodies remained, with the notable exception of one gorgeous blackjack table for $625, all purple velvet with leather trimming. It was the perfect shape for a nifty bar or eating counter, and life would only be enhanced if you could come home after an arduous day of work and serve yourself a cocktail over the reassuring words: "Dealer Must Hit Soft 17." Alas, we live in a 550-square-foot apartment, so for the foreseeable future, this dandy souvenir would have had to join our other surplus stuff in my in-laws' basement. I reluctantly moved on.

I helped one family carry eight keno chairs to their truck. They reminded me of my junior high school's chairs, with their little writing surfaces attached, except these had a cup holder. What could I buy? Portable curios were few and far between. The options were nondescript drinking glasses that didn't even have the hotel's name on them (pointless), botanical conditioner, or a guest room phone. Seeing the crates of conditioner, unaccompanied by shampoo, was deeply reassuring. Sometimes I fear I alone don't use the stuff. But this was no contest; the solid old phones beckoned. Besides the Aladdin name, printed on the dialing pad were the extensions for messages, massages, and room service. If I could get all these features to work back home, the phone would be my wisest $7 acquisition ever.

An amusing disclaimer below the dialing pad, one I'd never seen on any hotel phone before, stated that "management assumes no responsibility for missed wake-up calls." You had to wonder: Had there been a nasty lawsuit, or had the Aladdin merely been refreshingly honest about the mediocrity of its service? I bought two of the phones, thinking one would make a nice present for some people who had invited us to dinner the following day. Better than bringing the expected bottle of wine.

Carrying my two bulky phones, trailing cords, I walked up the Strip to Caesars Palace, where I was scheduled to pick up my rental car. The prospect of having wheels for the rest of my odyssey was exciting, as I never get to drive in Manhattan. I watch car ads on TV in the pained, tense silence of a destitute gambler watching Paycheck Bonanza ads. The Caesars valet-parking attendant who brought up my car eyed my phones suspiciously, but was far too polite to say anything. I guess he decided it wasn't his job to stop guests from stealing phones. I almost reassured him, but in the end decided it would be more fun to leave him wondering.

The green Chevy Malibu had me stumped. I always turn the letters on a rental car's license plate into a mnemonic so I can remember it and make the driver-vehicle relationship a bit more personal. But "601 EJY" didn't offer much promise, not until five blocks later when I came up with "Endeavor to Justify Yourself." Yup, this would be the Endeavor, I told Kat as I swung by the Hard Rock. We then headed west to check out where the natives live.

♣ ♦ ♥ ♠ People go to Paris to see Paris, much as they go to San Francisco to pay tribute to San Francisco, but they travel to Las Vegas for more self-centered reasons. The city has always been a therapeutic destination for needy travelers. The needs change, of course, and so does Las Vegas. In the old days, a lot of people came to get a quick divorce. Now they flock here to gamble, take in varying sorts of sexual entertainment, show their wares at conventions, watch the Super Bowl, or bid farewell to the single life. What most of these needs have in common is an escape from reality, and so it is not surprising that Las Vegas has long nurtured its image as a place lacking a reality of its own.

We cling to this myth. We want Las Vegas to remain a mirage where mobsters build hedonistic palaces surrounded by nothing but tumbleweeds and marauding coyotes. At Luxor I'd even heard a woman ask one of the dealers if he lived in the hotel, as if we were on a cruise ship.

But the nasty secret—that on their way to the Strip, casino dealers must commute past the same Office Depots, Taco Bells, Borders bookstores, Chilis, and other commercial clutter as do Americans elsewhere—is getting out. There are only so many times a newspaper or a TV newsmagazine can shock its audience by trotting out the same "Surprise, there are real folks living in booming Las Vegas" story. I can still remember the shock at my own first viewing of God-fearing Las Vegans going about their nongambling business in the booming metropolis on ABC's *20/20* in the early 1990s. For a decade, Las Vegas has been the fastest-growing major metropolitan area in the nation, its population having tripled since 1980, to some 1.3 million. Roughly six thousand people pour in each month. In 1995 *Money* magazine put Las Vegas on its annual list of the ten best places to live, and in 1998, astonishingly enough, *Fortune* picked Vegas as the nation's second-best city in which to do business. None of this makes it any easier to sustain the myth that Las Vegas is in the middle of nowhere.

Despite much recent talk among local politicos about the need to manage growth, the Feds may ultimately provide the only serious threat to the unfettered sprawl for which Sunbelt cities are renowned. That's because much of the desert surrounding the valley is in the hands of the Bureau of Land Management, and not intended for 7-Elevens. But that collision won't happen for another couple of decades, when the population will probably exceed two million.

Until then, there's plenty of room to sprawl. Across the valley, some twenty-seven square miles of land is under construction. Builders finish fifty-five houses a day, and the strip malls follow, pushing farther into the desert, as the county struggles to build enough roads and put up enough schools. Traffic everywhere is a mess, and on most days the dust makes it difficult for the valley to meet EPA air-quality standards. Then there are those perennial questions about water.

To explore Las Vegas's booming suburbia is to get a taste of life on a perpetual construction site. Major avenues never seem to end; they just fade away into the desert, a trail of billboards festooned with balloons—plugging condos "from the $80s"—in their wake. Residential developments appear intent on topping one another with the dopiness of their names. Oasis del Mar? Come on, guys, get over your water envy.

Later I'd visit the command center of Las Vegas's frantic battle to cope with its Third World–like growth rate: the office of the Clark County school district superintendent, Dr. Brian Cram. Cram oversees the nation's eighth-largest school district, which grows at a rate of twelve thousand to seventeen thousand kids annually. In the most recent school year, he put up a new school every twenty-eight days on average, and he just hired seventeen hundred new teachers for the coming school year.

As part of his job, the superintendent with the Dickensian name studies economic trends across the nation and targets struggling areas for recruitment, promising insecure teachers a Shangri-La of eternal growth, where some five hundred administrative positions will be created in the next few years alone. District officials would hit forty-three states in their recruiting trips in 1998; teachers across the country can access the district's website to check out pay scales and the like.

The first thing Cram tells arriving teachers, and nosy journalists for that matter, is that he's in the phone book, he's that kind of guy. Cram is a widely admired (has your superintendent been in office ten years?) no-nonsense Mormon who thrives on the challenge of staying one classroom ahead of the immigration tidal wave. He told me that Las Vegas schools perform above the national norm, but lose too many kids. Cram calls casinos the region's "steel mills," luring students away from education with their decent-paying jobs. He is working with Mirage and other casinos to offer employees on-site continuing education. Closing in on 10 percent, Nevada's is the highest high school dropout rate in the nation, and only 38 percent of those who do graduate go on to college, compared with the national average of 65 percent. Why go to college when you see casino valet-parking attendants making what accountants make elsewhere?

♣ ♦ ♥ ♠ Summerlin, the nation's largest master-planned community, built where Howard Hughes had wanted to base supersonic jets, seeks to be an orderly antidote to Las Vegas's chaotic sprawl. Kat and I had no clue what a "master-planned community" was, but it sounded intriguing, if a bit scary. We took the four-mile Summerlin Parkway, built by the Howard Hughes Corporation, west from the interstate to the Promised Land and followed signs to a "Home Finding Center" for our indoctrination. Here a sweet woman sat us down in front of a short video extolling the virtues of Howard, of the dramatic red rocks that supply the backdrop to the community, and of life on the "sunny side of the street." Like every hard sell in America, it was all about kids. Happy kids kicking around a soccer ball, happy kids attending an outdoor symphony concert, and happy kids going to the community's schools: It was all so darned happy.

At present Summerlin's 35,000 residents live in ten discrete villages, broken into neighborhoods built by different developers. Some of these boast condos priced at less than $100,000; others offer million-dollar custom houses sitting on a golf course. Parks, churches, and schools are spread out among the villages, and a walking trail cuts through the entire community, while broader needs are addressed by facilities in the Town Center. There is a striking modern library, a medical center, shopping, and some offices. The "master plan" is to have thirty villages by the year 2015, when the entire 22,500 acres will have been developed. By then, Summerlin will be home to 160,000—happy—people.

Kat and I drove around, peeking into model homes, which got a bit depressing after a while. Coming from New York City, the last thing you want to see is a new, two-story three-bedroom house with stunning views selling for $130,000. It was apparent that people here, and this must be true for other booming Sun Belt communities, shop for houses the way the rest of us shop for cars. The expectation is that you'll get a new one, and it's about as easy. To avoid the hassle of driving a few minutes between developments and to bring what it calls a "mall mentality" to home buying, Summerlin was building another House Finding Center where, incredibly, you could take a "Homewalk" and check out some twenty models from various Summerlin developments, all in one spot. God forbid it take you more than an hour to buy a home.

Summerlin provides lonely newcomers with an instant, if slightly contrived, sense of community, as do other planned communities sprouting up across the country in this transient age. There are clubs, sports leagues for the kids, plenty of shared recreational space and perhaps a slightly higher sense of obligation to say hi to strangers you meet along the walking trails. Residents also share a "Summerlink" intranet, like those found on college campuses.

Summerlin and the other planned communities sprouting up across the Sun Belt are a response to the absence of sound urban planning; call it the privatization of zoning. Summerlin residents still pay taxes, vote in presidential elections, and moan about how slow the mail is; they haven't seceded from the rest of us. What they can't do is paint their houses purple, keep their garage doors open or mess with their landscaping. Such things are *verboten* by covenants and restrictions, the guardians of so-called design integrity. Much of Summerlin is actually in the city of Las Vegas, though it's a designated Special Improvement District that assesses a modest fee of all property owners to pay for all the happiness.

♣ ♦ ♥ ♠ Dan van Epp, president of the Summerlin division of the Hughes Corporation (itself a Rouse Company subsidiary since 1996), speaks passionately about the importance of his community's "social infrastructure." By that he means the need to break the pattern of suburban life and design physical space in such a way that people will actually meet. "We need to think about what a community lives like, not just what it looks like," Van Epp later told me. It is tempting to mock any such "planned community" on principle, but that would be a tad hypocritical. If I had to live in Las Vegas, I would probably opt to live in Summerlin, which does exude a certain tastefulness, or in another such planned community. I'm bourgeois enough to appreciate a tidy neighborhood, and far too boring to want to paint my house purple.

At one telling point, on Vegas Drive, one of the boundaries between Summerlin and an adjacent residential area, Van Epp contrasted his community's low, textured adobe wall and the landscaped walkway on our left to a high, unseemly concrete wall on the right. "Do we want all of Las Vegas to look like a jail?" he asked. He had a point, although the very fact that we were critiquing *walls* was a depressing commentary on the Sun Belt's new fortress-chic suburbanism. Whatever its virtues, Summerlin shares some of the city's larger blemishes. High on that list: a lack of the more poetic adobe-inspired desert architecture found in Arizona and New Mexico. Van Epp agreed with me on this point, and said he is trying to get builders to move away from the southern Californian faux-Mediterranean look.

By sheer coincidence, James Kunstler, a former *Rolling Stone* editor who is an urban planning critic, was in town talking to a group of UNLV architecture students and faculty while Kat and I poked about Summerlin. He reportedly called Las Vegas "the most depressing, demoralizing town in the United States . . . where the American spirit comes to die," then proceeded to criticize the city's housing, which he deems not only monotonous, but badly built. All of this led me to one conclusion: His place back in New York must be a lot nicer than mine.

♣ ♦ ♥ ♠ After dinner at the Hard Rock, Kat and I tried once more to win the Megabucks jackpot, but we simply couldn't get any traction. We ended up contributing $60 to the cause, then moved over to more profitable endeavors. We won another $2,275 at blackjack.

Nest egg: $66,196

5

CAESARS PALACE

Westerners call what they have created a civilization,
but it would be more accurate to call it a beachhead.
— Marc Reisner, *Cadillac Desert*

Wednesday, April 15

♣ ♦ ♥ ♠ "It got to the point where I'd drive home from the casino and stare longingly at my gun, wishing I had the guts to pull the trigger," Roger told me over breakfast. We sat at a booth at the Country Inn, a cozy restaurant on Rainbow Avenue that strives to make patrons feel as if they are back in Virginia, with plenty of maple syrup, warm wood, leafy wallpaper, and a fireplace.

Roger hasn't made a bet in almost two years, but he scoffs at the notion that he is a recovering addict. Once a compulsive gambler, always a compulsive gambler. "I drive past Texas Station, where I used to play, and wish I could go in, play a roll of quarters, and gamble like most other people—you know, just enjoy myself for a time," he said. "But I know I can't. Once you cross certain invisible lines, there's no going back."

Roger and his wife moved to Las Vegas in 1990 from Ohio, where he worked as a fireman until he retired after being diagnosed with multiple sclerosis. In addition to his disability payments, at that point he had roughly $20,000 in cash and $60,000 in investments, and considered himself a responsible person.

Roger was first taken to Las Vegas in 1971 by relatives he visited in Salt Lake City. It was, as it is for so many visitors, love at first sight. "We pulled up to the Hilton," he recalled, eyes widening at the memory, "and I thought there was no way on earth we could afford to stay at such a magnificent place." But they could. After that, Roger vacationed in Las Vegas every year. He mostly played black-jack, always sticking to a budget.

Roger and his wife felt like royalty in their new hometown. The apartment complex they moved into was like a resort, with two pools and palm trees. They hit the casinos for $1.99 steak-and-eggs specials and 99-cent shrimp cocktails. A year later, they bought a house. His wife took a job in an insurance office, while Roger's daily routine began to revolve more and more around casinos.

Almost a quarter of local residents gamble at least once a week, according to the most reliable survey on the matter, directed by University of Nevada, Las Vegas, sociology professor Fred Preston, and roughly 6 percent say they have a gambling problem. Not that locals hang out at the Mirage, Luxor, or other Strip resorts. Gambling venues in town fall into one of four categories: Strip resorts, locals' casinos, neighborhood bars, and convenience stores. The latter two only have machines, under what's called a restricted gaming license. Roger did most of his gambling at the increasingly sophisticated off-Strip casinos.

He'd drop in at Arizona Charlie's for the $1,000 noon drawings and some video poker. You know, to take the edge off the day. In his second year in town, Roger crossed what he now calls the invisible line between recreational and problem gambling. He began taking cash advances on credit cards when he'd run out of his bankroll. And, like most other gamblers who have gone too far, Roger made sure to censor the mail each day, lest his wife discover the extent of her husband's passion from a pestering creditor. It helped that he had always been the one to handle the family's finances. But life overall was still good. He had some big wins and ate free most of the time, comped at a number of casinos where he was a big shot.

In time, video poker began to rule Roger's life. "It was like I was having an affair with that machine," he recalled. He thought he loved to gamble, a notion he now laughs at. "Imagine loving a woman who takes every last dime you've saved and then forces you to max out on all your credit cards."

Like most devoted gamblers, Roger clung to a series of rituals, trying to impose order upon the chaos of a casino. No matter how much money he'd ultimately go through in a session, Roger always walked in the casino with $60. "It seemed like the right amount, you know—it doesn't take that much to win." He laughingly recalls that it would take him three decent payoffs, breaks in the frantic action, to light a cigarette. At the first win, he'd reach for his cigarette; at the second, for his lighter; only upon the third win would he light it. Until the bitter end, inside the casinos Roger played the stoic gambler, looking down at the rubes who got visibly upset when they lost, those who swore at the machines as if they'd been betrayed. Roger saved his tantrums for the parking lot and the drive home.

Oddly enough, on his way down Roger took some steps to protect himself from, well, himself. He squirreled away some money in an old-fashioned downtown bank that didn't have ATMs, so as to make it harder to get at his money. One day he went to his inconvenient bank to pick up $1,500 in cash for a big vacation. Then, passing Binion's Horseshoe casino, he talked himself into playing $20. What's twenty bucks when you're carrying $1,500? Answer: about five minutes' worth of entertainment. Another $20 couldn't hurt. Nor another $120. Next door he lost $500 more. His vacation money was almost half gone. Now what? It was dawning on Roger that maybe he had a real problem.

His car provided another sweltering clue. He was driving an old Buick LeSabre whose air-conditioning had gone out a while back. This is not a good thing in Las Vegas. "I can't tell you the number of times I'd be sweating to death in that car with thousands of dollars in my pocket, but do you think I'd bother fixing it?" That's typical of gamblers, ever vigilant lest mundane expenses dilute their bankrolls—hence the beauty of comps.

Then there was Mom's Cadillac. Roger once fantasized about

winning a lottery, going so far as to make a list of what he'd do with the money. Near the top of the list was a brand-new Cadillac for his mother. But when he came to the last item on his list, a gambling allowance, he decided he needed $1,000 a day. That meant having to readjust the rest of the list, and, suddenly, Mom was out a Cadillac. Roger looks back at this little fantasy as an illustration of the frightening magnitude of his addiction.

At a point when he was at least two months behind on all the household's bills, in the fall of 1995, Roger's parents celebrated their fiftieth wedding anniversary. It was a humiliating milestone for their once responsible son, who was so broke he couldn't afford to fly home for the party, let alone buy a present. A neighbor bailed him out with a $5,000 loan, postponing the inevitable crash.

Then came D-Day, June 6, 1996, the day Roger gave up. Luckily, some residual inner strength allowed him to give up on gambling before giving up on life. That evening he and his wife, who considered herself a recreational gambler and never dreamed her husband was any different, had gone to a casino. Driving home, Roger suddenly blurted out that he "couldn't take it anymore," and that he'd call Gamblers Anonymous the next day.

"But you don't have a problem," his surprised wife responded.

The next evening, Roger sat through his first Gamblers Anonymous meeting. In the weeks and months ahead, he couldn't stay away. Some days he'd attend two meetings. It was so comforting to hear his story from others. "We all think we're unique when we're out there and when we first come in," he said, "but then we feel this immense relief when we start hearing our story over and over again, from so many people from so many different walks of life."

Discovering how crowded their seemingly private hell is helps compulsive gamblers embrace the first of GA's Twelve Steps, admitting that they are powerless over gambling. By the end of that first week of quietly sitting through meetings, Roger could stand up in a room full of strangers and, between sobs, introduce himself: "Hi, I'm Roger and I'm a compulsive gambler. . . ."

A few weeks later, he revealed the extent of their financial ruin to his wife, who was understandably shattered. Ironically, Roger's recovery may have placed more stress on his marriage than his hidden illness ever did. GA became an all-consuming affair for Roger, and his wife wanted no part of it. He chaired four GA meetings a week, manned a problem-gambling hot line in the mornings, and sponsored new arrivals; all this seemed a bit self-indulgent to his wife. He says he was growing, and she didn't want to follow. They separated last month, but are trying to work things out.

I asked Roger the obvious question: Why would a gambling addict stay in Las Vegas?

"Why leave?" Roger challenged back. "You can't blame your surroundings for your compulsion to gamble." Does the alcoholic blame bars for his drinking problem? Roger's a firm believer in personal responsibility; he acknowledges that for most people, casinos provide nothing but healthy recreation. A destructive gambling addiction, GA teaches, is a symptom of an underlying problem. You don't leave town to deal with the addiction; you look inward. On a more practical note, Roger added, this is the most supportive environment for a compulsive gambler. There are some seventy GA meetings around town in any given week, enough to allow people to choose between smoking and nonsmoking sessions.

♣ ♦ ♥ ♠ It was time to move on to Caesars. Our Hard Rock casino host, R.J., couldn't have been more effusive in congratulating us and in begging us to come back. He swiped more than $1,000 off our bill, leaving me to pay only for tips, and yes, those damned local phone calls. I then emptied my safe deposit box, making sure not to leave behind any pink chips. We had quite a collection. Instead of taking all the money in cash, I asked for a check. It seemed the prudent thing to do. Who knew? At the rate I was going, I wouldn't need to cash it until I got home. I walked out the door with $35,000 in traveler's checks, a $16,500 check from the Hard Rock—with funky guitars printed in the background—and some $13,000 in cash stuffed into my jeans' front pockets. And the funny thing is, I didn't even feel like a criminal.

♣ ♦ ♥ ♠ Caesars rained on our triumphal parade. After standing in a long line, we were informed by a rude clerk that our room wouldn't be ready until five, four hours away. After all we had accomplished, this was annoying. Something had gone terribly wrong in my planning for this odyssey. At every stop I'd arrived incognito, just another nobody who'd dialed the 800 number, then built a heroic reputation only to, well, leave. And, contrary to the fervent desires of a growing legion of casino hosts, there would be no tomorrow, no opportunity to enjoy my exalted status. I would never arrive to a gracious welcome, to a glass of chilled Chardonnay at the plush VIP check-in lounge, and to an obsequious host asking if I'd take the usual suite. It all seemed so tragic.

Kat and I went exploring. Built by Jay Sarno and his Miami architect, Melvin Grossman, in 1966, Caesars is the quintessential Las Vegas hotel, marrying a touch of class with a truckload of kitsch. If you venture into the most remote Burmese village and say, "Las Vegas," to a villager, he is likely to reply, "Caesars Palace," with a glint in his eye. This is still the most recognizable "brand" on the Strip, memorialized in countless movies. I was so excited to be here, within minutes I'd gone to the gift shop and bought some boxers bearing the emperor's profile.

Caesars has expanded in every decade, so you walk around like an archaeologist, peeling away layers of history, from the spacious new Palace Tower to the cozy old oval casino and the well-endowed faux statue of David, Vegas's nod to art before the town acquired pretensions. To poke around Caesars is to wander through a sprawling candy store, never knowing what delights await you at the end of each meandering corridor.

The newer casino in the back gives way to the Forum Shops, the nation's most successful mall (measured by revenue per square foot), and what has to be its weirdest. Where the mall seamlessly turns into Caesar's casino, two scantily clad Cleopatras posed for pictures and peddled applications to Caesars' frequent-gambler club. As we walked by, the Hispanic Cleopatra was confiding in her blonde colleague that she'd decided to ask her boyfriend to move out of her apartment because he was "a nightmare." Does Mickey grouse about his personal problems while on the clock at the Magic Kingdom?

Less amusing was the sight of slot machines a mere twelve feet from the entrance to the Warner Bros. store. That's the sort of dumb move, dangling slots in front of kids, that makes you wonder whether the people who run these casinos, emboldened by success, may have grown arrogant enough to court future troubles.

But the mall itself is wonderful, a faux outdoor Roman street, complete with a changing, computer-generated sky, fountains, and a bustling sidewalk café. This being Las Vegas, the fountains' statues put on a show on the hour. In addition to the Palm steakhouse, the tiresome Planet Hollywood, and a Cheesecake Factory, the Forum Shops is home to Wolfgang Puck's Spago and Chinois. The retailers lean toward the impractical and exorbitant, though FAO Schwarz, Virgin records, and Niketown are quite entertaining.

Over a cappuccino at the "outdoor" café, Kat and I decided to renew our wedding vows while in town. It was an impetuous decision, no doubt informed by the spray of the fountains, the beauty of the painted puffy clouds overhead, and the thrilling sensation I always get when saying the word "cap-puc-ci-no." I got on the phone and set it up for Saturday. After briefly considering a $229 helicopter ceremony, we decided to settle for something a little more traditional at the Little White Chapel on the Strip. We even put in an order for Elvis.

When ready, our room turned out to be in the new twenty-nine-story Palace Tower, the most dramatic on the Las Vegas skyline. Mussolini would have loved this massive white tower with its fluted Corinthian columns capped with three pediments (a handy word I've never before had a chance to use). The center one bears a gilded profile of Caesar, framed by a golden-leafed laurel. A horse-and-chariot statue reminiscent of the Victor Immanuel monument in Rome sits at the base of the tower, overlooking the pools. It's cool stuff.

Inside the new tower, everything reeked of luxury, from the gilded elevator doors to the nine-foot-high ceilings. Our seventeenth-floor room was by far the nicest nonsuite I'd see during my entire stay in Las Vegas. It had a little foyer with a mirror framed in ancient coin patterns, a refrigerator, floor-to-ceiling windows, a massive desk, and a marble bathroom I could have run laps in. The toilet was hidden away in its own separate little bathroom-within-a-bathroom. And, get this: Next to the toilet, in addition to a telephone, was a glass shelf offering a writing pad and pen. Who knows when inspiration will strike? I'd never before seen this writer-friendly touch.

I sat down for a minute in the armchair to read the day's *Review-Journal* before heading out to dinner. In a disturbing story that brought Roger's addiction to mind, a woman had pleaded guilty to embezzling $115,000 from her employer, the Nevada chapter of the Juvenile Diabetes Foundation International. She'd taken the money over a three-year period in order to feed a video poker habit.

More pleasant was one of the most satisfying headlines I'd ever seen in a newspaper: "Casino Winnings Nosedive." So this was what it was like to read about your exploits in the news. Not exactly: The article dealt with February's results, the latest reported by the state's Gaming Control Board. Nevada casinos as a whole won $588.2 million, down 7.3 percent from the previous February, the worst decline in memory. I smiled conspiratorially and told Kat April's decline would make of February a pleasant memory for these casinos. She didn't look convinced.

Baccarat was the culprit. Casinos on the Strip saw their winnings fall by 15.8 percent, to $276.3 million, because, as some analyst put it in technical terms, "players were winning at baccarat." If you took out baccarat, statewide casino winnings would have been nearly flat, down 0.1 percent, and the Strip's would have been down 3.2 percent.

This was unbelievable. *Baccarat?* Not only had I never played the game—in two weeks of living in casinos I hadn't been aware of any-one else doing so either. I'd seen signs pointing to the intimidating baccarat pits, to be sure, and knew it was a high-roller game, James Bond's favorite and all, but those mysterious tables always looked empty. What's more, there was so much other action in a casino—craps, roulette, slots, blackjack, you name it—that it strained credi-bility to read, as I did then in my classical Roman abode, that "many months baccarat is the driving force on overall state numbers." I'd been playing the wrong game.

♣ ♦ ♥ ♠ John and Lisa Costa, old friends of my buddy Greg's, had graciously invited us over for dinner, so we could see how "normal" folks live in Las Vegas. The Costas, who'd moved to town only in December 1997, could be poster children for the chamber of commerce's dream immigrants: young, highly educated professionals who don't work for casinos. And their two-year-old daughter, Stephanie, is pretty cute, too.

John's employer, a Midwestern bank that has a presence across the Sun Belt and would like to expand its commercial lending busi-ness in Las Vegas, transferred him to Las Vegas from the Detroit area. Lisa landed a job as a comptroller for a title-insurance com-pany. They live in a gated community down the road from Sum-merlin in a comfortable, vaguely Mediterranean house with a two-story foyer and a pool out back. Maybe James Kunstler would find fault with the place—it looks like every other place on the block, he might complain—but me, I make it a rule not to condemn the living arrangements of anyone whose pool is larger than my apartment.

Though we subsequently became good friends, I shudder to think of the impression I must have made that night, bearing an Al-addin phone as a present. All the Costas knew about me was that I was a former attorney hanging out for a month in the town's casinos.

This must have left John, a conservative banker, with only one question: Where does Greg come up with these people? Thankfully, I had my better half along to make me look somewhat respectable.

John seemed a bit apprehensive about the local economy's apparent slowdown—understandably so, given that he'd left home for Boomtown USA to advance his career. The financial meltdown in the Far East was depriving casinos of their best customers, and domestic visitors were finding it harder to make their way to Vegas because airlines were cutting flights in and out of paradise. It wasn't so much that the demand wasn't there, but that the airlines, stretched thin in good times, were eager to use the planes on higher-yield business routes. While passenger traffic at McCarran was up 64 percent since 1990, it had dropped slightly in 1997. "Build it and they will come" is a religion out here. But how will they come?

That question prompted Jason Ader, the premier Wall Street analyst covering the industry, and therefore a man as influential in town as Moe Dalitz was in his day, to downgrade casino stocks in February. They'd been on a downward spiral since, which had John worried. I tried to cheer him up, in part because I was bullish on the place's future and in part because I felt bad that the Aladdin phone didn't work.

People have been moaning about overcapacity here since the 1950s, I said authoritatively, as if I'd been around back then. Even as late as 1983, a *Business Week* article about the slump in Las Vegas noted that "most concede that Nevada has seen its last frantic building boom." Ha. Look down the Strip's flamboyant skyline and it's hard to find any buildings that date back to 1983. What always gets lost in the debate is that each new generation of resorts creates new demand. That's the beauty of Vegas's strategy: If you haven't seen the newest five hotels, you ain't seen nothing.

John just grunted, not exactly sharing my quasi-informed optimism. While I'd seen nothing but ravenous hordes on a video-camera rampage, he'd seen all sorts of balance sheets and other scary data. But a year after my stay, amid the hype surrounding the new hotels, the picture would be considerably more bullish. Traffic into McCarran was way up, casino stocks had sharply rebounded, and John was a lot happier. Even if his Aladdin phone still didn't work.

♣ ♦ ♥ ♠ I was determined to get to the bottom of this baccarat business. Kat and I went up to the baccarat mezzanine off the main casino floor, where a solicitous attendant sat us at the table and took our drink orders. The gamblers were an interesting mix: two Argentineans betting no less than $5,000 a hand, an elderly Taiwanese couple sipping tea, another Chinese gentleman, and, seated to my right, a gaunt man of indeterminate nationality, with flowing silver hair. He wore one of those black Caesars warm-up jackets slots players covet and reminded me of pictures of Howard Hughes in his final years. He appeared far too frail to carry his imposing stack of yellow $1,000 chips.

The whole ambiance was a couple of notches more civilized than that elsewhere in the casino. In addition to the four dealers, three supervisors hovered. Unlike pit bosses elsewhere, who are mainly interested in keeping an eye on the game, these guys also seemed eager to serve. And, as at every other self-respecting baccarat operation in town, there were Spanish and Chinese speakers on duty.

I'd done a cursory review of my dog-eared *Idiot's Guide*'s chapter on baccarat, but I was still lost. Reading about combat never really prepares you for the real thing. The dealers, however, seemed delighted by my befuddlement; it was as if they hadn't seen a baccarat beginner in a decade. I kept dealing from the shoe (one of the thrills here is that players can deal) when I was betting on the Player; this, as a matter of table etiquette, is like betting against yourself. But unlike at the blackjack tables, ignorance in baccarat can't hurt you. The only decision is whether "Player" or "Banker" will come closest to 9, and fixed rules determine which hands draw an additional card after the first two have been dealt.

It's that simple. So simple I felt cheated. Despite all the hype surrounding baccarat—its separation from the rest of the casino, the James Bond associations, the phenomenal sums of money involved—this was like betting on a coin toss. In the case of the people around us, betting a lot of money on a coin toss.

Amusingly enough, everyone at the table kept score on the provided sheets and pondered at great length before deciding whether to bet Banker or Player. Baccarat is about discerning a pattern, an overarching truth amidst the chaos. Try this with a coin toss. If you throw three consecutive "tails" in a row, followed by three consecutive "heads," on which side would you bet on the seventh throw? The dealers politely waited for my colleagues to see the light. This was one place where the bettors, not the house, set the pace. I used the time between hands, as well as the scorecard, to perfect my abstract sketch of Trotsky's silhouette: pointy ears, strong whiskers, whimsical tail.

The highest bettor on each side is dealt the cards facedown. Turning them over, too, can become a protracted ceremony, as experienced baccarat players love to blow on the cards, fondle them, and ultimately destroy them, all before even looking to see what they add up to. You can get away with these antics—which make blackjack veterans squirm, waiting for the guns to go off—because in baccarat cards are only used once.

I was dealt the Player cards on my $100 bet a couple of times, when everyone else had bet on the Banker. I would irreverently flick them over without further ado, much to my neighbor's disgust. His thing was to superimpose one card on the other, with the top card showing, and then slide them in opposite directions. He did this with such glacial dispatch that I could see the top card, go to the bathroom, fix myself a fruit platter from the little buffet (I'm telling you, baccarat is where it's at) and still get back to my seat in time to watch him unveil the bottom card.

Over by the railing, a number of people stood watching, transfixed and intimidated by our silly game. They had bought into the game's aura and were too far removed to realize that watching a baccarat game is about as exciting as watching CNBC when you're totally broke.

Because of certain quirks in the rules (the Player doesn't draw on a 6, for instance), the Banker has a slight built-in advantage. The house rectifies this and pays its bills by charging winning Banker bets a 5 percent commission, which brings the house's edge against both Player and Banker close to about 2.5 percent. The house also holds a staggering 14 percent edge on suckers who bet on a tie, which pays 8 to 1. This is why baccarat dealers are trained from infancy to sell those ties: "Make your tie bets. . . . Ties do repeat. . . . Skip-tie bets, anybody?"

I bet the Player every hand, fourteen straight until we were done with the shoe. The terms, I realize, were meaningless, but still, how could I bet on the Banker? In my mind, the Player was Luke Skywalker relying on the Force; the Banker was the Empire's Darth Vader. A juvenile notion, I know, which would prove quite costly in time, but that night it didn't get in the way of beginner's luck. An hour after we sat down, when we were informed it would take twenty-five minutes to prepare the new shoe, we were ahead $900.

Looking at my watch, I realized we had fifteen minutes before midnight, when the Forum Shops closed, so we abruptly departed. We rushed over to the Kenneth Cole store to buy Kat a sleek black $450 leather jacket she would never ordinarily have splurged on. I paid cash, as proud as Dick Carson must have been when flying his family to vacations on a Learjet. This will forever be known in family lore as the Baccarat Jacket.

Nest egg: $66,596

Thursday, April 16

We woke up bright and early, well before ten, put on our best touristy shorts, grabbed our camera, and headed southeast to visit one of the wonders of American engineering: the Hoover Dam. It was an entertaining forty-minute drive away, through the thriving suburb of Henderson, the charming town of Boulder City, and, as always, the glorious desert. Where you exit the southeast corner of the valley headed for the dam and Arizona, the mountains appear especially crumpled, bringing to mind a lunar landscape.

There are three things every Las Vegas resident will knowingly tell a tourist. First, six thousand people are moving into town every month. Second, life was better back when the Mob ran things. And third, the new visitor center and parking lot at the Hoover Dam took longer and cost more to build than the actual dam did. I'm never quite sure whether the last nugget, though only half true (the dam cost more, even before adjusting for inflation), is offered primarily to denigrate any contemporary undertaking by the federal government, or to lament the passing of a more heroic era. Probably both.

Even before it was completed, the Hoover Dam became one of the West's most popular tourist attractions. Scrappy Las Vegas hoped to ride the dam's coattails; the chamber of commerce took to billing the town as "the gateway to Hoover Dam."

It's impossible for someone my age, the product of a cynical era, to appreciate what something like the Hoover Dam, as a monument to boundless optimism and faith in technology, must have meant to a nation emerging from the Great Depression. Almost one hundred workers died building the 726-foot dam, "to make the desert bloom," as the memorial atop it reads. In addition to cheap electricity, flood relief, drinking water, and the nation's largest man-made lake, the Hoover Dam provides a stream of mind-boggling stats. It is 660 feet thick at its base and 45 feet wide at the top. Its building required the drilling of four 56-foot tunnels through the surrounding canyon walls to divert the mighty Colorado River. More than five million eight-cubic-yard buckets full of cement were lowered to plug the canyon. That is enough concrete to pave a two-lane highway between Miami and Los Angeles, and it's all held in place between the canyon walls by, er, gravity.

Because nothing of this magnitude had ever been built, the Six

Companies consortium had to design and build all the construction equipment, as well as lay railroad tracks from the nearby town of Las Vegas (population, 5,200). The federal government built Boulder City to house the five thousand workers involved in the project. Announcing the building of its new "company town" in 1929, the secretary of the interior wrote: "Instead of a boisterous frontier town [read, Las Vegas], it is hoped that here simple homes, gardens with fruit and flowers, schools and playgrounds will make this a wholesome American community." To this day, Boulder City, with its charming main street and WPA-inspired architecture, remains an unboisterous place. Its residents are notoriously engaged in their public affairs, ever vigilant to keep theirs the only community in Nevada where gambling is not legal, and one of the few where growth for growth's sake is not a religion.

The flow of water per second in one of the dam's intake valves, I learned during our hard-hat tour of the dam's bowels, could fill 640,000 cans of your favorite soda (a tour guide after my own heart), and each of the seventeen generators provides enough electricity for 100,000 single-family homes a year. I would drown you with even more staggering dam specs, but my notes from this point on were indecipherable. I couldn't keep up with our guide's rapid fire. I wrote something about "terrazzo floors," "American Indian designs," and, most intriguing of all, "six roundtrips to the moon," as if this would all be abundantly clear to me weeks later back in New York.

I tried to engage him in some pleasant small talk—at my own peril, for he had nearly brought a Japanese couple to tears for not picking up earplugs at the outset of the tour, as instructed. Our guide, who'd been leading groups through this engineering marvel for four years, had the deliberate walk of a night watchman, and rhythmically swayed his long black flashlight.

"Is this the first time you've worked for the government?"

"Yeah, I used to be in the army."

"Well, that counts; it's the government."

"It was quite different. They gave me a gun."

"I see."

♣

♣ ♦ ♥ ♠ We had dinner in Henderson with the Ericssons, more friends of a friend. Tom had gone to law school at Berkeley with Scott Feldman, a brainy conservative with whom I'd shared an office as a summer associate at a Dallas law firm. It's a good thing we argued politics and abused the free-soda privileges all summer instead of doing any real work: The firm perished soon thereafter.

Tom and his wife, Susie, both went to college at Brigham Young, but met in Sweden, of all places, where they were doing their two-year missionary stint for the Church of Jesus Christ of Latter-Day Saints. I've long admired the Mormon tradition of sending the young out into the world, to go door-to-door in a foreign language. Talk about a character-building experience, particularly in Sweden, so secular in outlook and culturally Lutheran.

Tom, a litigator at a downtown firm, is a bishop at his Henderson congregation. He graduated from Berkeley in 1993, the absolute worst year in recent memory to graduate from a California law school, he joked. He interviewed in San Francisco, San Diego (Susie's hometown), and Las Vegas (where he had family). The contrast between recession-weary California and booming Las Vegas was reflected in the quality of the offers he received. Las Vegas's far lower cost of living was another reason he and Susie decided not to stay in California.

After behaving exceedingly well throughout dinner, the Ericsson boys, led by karate prodigy Taylor, "arrested" me and locked me up in jail under the table after dessert. McKay, four, told me he wanted to go see the Reserve, a new casino with an African safari theme, just down the freeway in Henderson. The place is decorated with monkeys, who sit atop the building as if on a cake, which has convinced McKay the place must be loads of fun. "Remember what I've told you, McKay, we don't gamble," Father said, smiling at the son who'd named the family goldfish Gold Strike. It's a perfectly ingenious name, shared by a local casino.

Gambling runs counter to his religious beliefs, Tom said, noting that he felt terrible guilt when he won an office NCAA basketball pool he'd agreed to enter for fear of not being one of the guys. He bought everyone lunch the day of his triumph to get rid of the tainted money as soon as possible, he said with a laugh.

Still, since the Ericssons live in Las Vegas, casinos play a role in their lives. You cannot work downtown, Tom said, and not go to lunch every now and then at the Main Street Station's buffet or at the California Pizza Kitchen, inside Steve Wynn's Golden Nugget. Closer to home, the kids celebrate their birthdays at Sunset Station's Kids Quest, a place for local gamblers to check their kids while they go crazy on the video poker. The place has the latest and most elaborate games, so why not? Sunset Station also has movie theaters.

I asked Susie if she had qualms about raising kids in Las Vegas. "Increasingly so," with more and more casinos opening beyond the Strip and downtown. "I have no problem with the Strip, and I realize that to some extent Las Vegas will always be about gambling, but shouldn't we have residential neighborhoods that are off-limits?" Recently, a small casino opened up on the edge of their development. "There are no more options in the valley if you don't want to live next to a casino; Boulder City is the last bastion."

Susie's concern echoes that of Las Vegas mayor Jan Jones, who likes to talk about making Sin City a more habitable, mainstream place to live. Early in the year, she floated the idea of taking all the slot machines out of convenience stores and groceries, an idea much applauded by the establishment. Chamber of commerce types want the town's residential areas to feel more like Phoenix, and the big casino interests wouldn't mind getting more of the locals' business. But intransigent Las Vegas libertarians, of whom there are many, value their inalienable right to play slots when shopping for groceries as much as some rednecks across the country treasure their supposedly constitutional right to bear semiautomatic weapons.

Gambling, however, is not Susie's biggest problem with Las Vegas. She is more concerned about the city's overall moral environment, particularly as it relates to sex and pornography. The Yellow Pages are a minefield; most taxis are moving billboards for topless joints; and you can't walk down the Strip without being offered call-girl flyers. Every time the family drives into town, Susie said, she has to figure out a new way to keep her boys from seeing the huge billboard on the freeway advertising the Riviera's thonged Crazy Girls. *What's that to the right, Taylor, a fire?*

It's tempting to ask the Ericssons the same question I posed to Roger, the compulsive gambler: Why are you here? But of course that would be a reaction born of ignorance, and a misguided belief that Las Vegans must by necessity be craps players who frequent the Olympic Garden.

The truth is that beneath the surface, Las Vegas, first established by Mormon missionaries and home of the world's fastest-growing Catholic archdiocese, can be a fairly conservative place. Any city home to more than a million people is going to be a patchwork of astonishing diversity, but that's a fact too often overlooked when it comes to Las Vegas. Along with the 72,226 other Mormons in the valley, the Ericssons represent an important strand in the community's heritage. As School Superintendent Cram, also a Mormon, told me: "Gambling is our town's industry, but it's not what we are about when we go home at the end of the day."

Nest egg: $66,556

Friday, April 17

Even on the most epic of odysseys, there comes a time when a man must set aside life's big questions and count his remaining clean pairs of boxers. That time had come, and the count drove me up Sahara Avenue in search of a laundromat. I was tempted to wash my own clothes because I think that's the best way to stay humble and avoid premature snootiness, and because the folks playing the laundry's slot machines seemed to be having such a blast. But, pressed for time (the rationalization behind most modern-day bourgeois indulgences), I reluctantly left my bundle behind and headed for the National Science Teachers Association convention, which had brought more than twenty thousand high school science teachers into town.

I spent all of twenty-five minutes roaming around the convention center before I was overcome by the same urge I'd felt in every science class I ever took—an urge to run. This time I did, back to Caesars. I longed to spend some time with Kat at the swimming pool.

It was past four on a Friday afternoon, time to relax after another strenuous week on the job, when Kat burst my bubble by saying, "This is so great, I keep forgetting you're not on vacation." Ouch. With that, I turned my attention to the paper.

The *Review-Journal* reported another stunning coup in Las Vegas's march to acquire highbrow culture overnight. Or, in this case, lease it. The Rio, which had so impressed me with its cocktail waitresses' buttocks décolletage, announced that it had struck a deal with Russian cultural officials to bring the largest collection of Imperial artifacts ever to leave Russia to Las Vegas late in 1998. The collection would be exhibited in the hotel itself. The Rio outbid some respectable Western museums for the exhibit, which would include such nifty heirlooms as the throne of Peter the Great and the Fabergé pen with which Nicholas II, the last czar, abdicated the throne. The resort has also agreed to build a twenty-thousand-square-foot hall replicating the Peterhof palace to house the six-month exhibit. That's one way to keep up with Wynn's Van Goghs.

You can't blame the Russians, voracious new capitalists, for coming where the cash is. The Rio will pay for some much-needed restoration of the Peterhof. Still, the cultural dignitaries from St. Petersburg must have cringed later in the year when Nevada governor Bob Miller, at a ceremony to hype the exhibit, was quoted in the papers as saying: "No country in the world has changed more in my lifetime than Russia. They've gone from czars to world leaders in communism, to democracy." Presumably the fifty-three-year-old governor thinks Czar Nicholas II was our World War II ally.

Speaking of the governor, he'd starred in an entertaining corruption story in the previous day's *Review-Journal.* Governor Miller apologized for failing to disclose some $60,000 in travel and other expenses that had been paid for by a slush fund "financed largely by casino interests," as the paper put it. The politician's defense (picture someone swimming in quicksand) is what makes these stories so entertaining. You see, Bob couldn't cover these expenses from leftover campaign funds, as he said he normally would, because that piggy bank was empty. So, facing additional costs as a result of his presidency of the National Governors Association, he hit up his political supporters for what Lyndon Johnson used to call some WAM (walking-around money).

None of this was inappropriate in the governor's eyes. His only mistake was a failure to disclose, he said, echoing one of the central tenets of American politics: Any institutionalized corruption can be excused so long as it is transparent. And here's the clincher: In describing his fund-raising technique, Bob turned the slush fund into a symbol of his fiscal prudence: "I said would you help us so we don't have to raise taxpayer dollars," he explained. But why stop there: Why not hit up casino interests for his salary and save each hardworking citizen of Nevada another few pennies?

♣ ◆ ♥ ♠ Caesars pompously calls its pool area the Garden of the Gods, and claims it's inspired by the Baths of Caracalla in Rome. Drink enough piña coladas and fry in the desert sun by these marble-tiled pools surrounded by columns, sprouting fountains, decorative urns and statuary of seahorses until your brain softens, and it isn't hard to picture yourself a hedonistic Roman senator living in the age of Caesar. What better place to read Marc Reisner's engrossing *Cadillac Desert,* my once again inappropriately heavy poolside reading? The book's subtitle: *The American West and Its Disappearing Water.*

Whether he is retelling the story of John Wesley Powell's heroic exploration of the Colorado River, or the less edifying tale of how Los Angeles raided Owens Valley for its water, Reisner's thesis is constant: The Southwest was never meant to sustain so many people. It took a "messianic effort" by Mormon settlers and later by the "dam-crazed" federal Bureau of Reclamation to green patches of the great American desert and obscure its aridity, to a large extent by using up nonrenewable groundwater supplies.

Reisner recounts that in the nineteenth century, a wacky school of meteorology, undoubtedly influenced by the ideology of Manifest Destiny, developed under the rubric "Rain follows the plow." The principle, most closely associated with the climatologist Cyrus Thomas, was that an arid region's moisture will increase along with its population. This was so, Thomas and his followers believed, because plowing the land exposed the soil's moisture to the sky, newly planted trees enhance rainfall, smoke from trains causes rain, and all the "commotion" associated with growth forms clouds. Drive around the modern-day sprawl that is Las Vegas and you start to wonder whether local planners may not still be clinging to these beliefs, in addition to subscribing to the decidedly more contemporary faith that, as Reisner puts it, "water flows uphill to money."

A nubile Caesars pool attendant sprayed me with her bottle of cooling mist as I read this ominous statement: "Only one desert civilization, out of dozens that grew up in antiquity, has survived uninterrupted into modern times, and Egypt's approach to irrigation was fundamentally different from all the rest." Draw your own conclusions.

Echoing Professor Moehring's point that this part of the country was nurtured by federal largesse, Reisner calls the western farmer "the embodiment of the welfare state, though he was the last to recognize it." The federal government's reclamation program, in Reisner's view, became "the worst perversion of the New Deal, subsidizing high-altitude desert farmers so they could grow the same crops farmers elsewhere in the country were being paid not to grow."

♣ ♦ ♥ ♠ Pat Mulroy shares her "good friend Marc's" contempt for California farmers' unquenchable thirst, but otherwise thinks

Reisner gets a little carried away. That's not surprising. In a town run by women, Mulroy, a widely admired, forceful blonde who grew up in Germany and studied German literature at Stanford, is the water czar, general manager of the Las Vegas Water District and the Southern Nevada Water Authority.

"Where does Marc want us all to go?" she asked when I met her on a subsequent trip to Las Vegas. "To Maine?"

Mulroy assured me that Las Vegas, contrary to the perennial (and wishful?) reporting of visiting journalists, will not run out of water anytime soon. Even under the most bullish growth forecasts and assuming the city gains no access to new water sources, Mulroy is confident the valley's needs will be met through the year 2030, thanks to recent conservation efforts and an agreement with Arizona brokered by U.S. Interior Secretary Bruce Babbitt that will allow Las Vegas to bank water in that state. Mind you, 2030 is an awful long time away in dog years.

Beyond then, Las Vegans will look to the Colorado River, that serene chiseler of magnificent canyons and provider of life to the Southwest, which at present accounts for a full 85 percent of the city's water supply. The arrangement embodied in a series of 1920s deals to allocate the river's bounty, the Colorado River Compact, constituted one of the most complicated interstate agreements ever. It's also one of the most outdated, according to Las Vegans. "As the West changed from its agrarian roots to being overwhelmingly urban, people moved, but the water hasn't," Mulroy said.

Under the compact's terms, the so-called lower-basin Colorado River states are entitled to 7.5 million acre-feet (an acre-foot equals 326,000 gallons, about a year's worth for two small families). Of that, California is entitled to 4.4 million acre-feet, Arizona to 2.85 million, and Nevada, home to little agriculture and only a few hardy souls seven decades ago, to a meager 300,000.

To remain sustainable, the desert Southwest simply needs to strike a new balance among the needs of its environment, its agriculture, and its cities, according to Mulroy. The West's perceived water scarcity is more political than real. The Colorado allotment for the Imperial Valley's farmers in southern California, she added by way of explanation, is ten times greater than the whole state of Nevada's, and there is absolutely no incentive for its irrigation districts to use water, the farmer's birthright, more efficiently. The West's mentality concerning water has long been "Use it or lose it," and under the law, the irrigation districts have first dibs on the water, ahead of Los Angeles and San Diego.

Mulroy led a water-coveting field trip earlier in the year; the Nevada delegation was astounded in the Imperial District by the sight of (among other signs of waste) unlined dirt ditches that lose water to seepage. Adding insult to injury, the *Review-Journal* reported during the trip, the Imperial District's chairman called Mulroy "a chick."

Mulroy is the first to admit that Las Vegas was slow to get on the conservation bandwagon in the 1980s. In the 1990s, however, per capita consumption has been cut by about 15 percent, and the water authority estimates that by the year 2010 a full 25 percent of the valley's water demand will be met through conservation. All this has taken a lot of prodding, Mulroy said, because "water is not a religion here as it is some places, particularly places with an agricultural heritage."

When Las Vegans, most of whom are immigrants from green states, turn on a faucet they expect water to come out, without giving it much thought. What's more, they traditionally haven't hesitated to create their own patch of green in the desert. What I'd noticed about the city's architecture applies to its landscaping as well: Unlike places like Albuquerque and Tucson, Las Vegas hasn't fully come to terms with the fact that it's sitting in the middle of a desert. That is why the water authority sports a spectacular desert garden exhibit, which people can walk through to contemplate life without grass. Roughly two-thirds of all water in the valley is consumed by residential customers, and of that roughly two-thirds is used to water lawns.

"I think Las Vegas still needs to make the transition from think-

ing of itself as a city that happens to be in the desert to thinking of itself as a great city *of* the desert," Mulroy said.

I was horribly disappointed to learn from her that most of the resorts' ostentatious aquatic displays on the Strip are less wasteful than
they appear. These displays are every self-respecting quick-hit journalist's favored symbols of the town's destructive hubris, and it's always a shame when facts get in the way of nifty symbolism. Mulroy
actually calls Steve Wynn—here we go again—a visionary because
he spent $2 million to install a wastewater treatment facility under-
neath the "bay" fronting Treasure Island. More than anything, Mulroy said, this sent a message to the rest of the business community
that it was time to get serious about water conservation.

♣ ♦ ♥ ♠ That night Kat and I ate one of the best dinners—crispy
Mandarin quail with mango-ginger sauce and spicy Asian greens—
I'd have in town, at Chinois. We had a choice table on the
restaurant's second floor, overlooking FAO Schwarz's three-story
Trojan horse. The food, the sounds of merry tourists wafting up, the
effects of an afternoon in the sun, and the delicacy of the Pinot
Grigio lulled us into a state of total contentment. After dinner, we
caught deadpan comedian Steve Wright's show at the Sahara.

Late at night Kat and I played some low-stakes Let It Ride, a popular poker derivative played on a blackjack-sized table. Let It Ride
is a dopey game, whose very existence testifies to the corporate
takeover of casinos. While games like craps, baccarat, roulette, and
blackjack all have a storied past, and were handed down to us by real
gamblers from a bygone era, Let It Ride was invented in 1993 by
Shuffle Master, Inc., a maker of automatic shuffling devices. Talk
about a classy lineage. As far as I could tell, the whole point of the
game, in which you don't play against your fellow gamblers as you
would in real poker, is to perfect the art of retreating. That's because
you place three separate but equal bets on each hand, and can withdraw two of them if your first four cards aren't so hot. People

seemed to derive great satisfaction from this. The game killed me, but more slowly than it might have if those Shuffle Master folks hadn't allowed me to keep raising the white flag.

We then moved over to the Megabucks slot machines (speaking of corporate gimmickry), which still hadn't hit. We didn't win the life-altering jackpot, but did walk away with $175.

Nest egg: $65,911

An Ill-Advised Intermission

6

ROMANCE

Love one another,
but make not a bond of love: Let it rather be a moving sea
between the shores of your souls.
—Kahlil Gibran, *The Prophet*

Saturday, April 18

♣ ♦ ♥ ♠ I awoke in a rebellious mood. My plan had us moving on to the sixth hotel, Sunset Station in Henderson, that morning, but I was fed up with my own demanding schedule. Moving to a new hotel every fourth day was starting to feel like—horrors!—a job. Besides, it made no sense to move out to the boonies, to a modest hotel no less, on the day of our marriage renewal ceremony, which was also Kat's second-to-last day in town. If only we could take a break.

And so, while I was still lying in bed, the elegant idea of an intermission came to me. Why not insert a weeklong break between my first five and second five hotel stays? I'd spend a couple of romantic days with Kat; then, after she'd flown home, I'd hop in the car and head out into the great Mojave Desert for some tranquillity, a few days out of earshot of a slot machine. I could come back the following Friday, and slide back my return date to New York. My editor would still get his full crazed month of gambling in Vegas. It wasn't as if money was a problem.

Exhilarated by this prospect, I reached for the bedside phone to call the front desk and let them know we wouldn't be checking out until Monday. Caesars was as good a honeymoon nest as any. I felt I'd hardly gotten to enjoy all the whimsical resort had to offer, and the idea of not having to pack seemed heavenly. Nobody picked up. I tried again fifteen minutes later; nada. That is the problem with these mammoth Vegas resorts. They can spend millions to build a hell of a swimming pool, put a Jacuzzi in the bathroom, or woo some famous chef. But at some point, once a hotel is larger than 1,367 rooms—and that is a precise ballpark figure—you can be sure there will be times when rooms aren't ready and phones don't get answered. I don't know how the Bellagio and the other huge, up-scale resorts being built will address this issue. There is simply no way to get around the fact that when it comes to a hotel's service, size does matter. On my fourth attempt, a brusque clerk informed me that my request could not be accommodated. The hotel was sold out over the weekend. Sadly, given my scant time at the tables, I couldn't even dial up a casino host to make a room suddenly available. It was time to pack.

I may not have had "juice" at Caesars, but I did across the Med-iterranean and down the Strip, at Luxor. This would all turn out for the best. Hadn't I been muttering just the other day about never ar-riving in style anywhere? I fumbled for Bob Miner's card and gave him a call. My bride was going to be pampered. So before leaving, I grabbed my Mirage money clip out of the safe deposit box and told Kat I wanted to buy her something to wear on our big night. I was getting into this sugar daddy role.

♣ ♦ ♥ ♠ I popped the question the first time we ever had a meal together. We were at V&T's Pizza with my roommate Michael Hein.

"So, are you going to marry this guy?"

"I think so, if he asks. I really thought he was going to propose last month, when we vacationed in Guatemala, but he didn't."

Mike grinned, gave me a "You're screwed" look, and reached over for another slice of pepperoni. A minute later we were back to talking torts.

Kathy and I (and Mike) met in the twilight of the eighties, weeks before the Berlin Wall came down, on a boat trip around Manhattan that was part of our law school's orientation. We became, by necessity, fast friends. I say "by necessity" because we were both (not you, Mike) seeing other people at the time; in Kathy's case, quite seriously. She'd been going out with a guy for four years, an unfathomable stretch of time to my impressionable young mind, which was why I popped the question.

So, as you can imagine, when in our premarital counseling sessions three years ago Father Taylor asked us how we'd come together, I cleared my throat and asked for some coffee. He was in for a long story.

I reflected on all this history, basking in my good fortune, as we made our way through the Forum Shops, going from one outrageous boutique to another, looking for an appropriately slinky dress for the evening's ceremony. Kat was humoring me, trying on things she'd never in a million years buy.

We laughed our way through Versace, DKNY, Emporio Armani, and Bernini. We'd walk in, I'd pick out the most outrageously impractical dress, usually something on the skimpy side, and Kat would try it on, usually while rolling her eyes. "You'd kill to find this in Milan for a mere thirteen hundred ninety-five bucks" was my line of choice, followed by "Come on, let's get it for the book." We did this loud enough to annoy more than one androgynous-looking salesperson. They all spoke with a contrived all-purpose Euro accent, and did not appreciate intruders from the real world, which we definitely were. Of course, the problem with Vegas, at least if you are a snooty salesperson, is that you never can tell who might be trying to unload a wad of C-notes.

I waved my money clip, pointed out that all the money would go to some casino mogul if not to some deserving designer, but with little success. As hard as I tried, I could not get Kat to buy something outrageous. Eventually she dragged me over to Banana Republic and bought a pretty sundress. On sale, no less.

It was up to me to go crazy. I had been looking at coats for the evening, but I already had a snazzy cream-colored silk jacket that was sort of Vegas, and nothing I saw really wowed me. Then, walking past a store called Vasari, I knew I'd found my place. The shirts in the window screamed "Gaudy jewelry not included." Some of them were actually pretty nice. "They're one hundred percent cupro," the saleswoman informed us as we admired a shelf of shiny silky long-sleeved Bertone shirts. "It's wood," she added, noting our blank expressions.

"You mean like tree bark?" This I had to get. A wooden shirt.

The most radical of these shirts would make quite a statement at the Little White Chapel; the more sedate, I could see myself wearing again. What to do? At $185 a pop (roughly the amount I'd spent for all the dress shirts hanging back home in my closet), practicality was a slight concern. This was a shirt, not a dress. I compromised, going for a royal blue number with a papyruslike feel. It was just right: Any Vegas hustler would feel proud to wear it, *and* I might find another suitable occasion for it. With tax, my wooden shirt made in Poland of Austrian materials came to a dizzying $197.95. I paid cash. All that was left was for me to buy some blue Hush Puppies.

♣ ♦ ♥ ♠ It felt good to walk back into the pyramid and come face-to-face again with the Sun God, Ra. I whisked Kat into the VIP lounge, where we were offered drinks and chocolate-covered strawberries. This was more like it. Bob had taken care of us, to be sure, even though the hotel was sold out. Our comped suite in one of the new towers was a real beauty. No slanting walls, but still plenty of kitsch. The living room's standing lamps were neoclassic columns; the carpeting had borders featuring Egyptian figurines, and the art depicted Cairo market scenes and the like. We had a wet bar, a dining table, and a sitting area. A huge fruit basket from Bob awaited us, with some Luxor souvenirs thrown in. The marble bathroom had four separate light switches, it was so immense.

We relaxed for a while, changed into our new purchases—I also put on my Caesars boxers and Hard Rock socks—and went off to dinner at the Top of the World, the revolving restaurant atop the Stratosphere hotel, in the seedy vicinity of the Strip's wedding-chapel row. I'll leave it to more philosophical minds to ponder why wedding chapels and topless bars have converged in the same neighborhood.

At 1,149 feet, the Stratosphere Tower, reminiscent of Seattle's Space Needle, is the tallest structure west of the Mississippi. It filed for bankruptcy protection less than a year after it opened, which is why I vetoed riding either the roller coaster (yes, the world's highest) or the Big Shot free-fall, which are above the restaurant. I make it a rule not to seek my thrills from high-speed, jerky-movement contraptions operated by financially troubled concerns. I'd take my chances on the food.

This was God's view of Gomorrah. The Strip looked reassuringly small amidst the vast desert. The restaurant oozed manufactured romance. As soon as we stepped onto the revolving platform and walked to our table, it became clear that most of the night's clientele was made up of prom-night couples wearing exquisitely uncomfortable outfits (no cupro in this crowd) and sipping virgin daiquiris while they nervously awaited their food. Outside, a small plane kept buzzing by—too close for comfort, I thought—trailing a banner that read, "Eydie, will you marry me?"

On our way down the elevator we ran into the glowing Eydie, sporting a new diamond, and her new fiancé, Gregory Gubner, CEO of a southern California software company and longtime Vegas fan. "When I first saw the plane, I thought it must be about that entertainer Eydie Gormé, because she's a Vegas personality who spells her name the way I do, but then I thought, isn't she married to that Steve Lawrence guy?" Eydie said. Finally, she got it, and said yes. The couple would marry in California the following spring and told me I could track developments at their eydieandgreg.com wedding website. Ah, kids today.

♣ ♦ ♥ ♠   The Little White Chapel is a Las Vegas institution whose marquee announces that this is where Joan Collins and Michael Jordan were married, presumably not to each other. Its other claim to fame, distinguishing it from the competition, is that it was the first to install a drive-through window, for those too lazy to leave their cars to get married. The chapel was bustling as we entered, some twenty minutes early for our nine o'clock, and we took our seats in the antiseptic waiting room. If not for the flowers we'd been handed—unlike our Elvis, these were included in our $150 package—I might have worried I was about to see the dentist. Couples filed in and out of two rooms. Some came alone; others brought an entourage. A group of bikers from Atlanta filled up most of the room, further reassuring me that I was not about to see a dentist. They told us they were in town for a pool tournament at the Riviera, and two of them decided to get hitched.

That's what's great about love in Las Vegas: You can be spontaneous. All you need for a wedding license is $35, none of that waiting-period or blood-test nonsense. What's more, the marriage license bureau, where couples swing by on their way to the kitschy wedding chapels, is open twenty-four hours on the weekends, until midnight on weekdays. Anyone doubting that this is the most remarkable of American cities should pause and reflect on this startling fact. Where else would a government office stay open around the clock to better serve its impetuous, often drunken, customers? More than 100,000 marriage licenses are issued each year in Las Vegas, and the Constitution's Full Faith and Credit clause leaves other states no choice but to recognize them as the real thing.

With so much love going around, it's easy to forget that once upon a time it was convenient divorces that first put Vegas on the nation's marital love map. Professor Moehring writes that "one cannot underestimate the publicity value gained in the late thirties from such celebrated media events" as the Clark Gable–Rhea Langham divorce. Mrs. Gable lured the national spotlight to Vegas when she moved here to fulfill Nevada's six-week residency requirement for a divorce. She whiled away her days dealing craps, roulette, and blackjack at Frank Houskey's Apache Club on Fremont Street and cruising Lake Mead on his yacht, and talking up the town to the national media. In subsequent years middle-class Americans came in droves, eager to consummate their falling out of love where Hollywood celebrities did.

As convenient divorces became more accessible across the country, in modern times Las Vegas has accentuated the positive, as the nation's all-inclusive bachelor party–wedding–honeymoon capital. In 1967, Joan Didion noted in the *Saturday Evening Post* that Las Vegas's wedding industry achieved peak operational efficiency between nine P.M. and midnight of August 26, 1965, an otherwise unremarkable Thursday that happened to be, by presidential order, the last day on which anyone could improve his draft status merely by getting married. Keep that in mind, single folks, when the next war comes along and you've no time to get a blood test.

It was 9:10, and Joseph and Sandra from Chicago were up next. They had known each other for nine years, but only decided to get married on Thursday night, after a night of drinking and soulful talk. They got on a plane to Vegas the next morning, and here they were. Having failed to find a hotel room, they'd spent the night sleeping in their rental car. Come to think of it, Joseph did look a bit disheveled. He wore Dockers and white tennis shoes. Still, he looked suitably anxious. They were catching a red-eye back to Chicago two hours after their wedding. "I hope we can get this done quickly, so we have time to get a drink before going to the airport," Sandra said.

When it became apparent that they had no witnesses, I volunteered to sit through their service and sign their marriage license. I even lent Joseph a prop to use during the six-minute ceremony—my

wedding ring. Kat stayed outside in the waiting room, waiting for
Elvis and enthralling the bikers, one of whom asked her to marry
him in my absence.

Clergy at these Vegas wedding chapels must get the same frazzled rush as do emergency-room doctors—you can only do so much
for so many and hope for the best. The Little White Chapel's Reverend Belinda Rhodes appeared serious in her dark business suit,
very Episcopalian, and her concise sermon, delivered in a firm yet
soft-spoken tone, was as moving and inspiring as any I've heard at a
wedding. I'm not sure what I'd expected to hear—"Go forth and
party"? Maybe I was simply surprised that the default service here
was, well, religious.

After wishing Joe and Sandra a good life and retrieving my ring,
we were on. Our Elvis, a.k.a. Jesse Garon of Dallas, was pumped.
He wore a sequined gold jacket and a black silk shirt and sported a
beautiful wall of white teeth, an impregnable wall of black greased
hair, healthy skin, and the most dazzling, self-ingratiating smile.
The first hints of puffiness were barely detectable under his chin. He
looked very much like the real thing, not to mention a young Bill
Clinton. We'd been given a choice between a young and an old Elvis
on the phone, and I'd gone with the "old" one, figuring him to be
more Vegas, but we got young Jesse. You can't always count on the
older Elvis, I guess.

Elvis walked Kat down the aisle to a cassette recording of the
Wedding March, past the cozy chapel's four empty pews, and presented her to me with a wide grin. She carried a bouquet and looked
as stunningly beautiful as ever in her sensibly priced Banana Republic outfit. Then Elvis stepped aside and serenaded us with a decent rendition of "Love Me Tender," which he finished off with a
spirited "Take it from there, Rev."

Elvis and the prim and proper Reverend Rhodes made an un-
likely team. One moment we were swaying to "Love Me Tender,"
and the next the minister was saying, "We're assembled here in the
presence of God to celebrate the rejoining of this man and woman
in the unity of marriage." God? Here? Was He also at the drive-

through window? Why not? I was touched to see that Elvis was earnestly looking down at the floor in a prayerful mode, hands clasped in front of him.

"No obligations are more sweet or tender [maybe they *were* a good team, after all] than those you are about to resume," Reverend Rhodes continued, as I noticed Kat's eyes turning watery. She then charged us, among other things, "to make a living space for each to be one's self, fully expressed," which I found both insightful and moving.

I grew up in northern Mexico an idealistic, romantic kid, the result of a tempestuous heritage (I have Scottish, Norwegian, and Spanish blood all swishing about in my veins) and too much spicy food. I was a veritable Quixote, firmly believing there is the One, somewhere, for each of us. I know, I know, it's a rather feminine notion—what can I say? At times—say, out on the dusty soccer field or on one of those interminable car trips we'd take to the border to gawk at a JCPenney—I'd torture myself with the thought: What if the One happens to be in Ulan Bator, or Penang? This isn't to say that I didn't make an ass of myself with local girls; I did plenty of that.

In time, I got over it. Throughout high school, college, and graduate school I remained quite the romantic, tending to be in serious, mostly wonderful relationships. The point of my liberal arts education was that there is no single all-encompassing truth, but rather a dazzling array of competing, meritorious truths. It's the same with women, I learned outside of class. There are many remarkable ones, Quixote, so get off your absolutist horse.

Getting to know Kathy on our strictly comrades-in-law-school terms resurrected the faith. The One for me existed. Kat is wise, generous, bright, fun, loving, patient, beautiful, nurturing, gracious, sexy, curious, and funny. Her eyes are luminous, large, alive; her neck graceful and elegant; her skin Mediterranean olive; her body sleek.

And here we were, once again at the altar. We exchanged vows ("I will continue to . . .") and the reverend proclaimed us (still) husband

and wife, "by the legal authority vested in me by the state of Nevada." This last part, I must admit, was a bit scary, because I'd thought a renewal of vows was merely symbolic, and all of the sudden the state of Nevada was somehow involved.

Elvis closed the ceremony with a stirring "Viva Las Vegas," with Kathy and me singing along. We then paid the chapel for the package—which includes a video memorializing the occasion—and went outside to check out Elvis's pink, mint-condition 1955 Cadillac. "Yup, she's my baby," he said, loading up his gear. I then tried talking to Jesse more about his life as a Las Vegas entertainer, his move from Dallas. But this seemed to make him uncomfortable. Elvis wanted to remain Elvis, even offstage. I handed him a crisp C-note, and he was off. We waved and watched him go. We'd really wanted to hang out with him, if you want to know the truth, but this was Saturday night in Vegas, and Elvis had people to see, places to go. Elvis belongs to all of us.

As we turned around, in the chapel's gazebo, an elderly Hispanic couple from Los Angeles renewed their vows, on their fiftieth wedding anniversary. Their adult children proudly looked on, and at least a dozen dressed-up grandkids ran around, playing in the night. It was a good Kodak moment. Or could have been, if not for the fact that the gazebo stands in the middle of the chapel's driveway. Kat and I got in the one of the chapel's limos and drove back to the pyramid, our marriage renewed.

Nest egg: $64,696

Sunday, April 19

To my mind, a day spent wallowing at the pool and spa would have made a suitable second honeymoon. But Kat was in a more adventurous frame of mind, and proposed that we do some hiking out at Red Rock Canyon, which our guidebook described as a "multicolored sandstone palisade only 15 miles from downtown Las Vegas . . . known to leave even *National Geographic* photographers speechless." How could I say no to that?

On our way out of the hotel, we stopped by to say hi to Bob Miner and thank him for taking such good care of us on such short notice. Bob was his natural gracious self, though he did look a bit crestfallen when I told him we were going out to Red Rock for the day. "But don't worry, we'll get our gambling in at some point," I said, feeling some guilt. Clearly, Bob hadn't put us up in a splendid suite for us to frolic in the desert. Whatever happened to that all-night blackjack fiend he'd been thrilled to meet a couple of weeks earlier?

It's criminal to go to Las Vegas and not visit Red Rock, it's such a stunning sight. Then again, it would be criminal if all thirty million visitors to Vegas came out, it would be such a zoo. The 62,000-acre recreational area, dissected by a thirteen-mile scenic drive that leads to dozens of trailheads, is a tribute to what God is capable of accomplishing with nothing more than a little petrification and a little erosion. It's also the site "somewhere near Las Vegas" Dr. Evil chose for his underground compound in the first Austin Powers movie. We climbed among the huge red boulders and in the narrow, cool steepwalled canyons. Other hikers were swallowed up by the immensity of the scenery, leaving us alone, amidst a stillness so profound and so serene it seemed impossible we could be less than a half-hour away from the Strip. It hardly seemed as if this place and a slot machine could exist on the same planet.

♣ ♦ ♥ ♠ It was a bittersweet evening, since Kat would be going back to New York the following day. We'd had such a blast together, and being alone in Las Vegas is unhealthy, though it's probably a bit unsettling to be alone anywhere people go primarily to play.

Nest egg: $65,246

1

FREE FALL

*If one is prudent, that is, if one is as though made of
marble, cold, and inhumanely cautious, then definitely
without any doubt, one can win as much as one wishes.*
                    —Fyodor Dostoevsky, letter to his wife

Monday, April 20

♣ ♦ ♥ ♠ Kat left early, around seven, and the phone woke me up
for a second time around ten. Mayor Gibson of Henderson was so
sorry, his assistant informed me, but he was going to have to
reschedule our lunch for another time. "Well, that's too bad, I was so
looking forward to discussing the challenges of growth with him," I
replied, doing a passable impression of someone who'd been hard at
work for hours. I went back to sleep, thinking *God is great*. I'd stayed
up far too late gambling.

When I next looked at the clock it was past two in the afternoon,
and my headache was gone. I got out of bed, ordered a waffle from
room service, and called the VIP folks to let them know I'd be staying another night. Then I set up a tennis lesson with Randy for five.
My plan had been to check out before going to Henderson for lunch,
and set out for the wilderness after that, but this no longer made any
sense. Better to relax, get a good (and free) night of sleep at Luxor,
and hit the road the next morning.

Driving over to the DI, I swung by a Borders—which I've always treated as a chain of libraries that happen to sell overpriced coffee—to decide where to go. I had three nights, through Friday, when I'd pick up my original trail at the Riviera Hotel. I read up on Zion and Bryce Canyon National Parks in Utah, but ultimately settled on Death Valley, which sounded appropriately desolate for my needs. Michael Berg had raved about it at our lunch, particularly about the Furnace Creek Inn. I then played inspired tennis, rejuvenated by the thought of leaving Vegas, not to mention by the fact that I'd woken up in the afternoon.

I dined at the Luxor's Asian restaurant, Papyrus. It being Monday night, the place was pleasantly uncrowded. I read up on Death Valley over a hot-and-sour soup and Mongolian beef. Then I ambled across the attractions level to the Swensen's in the food court and bought myself a scoop of raspberry sorbet on a waffle cone. I felt clean, rested, well-fed, and oddly at home as I surveyed the King Tut museum, the Egyptian artifact stores, the IMAX theater, and the rest of the attractions floor. Not for the first time on this odyssey, I also felt unbelievably free.

The question, as always, was whether to gamble. I decided to go for it, "for a while." The solicitous young clerk who helped me into my safe deposit box looked longingly at my cone and asked how much they charged for one "up there." She was soon going to go on break and could use one. I'd paid $2.65, which seemed to disappoint her. "Oh, that's too much," she replied matter-of-factly, then turned away to give me some privacy while I retrieved fistfuls of cash from my box. I felt ashamed. Here I was, a wastrel throwing money around, while this poor woman worked nights to cobble together a living. Worse, she had to cater to the likes of me. For a moment I thought of confiding in her that I wasn't one of *them,* but I thought this might alarm her. I also toyed with the idea of buying her some ice cream, but decided this, too, might make her uncomfortable.

I walked around the casino, taking in all the action. I tried to see things through the eyes of the fresh new hordes of gawkers wandering about, but it was difficult. Las Vegas provides visitors with a thrilling forty-eight-hour roller-coaster ride. That's its thing, really—taking impressionable, upstanding citizens from across the country for forty-eight hours (seventy-two, tops) and jolting them as if with an electric shock. They then go home, and for a week or so walk around like zombies, a glazed look in their eyes, babbling on and on to co-workers and fellow PTA members about the wonders of El Dorado, intriguing them into joining a future class of inductees. You are not supposed to stay on for a couple of weeks, as I already had, lest life on the roller coaster begin to feel normal.

I nodded to Dianne, the friendly cocktail waitress; to Juli, the pit boss; and to a number of the dealers; most of these faces had become familiar. I even pointed an old lady to the nearest ATM machine, and warned her not to inadvertently fall instead for the credit-card-advance gouger, as I had seen so many other old women do. I paid my tribute to the Megabucks monster, hoped for the elusive 22 over five spins at a roulette table, and then slowly, almost reluctantly, made my way over to the high-roller temple.

Sitting down at one of the empty $100 blackjack tables, I felt something other than the usual adrenaline rush that precedes combat. I was struck by a certainty that left me cold. Tonight would be The Night, my luckiest. Funny, I wasn't even supposed to be here; I was supposed to have left for my desert interlude. I was sneaking up behind fate's back, and would take her unawares.

Gamblers are master storytellers, always able to divine grandiose theories as to why karma should be on our side. We're due to win because it's the seventh hour of our seventh gambling outing; because the dealer is from the country we honeymooned in; because we wear the right shade of blue; because we fondle that lucky money clip; because we were good and ate our veggies at lunch, or, in my case, because I wasn't even supposed to be in the casino. When we're proven right, we are masters of the universe, and our stories acquire the halo of oft-repeated lore, passed on from generation to generation. "Imagine, son, I wasn't even supposed to be there that night, but the mayor of Henderson canceled on me, and I never got going...."

When we lose, there is no story. There may be irritations—a man puffed smoke in my face, the dealer was obnoxious, I was hungry, they wouldn't stop playing that damned *Titanic* song—but there's no transcendent story. When you gamble and lose, you just gambled and lost. And soon you forget. As Randy told me on the tennis court, great athletes remember their most painful defeats far more vividly than their sweetest victories, but an inveterate gambler will only recount his wins. To linger over a loss is to stop being a gambler.

A fainter heart or a jittery rookie would have seen his confidence rattled by my first three hands. Actually, the problem wasn't so much what I was dealt—20, 20, 19—but what the dealer, Cindy, had dealt herself—blackjack, blackjack, and a 20. Our timing was exquisite. Cindy had been sitting there idle for an hour or so, her two consecutive blackjacks cooling their heels, waiting to collide with my rosy certainty, on which I'd staked a bundle. On those three hands I bet $500, $1,000, and $1,000. Within ninety seconds, I'd already dug quite a hole for myself. But no sweat, this was only a test. To be deserving is to be patient, and the keepers of the temple were merely trying to scare me away before the money faucet was turned on, full force. My certainty was only strengthened by those first three mocking hands.

I ordered a coffee with Kahlúa and settled in for a long night. I cut back my bets and alternated playing one and two spots, depending on Cindy's momentum. But no amount of gimmickry seemed to work. I was like a feeble guerrilla force going up against a formidable army. Finally, down more than $6,000, it was time to retreat into the jungle—or, in this case, back into the comfy high-roller alcove with the fruit juices and yummy Chinese-food spread. My certainty was definitely rattled.

When I reemerged onto the battlefield, having regained my composure, I noticed that five people were playing that loopy game of baccarat. Having had my fill of blackjack, I decided to join them. As had been the case at Caesars, the four dealers at this table were the casino's crème de la crème—winsome, charming characters you'd want to hang out with after work; winsome, charming characters who'd give me gobs of money. Backing them up, more than one supervisor scurried about, doling out scorecards, credit, and gossip.

My fellow players were all Chinese. Four of them drank tea and studied their scorecards intently, as if a proof of Fermat's last theorem could be discerned in the intriguing string of black B's and red P's. I asked one of the dealers if keeping score makes a difference. "Not a damned bit," he replied, which brought to mind the narrator Alexey's take on roulette in Dostoevsky's *The Gambler*:

> It seemed to me that calculation meant very little, and had by no means the importance attributed to it by some players. They sit with papers before them scrawled over in pencil, note the strokes, reckon, deduce the chances, calculate, financially stake and—lose exactly as we simple mortals who play without calculations.

I took my seat at the table, and, trying to fit in, dusted off one of four Chinese expressions I recalled from my distant past. "Ni hao, ma, tongshr?" I asked the man to my left, a Mr. J. I thought I'd said, "How are you, comrade?" but the man looked annoyed. "Our friends don't know the term 'tongshr,' as they are not from the People's Republic," a dealer explained politely. The gentleman did seem to know the term, though, judging from his growl; he was from Taiwan, and didn't appreciate the Communist greeting from a stupid *meiguo ren*. The two couples at the table were also ethnic Chinese, but from Southeast Asia.

The great Chinese diaspora produces the world's wealthiest gamblers and most avid baccarat players, which is why Asia's financial crisis has hurt Las Vegas's casinos as much as it has any other American industry. A Luxor official told me the hotel had seen an alarming increase in the number of bounced checks from some of its best Asian customers; the Mirage had reviewed every customer's line of credit, and across town a number of casinos were attributing lower earnings to the slowdown in high-roller Asian business. But all such troubles seemed far removed as we closed in on midnight. To quote Dostoevsky again, "Only in gambling does nothing depend on nothing." Hence the sense of utter freedom. We were here, each one of us with a formidable stack of chips—some black, some pink, some yellow, and some brown—and that was all that mattered; we were in action. Whatever machinations we'd gone through to put our chips on the table—lying, embezzling, saving, stealing, working, inheriting, speculating, or, as in my case, dreaming up a nutty book concept—no longer mattered. In Luxor's eyes, we were all moral equals, all free.

In my case, free to bet on the Player all night. I persisted with my juvenile notion that somehow the Player was the noble bet, and I was going to have nothing to do with the Banker. My obstinacy pained my neighbor, the elderly Mr. J., who in time came around to the idea that I was not some kind of Communist ogre. After the Banker won twelve hands in a row, with me the only person betting on the Player for the last eight, Mr. J. leaned over to me and said: "You know, this game isn't meant to be a loyalty test." His accent was that of a foreigner who has spent much time among the English, always a delicacy to American ears. He took a sip of his piping hot salted water—that's all I saw him drink, and he tipped Dianne $5 a shot—and proceeded: "If it's thinking you're averse to, may I suggest you simply bet each time on the previous winner." Mr. J. said this in all seriousness, without cracking a grin. He wore a pinstriped suit, thick horn-rimmed glasses, and what in the eighties would have been described as a red power tie.

I liked the man's style, if not his choice of beverage. Offering advice to total strangers—advice on how to wager hundreds of dollars on a coin toss, no less—is always a delicate task. But prefacing it with the statement, "If it's thinking you're averse to . . . " was endearingly audacious. Or perhaps it was a territorial matter. Perhaps he felt an obligation to set straight any American who wandered into the baccarat pit, the way some hospitable American might have once felt obligated to explain baseball to him.

When it came to his own gambling, Mr. J. liked to have the last word at the table. He delayed making his bet until everyone else had. He would study his scorecard, sip his salt water, close his eyes, and slowly roll his neck around, all the while humming, ever so softly. This could go on for a few minutes, as the two couples at the other end of the table from us liked caucusing between hands. Meanwhile, the dealers would be going on about the likelihood of an upcoming tie. My bet, of course, would have been out there for what seemed like ages—defying the others to hop on the Player band-wagon—by the time Mr. J. was prodded by one of the dealers to either place a bet, after everyone else had, or miss a hand. Then he'd invariably throw out a yellow $1,000 chip with an apologetic mumble, as if he'd been distracted and not strategizing till the bitter end. Once, when the younger of the two gentlemen at the other end of the table changed his bet at the very last instant, Mr. J. icily stared at him for a good minute thereafter. For once, he hadn't had the last word. But it never happened again.

Despite his natty attire, Mr. J. had no right to demand anything of those other players, the C. and K. families. Each of those couples bet between $5,000 and $10,000 a hand, to Mr. J.'s never-changing grand. I was all over the map, betting anywhere between a couple of hundred and a couple of grand, depending on the Player's momentum.

When Mr. J. was dealt the cards because he happened to be the highest bettor for a side, typically when he was the sole bettor on the Banker, he produced a purple marble, with which he'd tap the cards before turning them over. This was a mild eccentricity compared to the protracted shenanigans that took place at the other end of the table before the cards were unveiled. The C.'s and K.'s would check out how many "sides" each card had, pound the table, rub the cards on the green felt, scream, "San bin!" (which means "three sides," as in the number of, say, hearts running down the side of a 7, 8 or 9, which you'd want if your first card had been a face card), and often tear up the cards in disgust. All this was done with such exercised drama that they emerged from each hand totally spent, which no doubt contributed to the length of their ensuing huddles. Worst of all for those of us trying to discern the numbers from afar, the younger Mr. K. had a knack for looking the most anguished, moaning the loudest, and tossing the cards the farthest when pulling a "natural" 8 or 9. It would therefore take a minute to realize that, contrary to all appearances, his side had prevailed. Needless to say, this proved more than a little annoying when he'd bet on the Banker. Throughout the night, their theatrics became more and more pronounced—fueled only by tea, I might add. I was the only one drinking.

On one particularly lengthy vigil, while we waited for the K.'s to stop fondling the cards, Al, a sympathetic dealer from El Salvador with whom I carried on in Spanish, told me that when he used to work at the Aladdin, back in the late 1970s and early 1980s, lots of Mexicans would come to play baccarat; they couldn't get enough of the game. "But now you don't see as many," he added sadly. Yeah, shit happens. Devaluations, oil crises, currency transaction requirements; where have all the good times gone? Still in Spanish, Al continued, "I miss the Mexicans, they were the best players, and great tippers." And they didn't do any of this bullshit, his tone implied, as the young Mrs. K., wearing a Mickey Mouse sweatshirt and sporting what one of the dealers claimed was a four-carat engagement diamond, sang what sounded like a lullaby before her husband turned over the second card.

Only once did I see the two couples (at first I erroneously thought they were related) bet against each other. When they did, all four of them individually bet the table maximum, $15,000. Surprisingly, in that showdown they didn't dither too long before turning the cards over. Would you believe me if I told you that hand was a 6–6 tie, that Mr. J. collected on it—the only time I saw him bet on a tie—and that I was starting to get into this game? As is true of life, baccarat's mechanics are deceivingly simple. There's plenty of drama.

The shoe ran out at about three in the morning, which meant it was time to call up new cards, check every one of them individually, and shuffle. The whole process takes about twenty minutes, so we all migrated to the bathrooms and then back into the alcove, where fresh goodies awaited. "I think this next one will be a strong Banker shoe," the elegant Mrs. C. whispered to me conspiratorially as we served ourselves fruit juices. Unlike her husband, who wore a nondescript brown cotton sweater and had a distracted professorial air about him, Mrs. C., draped in a Hermès scarf, was dressed as if for high tea at the Ritz.

For the moment, Mrs. C.'s charm was entirely focused on getting the message across to this oafish American that baccarat was about tapping into currents, about surfing between the conflicting magnetic forces of our universe. My static play—sixty-one Player bets in a row, so far—was deeply unsettling to all those around me. "No, ma'am, I believe it will be a strong run for the Player," I told her, in an even softer whisper.

I sure needed it to be. On top of the $6,000 I'd lost at blackjack, moody baccarat's seemingly gentle ebb and flow had taken another $4,000 bite out of my nest egg. I only had about $2,500 left in chips, which should suffice, I reckoned, to turn the tide. *To be deserving is to be patient.*

Still waiting for the new shoe, I asked Mr. J. if he played any other casino games. "No, this is the only one for me," he said, grimacing at the sight of the blackjack tables I'd vaguely pointed toward. "Those games are for cowboys, and I am not a cowboy," he went on. "Craps and blackjack are about action, like a good Hollywood action film, where you try and overpower fate, guns blazing, while baccarat is no verb, but rather a state of mind where you must isolate yourself from the physical in order to interpret fortune." *That's enough salt water for one night,* I thought.

"What do you do when you are not in that nonphysical place?" I asked him, not meaning it to sound so sarcastic. But such polite inquiries, so routine at a $5 table, were bad form here. "The key to baccarat, you'll learn," he continued, disregarding my faux pas, "is not so much to read the past as it is to read the people around you. There is a lot of money to be made in overlooking your fantasies of being the anointed one, identifying the person who really is the anointed for the moment—because someone always is—and acting on that information."

Back at the table, I was surprised to see Mr. J. abstain from betting on the first hand (a 7–5 win for the Player); on the second (8–0 killing for the Player); and on the third (a lousy 3–2 win for the Banker). Perplexed, he stood up, and said he saw something he did not like and was therefore retiring for the evening; tomorrow would be another day. One of the suits appeared from behind, offered to deposit his chips into his account, and brought him a receipt, which indicated that Mr. J. had more than $200,000 on deposit. And with that, he was gone. I'd miss him. What the hell had he seen, anyway?

For the next hour or so, I settled into an adversarial relationship with my remaining colleagues, because they insisted on tilting more and more toward the Banker. This "them-versus-um-me" sense was magnified by the fact that we sat on opposite halves of the large table, facing each other, with the four dealers between us, two across from each other, as if marking a DMZ line. Mrs. K. smiled graciously at me every now and then, as if to say, "This isn't personal, dear, why don't you come over to our side?" Mrs. C., who looked no older than twenty-five and was rather attractive, would fix me with a spiteful leer, rendered almost playful by the giant Mickey on her chest, after each 8 or 9 for the Banker. Her large dark eyes would widen, her dimples and perky nose shining through the smoky haze of her sleepy husband's Marlboros. Mrs. C. was loving this; to this vixen, "baccarat" was most definitely a verb.

The shoe was indeed turning out to be one for the Banker. Half of its first ten hands went to the Player, but by the twenty-fifth one, the Empire was crushing the Rebellion by a score of sixteen hands to nine. And on the twenty-eighth hand, I was out of chips and out of cash. Feeling rather sheepish, I stood up, promising to return. It was obvious I was leaving to scrounge up some money, a rather undignified position to be in at a baccarat table, where most can summon a marker without getting up—as Mr. C. had done about an hour ago, for a cool hundred grand—from one of the solicitous executives monitoring the game. I crossed the casino and went back into the safe deposit box room, signing in at 4:02 A.M.

"You still up?" the clerk asked me, and I realized that since toying with the idea of buying her a raspberry sorbet six hours ago, I had blown enough dough to buy her 4,717 waffle cones. This was a stunning realization. In there, in the temple, the money isn't real. To gamble, most of us need to insulate ourselves from the reality of the sums involved. We do this by first transporting ourselves to a pyramid or a pirate cove. Then we exchange our scary cash for plastic chips that feel good to the touch; live ammo in the battle to haul in a tidy fortune. A gambler's bankroll is a means, not an end; otherwise, no sane man could stand to lose the monetary equivalent of 4,717 ice cream cones.

Shit, maybe I'd lost because I resisted the urge to do something nice for this hardworking woman. I stopped myself: *Don't do that.* Remember, gamblers don't weave fanciful stories about their losses, or they're done. Through sheer determination, I'd win back my losses, and then some, as I had at the DI, even if it meant leaving for Death Valley a little later than I'd anticipated. I walked over to the cashier and cashed $10,000 in traveler's checks for chips.

The next hour and a half was an anguishing blur. Instead of going straight back to the baccarat pit, I tried blackjack again, then craps, roulette, pai gow poker, anything. I was getting my ass kicked everywhere. Blackjack had been particularly harsh all evening. Could I really have lost twenty hands in a row, or did it just feel that way? I was running out of casino games to turn to. Couldn't we get a Risk game going and bet on that: "Kamchatka attacks the Irkutsk for $2,000"?

At six I hobbled back to baccarat, where a new crew of dealers presided over the chummy C.'s and K.'s, who still sipped their tea and whose stacks of chips had appeared to grow. This time they all greeted me with encouraging smiles. I had a mere $827.50 left, and the severity of my fall must have been written all over my face. Trying to sound encouraging, the once-combative Mrs. C. told me the

Player had been doing well lately. Great, I'd missed a run for the good guys.

Desperate times require desperate measures, and I was frazzled enough to act the role of a true gambler going down. Think Butch Cassidy and the Sundance Kid rushing out into that square in Bolivia . . . or maybe it was Che who bought the farm in Bolivia. There was only one honorable course for a man in my condition to take, and that was to bet on a tie, the sucker bet that paid 8 to 1. Player drew an 8 and a 7, for a 5; the Banker, an 8 and a 5, for a 3. Shit. But then it happened. Mr. C. unveiled the third card dealt the Player, another 8, and smiled at me, even though he'd hurt himself. A 3–3 tie! And though I was still down a staggering $21,000 or so for the night, this bet, because of its timing and sheer audacity, was one of my more memorable triumphs. You could smell lore forming.

I was still in the game, and anything could happen. As Dostoevsky in 1867 wrote his wife during one of his gambling trips to the German spa of Bad Homburg: "Here is my definite observation, Anya: If one is prudent, that is, if one is as though made of marble, cold, and inhumanely cautious, then definitely without any doubt, one can win as much as one wishes." That's right, as much as one wishes. Maybe this would be my night, after all.

My luck continued. The Player was prevailing. After about an hour of being back at the table, I decided it was time to make my big break for it. When the Player won three hands in a row, I raised my bet back up to $1,000, which at that point was a third of my bankroll. We won three more in a row (the C.'s and K.'s were with the Force, too), and on the hand that would have been the seventh win, I put down $2,200 on the Player. Gamblers are funny that way. We can even become superstitious about the amounts we wager, and I thought my old friend 22, Kat's birthday, would bring added good karma on this significant seventh hand of the streak. There was no way the Player could fail to win a seventh consecutive time.

My Chinese friends hadn't gotten the memo, though, for after a lengthier-than-usual caucus, they all switched over and bet on the

Banker side. The bastards. I was handed the first two Player cards. I picked them up, hiding one behind the other. The visible card was a 9, making me want to burn the second, unnecessary one. Slowly, I slid the cards apart and let out a sigh of relief at the sight of a king of hearts. A natural 9; I could not lose. "Player stands with a natural nine," the dealer announced, arranging the cards before him after I'd tossed them back. Mr. C. had bet $10,000 and wasn't looking too happy. I wondered what that amount meant to him back in the real world, what the equivalent figure would be back in my real life. Twenty bucks?

The first card he turned over was a 9, too, which got us all a bit agitated. He waved it at me with a big grin, yelling across the table, "Too bad, nobody tie-bet!" Then both the wives starting blowing on the second card, which he'd left facedown on the table. I think the vixen even drooled a bit on it, but I'm not sure; it was hard to tell from where I sat. We were all pretty tired. They needed a "monkey," or face card, to match my natural 9, but they didn't get it. As soon as Mr. C. folded over the card to see how many sides it had, he knew it was low and the game was up. He tore up the card without even looking at it. I was paid my $2,200.

It was time to show some restraint. I was flying high, in tune with the invisible currents swirling above. My bankroll had surpassed the $10,000 mark. Somehow I knew the Player didn't have an eighth consecutive win in it, so I staked a mere $100 on a tie. Encouraged by my retreat, the two couples pressed their bets on the Banker. Ludo, my college probability prof, would have been aghast at our behavior. The dealer unveiled a respectable 7 for the abandoned Player, and Mr. C.'s first card was a 6. No margin for error here: He needed an ace to tie it up, or a 2 or 3 to win. Then, when I thought I'd seen it all, his wife started waving a lit match over the second card. Mrs. K. joined in with her Zippo lighter. Even the jaded dealers raised their eyebrows at this. How does the Nevada Gaming Commission feel about pyromaniac whales? Mr. C. flicked over the toasted card, a 3. The Banker had broken the fever. I felt as triumphant as if I'd betted with them, having wisely refrained from giving back my recent winnings. I had read and timed the game perfectly.

We skirmished for another hour or so, as the shoe fell back into a choppy game. Player and Banker each had their moments, but in no discernible pattern. I think we were all relieved when the dealer announced that only two hands remained in the shoe. We could use the twenty-minute break to grab a bite to eat, stretch our legs. When the shoe ended, I counted out $16,800 in front of me. It was almost nine A.M., and I had narrowed my loss for the session to a less-than-catastrophic $5,700. I couldn't think of quitting now. I was back from the dead, in control. I had grown the $827.50 I'd sat down at the table with a few hours ago by a factor of 20. If I did that again with what I now had in front of me, I'd walk away from the table with $325,000. It was that simple. *Carpe diem.*

I got up from the table as the dealers starting unwrapping the new decks of cards and one of the game supervisors rushed over to cover my chips with a transparent plastic box. It looked like something you'd use in a biology experiment; perhaps in my absence my chips would grow in this biosphere. It would be bad baccarat form to suspect that they would shrink, so I left them there. It being a bit chilly, I ran up to my suite to grab my Hard Rock sweatshirt.

Coming back down, I shared the elevator with Anna Coleman from Detroit. She blurted out—Vegas being immune to that otherwise universal rule that thou must remain silent in an elevator—that she'd fallen in love. How wonderful, I said, meaning it. "Nah, it's not like that," she said, laughing. "I mean I've just fallen head over heels in love with this place." Anna owns a gift basket business, and was in town for a lingerie convention. She'd lost $50 on the slot machines, she confessed, lowering her voice. What would she make of my Las Vegas? Seeing her enthusiasm for the place and her thrill at risking $50 brought home the craziness of what I was up to. And I couldn't tell what was crazier, the fact that I had $16,800 worth of plastic chips—picture a brand-new car!—or the fact that I'd left such a tidy fortune unattended, under the cover of plastic.

The dealers were ready to go. But I was stunned to see that the

C.'s and K.'s had left. Even their teacups and ashtrays had been cleared. The only remaining evidence of our heroic night was my incubated tower of chips. "Where did they go?" I asked stupidly. Change was not good, not when I was in the process of growing my eight hundred bucks into a fortune. Come back, we'd only taken a quick break.

But they were gone for good, so I sat down to play, alone. The show had to go on. Playing baccarat alone is one of life's great indulgences, what with your own team of tuxedoed dealers and back-up staff. As we were about to get started, a casino host named Kent Houston came by to introduce himself, and asked if there was anything I needed. "Come to think of it, Kent, I probably ought to extend my stay another night," I told him. I'd be in no condition to drive out to Death Valley anytime soon. "It's taken care of, sir," he said.

Kent's card identified him as the "East Asian Marketing" guy, so I was more than a little flattered that he'd deigned to schmooze with me. I'd become an honorary member of the diaspora. But what about him? Kent looked about my age, had a clean-cut glow about him, and, well, wasn't Asian. "You speak Chinese?" I asked him. "Yes, I learned it"—you'll love this—"while doing my missionary work for the Mormon Church in Taiwan." I'm sure the church elders would be proud to know Kent was applying the language and cultural skills he'd acquired during his mission in his professional life.

I bet $1,000 on the Player, and we were on our way. I wish I could recount to you in riveting detail how for the next few hours our gallant hero mustered savvy tempered by prudence to stay the course and grow the nest egg into a lifestyle-altering sum. But, alas, I cannot. My earlier bravado notwithstanding, I was like a ship at sea that loses radio contact with shore after being hounded by a ferocious storm; the next few hours are a bit of a mystery. What's known is that I'd been gambling for more than twelve hours, which meant I no longer felt any pain, and had bounced back from the dead, which meant I no longer felt any fear. Those are dangerous forms of immunity.

I kept tumbling. Why I persevered, sitting there all alone, I cannot explain. A chain of events had led me to believe in the inevitability of my full recovery. You don't take $22,500 down to $827.50 and climb all the way back to $16,800, only to start drifting south again! Do you? So I accelerated my free fall. As Dostoevsky writes of being slammed in *The Gambler*: "When once any one is started upon the road, it is like a man in the sledge flying down a snow mountain more and more swiftly."

At noon, the day shift arrived. They were my third set of dealers at this table, and the whole lot of them seemed so awake, so eager to please, yet so indifferent to what had here transpired. They didn't know about the four-carat vixen or cool Mr. J., or how I came back with mere rags to win a tie bet and launch one of the great comebacks in baccarat history. Near-comebacks, I should say. The day shift was here to finish me off. My eyes were scratchy, my mouth was raw, and I no longer had the stamina to keep up with their conversation. "What do you do back in New York?" one of the new dealers, a blonde with fine Scandinavian features, asked pleasantly, but I wasn't in the mood. Hadn't we done this routine around midnight?

Mr. L., a bundle of muscles, a Gold's Gym habitué no doubt, sat down a couple of spots to my left at some point, and it soon became clear that his sole mission in life was to ruin me. He was a Californian of Chinese origin. His forehead would have made a decent movie screen, it was so broad and flat. Mr. L. was a big Banker fan, and he relished taking hold of the shoe—which none of us had opted to do all night—and dealing himself terrific cards. He seemed to will those natural 8s and 9s into being. He crushed me, all the while charming the dealers and waitresses. They were all in his corner; my time was long gone. Bring back my friend Al!

Toward the very end, I disregarded every lesson I'd learned on my odyssey. Simply put, I defied momentum. The tide was due to turn, I told myself, increasing my bets as I plummeted. There was a final hand—there always is—on which I busted. Player had a natural 8, a seeming winner, only to have my buddy reveal a 2 and a 7. And that was that. Dazed, I looked down to see that I had $82 in chips, less than the $100 table minimum. It was time to go.

On my final hand I'd lost $1,500, almost twice the amount with which I'd first returned to the game in the early morning hours. Back then, wits still about me, $800 had been enough of a bankroll on which to launch a counterattack. Hours later, worn out, I'd surrendered twice that amount, long after it was clear I'd been vanquished by the muscle man from Orange County. Strange how that works.

I scurried away from the table, but not before tossing the $82 to the dealers. A sarcastic tip. I then walked out into the dazzling sunshine. After more than fifteen hours in the casino, the brightness was blinding. I sat by the pool in a lounge chair, still wearing my damned Hard Rock sweatshirt and my khakis, the way you see gamblers drying out poolside at any Vegas resort, like fish at market, though usually decked out in polyester. I closed my eyes and focused on the sounds of the kids splashing about in front of me, playing Marco Polo. I envied their innocence.

Passing snippets of conversation intruded on this catharsis, particularly that of one woman in the Jacuzzi who told her husband: "I'm so excited to be ahead $120 for this trip, honey, do you think I should stop?" This made me want to cry. Since my last meal, I had lost $22,500, an incomprehensibly vast sum (8,490 waffle cones) when contemplated out here by the pool, in the light of day, surrounded not by inveterate gamblers but by wholesome vacationers. I could have thrown up, had I any energy left. I had to get to bed.

♣ ♦ ♥ ♠ I woke up at eight, feeling sore all over. There is such a thing as being hungover from gambling. I had a hollow feeling in my chest, as if I'd lost an organ or two in some gruesome surgery and had not been sewn back together. It took me a moment to get oriented. Could this be the same suite Kathy and I had stayed in, where we'd laughingly dressed up for our vows-renewal night, in happier times, in what was supposedly going to be a weeklong break in the gambling frenzy? Was it morning or night? I reached for the remote and flicked on the bedroom TV. The answer was night: *Mad About You* was starting. I dialed room service and ordered some pasta, and lay there watching Paul and Jamie go about their neurotic New York lives. Sitcoms can be a soothing tonic. *NewsRadio, Frasier,* and *Lateline* would follow, and, with luck, I could find other sitcoms in syndication after that—anything to keep me from being alone with my thoughts, to keep me from dwelling on what I'd done.

My remorse was so overpowering I could barely eat. I think it was one of the DI's dealers who had told me that when he has one of his "shit-kicking" gambling outings he always asks to have the comped meals he earns a week or so later. It takes days to recover from a massive loss, he'd explained, days before you can eat with gusto again. I thought of him as I picked at the pasta.

But mainly, I just lay there, trying to think of anything else in recent memory that had been this painful. I couldn't.

Nest egg: $43,271

Wednesday, April 22

They say a drink or two helps soothe a wicked hangover, which might explain why I felt compelled to gamble a bit that morning before hitting the road. I was no longer intent on winning it all back in one sitting, but simply wanted a nice little pick-me-up to leave town on a positive note. At least enough to cover the Furnace Creek Inn, which didn't comp and wasn't cheap. I cashed in $5,000 in traveler's checks—I had all of $8 in my wallet—and sought out a $5 blackjack table I'd never played at. This wasn't easy, given how I'd been around. Despite my intention to take it easy, I couldn't bring myself to play less than $100 a hand. I lost $2,980 in an hour. Brilliant. The Furnace Creek Inn wasn't *that* expensive.

I walked back over to the scene of the crime, to the baccarat table, and took a seat. Did the dealers greet me warily—would the guy totally lose it this time around?—or was I getting paranoid? I bought in $2,000 and cashed in $6,500 forty-five minutes later. It's an easy game when it wants to be. But I wasn't in a reflective mood. I didn't dwell on the fact that I'd managed to triple $2,000, but not $16,800, nor did I fantasize about extending the roll. No, I was just grateful for the dead man's bounce and eager to get the hell out of town, forty-eight hours after I should have.

As I was preparing to leave, Bob Miner wandered into the temple, looking for me. We shook hands, and I thanked him again for everything, which seemed a little ridiculous under the circumstances. I felt like the losing quarterback being interviewed after a tough loss. *You know, Bob, we thought we'd make a comeback there in the third quarter, but in the end, we just couldn't survive those turnovers; that's football.*

Bob wore an appropriately mournful look, having checked the score on his tell-all computer screen. "I know you didn't do too well, and we always hate to see that." Bob's a sweet guy, but I wonder who else in Luxor's corporate ranks hated to see me drop twenty grand. "Is this when you hand me back a fifth of my losses?" I asked him. Casinos around town do offer such rebates to their best customers, the whales who lose millions, but these are typically negotiated beforehand. I knew this, and was just teasing Bob, to show him I was unfazed by my loss.

"Why don't you show me your ticket, so that I can reimburse you for your airfare? That's the least I can do," Bob said, after a moment of awkward silence. This was tempting, but probably a bad idea. My ticket didn't have me leaving town for a few weeks, which would be hard to explain. I didn't want to get into the book right now, so I simply mumbled something about having used a free ticket, but thanks anyway.

There was one more thing left to raise. "Say, Bob, how about taking care of my local phone calls this time?" I suggested, no longer teasing. It was Bob's turn to mumble, something about how that almost never happens, it was handled by another department, and so on. Amazing. I could get the casino to cover my airfare, but not local calls. This was getting personal.

Before I left, Bob reminded me to send some of my fellow New York "constituents" his way. I tried not to chuckle at his image of my circle of friends. *Paul, Kim, if you guys ever want to go to Vegas and blow a few grand, I can set you up with a host.*

Feeling blue, I stopped at Borders on the way out of town to pick up some inspirational literature, the equivalent of a rousing halftime locker-room speech. I made a beeline to the self-help shelf, which in my old life I used to snicker at, and surveyed the options. Buying a book on overcoming an addiction or finding the right career seemed a bit premature, so instead I focused on broader get-your-shit-together titles. Stephen Covey is about the nearest thing we have to a national coach, a corporate Yoda who gets $75,000 per appearance for peddling cleverly packaged common sense, so I picked up his *7 Habits of Highly Effective People.* Presumably this would turn me into a *highly effective* gambler upon my return to town.

I stopped for a late lunch at a Burger King, settling into a booth with my Whopper Meal—I'd even sprung for the extra 39 cents to go large—and the *Review-Journal.* I'm not mathematically adept as a rule (as if you hadn't noticed) but my mind was in a cruel number-crunching mode, the result of my numbing guilt. As soon as the clerk informed me that my total would be $4.15, the number 5,421.68 popped into my head. As in, I could have bought 5,421.68 Whopper Meals with what I pissed away in one night of baccarat! Or 5,921, if I hadn't gone large. All the ads in the paper resulted in the same mathematical idiot-savantism. Take your pick: I'd lost 32 cruises down the Mexican Riviera, 3,461 movie tickets, 174 round-trip plane tickets to Albuquerque, 1,505 bathing suits at Mervyn's, or 56 months' worth of a lease on a snazzy BMW.

The paper had an amusing story involving our own Little White

Chapel on the Strip. A Los Angeles housepainter, suspected of swindling a senile eighty-year-old widow out of $300,000, was arrested. Turns out the fifty-three-year-old gentleman had married the widow at the chapel's drive-through window in 1996, and had soon thereafter transferred her property to his son and daughter-in-law. A detective in the case was quoted as saying that the old woman "probably thought she was going through the McDonald's drive-through." That's the problem with our free society. We set up these wondrous conveniences to make our lives easier, and someone always comes around to abuse them. I wondered what the prim and proper Reverend Rhodes thought of all this.

My late-afternoon drive to Death Valley was a real treat. The desert was blooming, thanks to the rainier-than-usual spring, and I had the highway to myself. I watched the Endeavor's shadow on the scrub alongside the highway for entertainment, pleased to be putting distance between me and Las Vegas. I cranked up the radio when Sheryl Crow's "Leaving Las Vegas" came on the radio. When I saw the "Welcome to California" sign, I was positively giddy.

I pulled up at the Furnace Creek Inn around seven. Built on a hill, the hotel, a stone-and-adobe landmark opened in 1927 by the Pacific Borax Company, overlooks a spring-fed oasis and the stunning valley beyond, with its eerie salt flats. But what most struck this refugee from Las Vegas was the hotel's sheer tranquillity. It was an odd feeling to stand alone in a hotel lobby, in front of a solitary check-in clerk, with no one else in sight. The dining room stopped serving dinner at nine, I was informed. There was no buffet, no food court, no Chinese place, no slot machines clanging in the background, no keno, no souvenir daiquiri stands, no way of getting comped. It was a brave new world.

Nest egg: $44,789

Thursday, April 23

Death Valley has been the nation's largest national park outside Alaska since 1994, when Congress passed the Desert Protection Act, and I was intent on seeing as little of it as possible. I wasn't here to sightsee, but for some peace and quiet. A sucker for superlatives, I did venture out to Badwater, the *lowest* point in the Western Hemisphere, which looked like a lunar landscape. In 1972 the Park Service recorded a ground temperature of 201 degrees here. Even in April the air felt like a hair dryer's blast.

I spent most of the day holed up in my room, mixing Dostoevsky and Covey. I also called my friend Greg in Houston. We'd clerked together for a federal judge after law school, but our lives have taken slightly different paths since then: Greg now represents people on Death Row. He filled me in on the latest developments in an appeal he'd filed. I filled him in on the rules of baccarat.

Late in the afternoon I went down to the pool and splashed about in the natural thermal waters. It wasn't much fun, on account of the wind. There are few things more demoralizing than a desert's springtime whistling winds, spraying dust every which way in order to remind people that they are living in what ought to have remained godforsaken country.

At five I had a massage from a guy called Stan. The hotel's lights went out—the winds had knocked down a pole somewhere—as he went about the hopeless task of unknotting all that baccarat tension in my shoulders. *Great,* I thought, *no* Seinfeld *tonight.*

Nest egg: $44,789

Part Two

8

RIVIERA

*We were stark mad with excitement,
drunk with happiness, smothered under mountains
of prospective wealth.*
—Mark Twain, visiting Nevada

Friday, April 24

♣ ♦ ♥ ♠ "Pahrump" sounds like the sound Paul Schaeffer makes off-screen when one of David Letterman's jokes misfires, but it's actually the name of a town halfway between Death Valley and Las Vegas, home to conspiracy-minded radio personality Art Bell and to a number of "ranches" of ill-repute. It's true: This seemingly sleepy little town is one of the world's prostitution hot spots. That's because prostitution is illegal in Clark County, despite all that suggestive advertising you see in Las Vegas. But here, in adjacent Nye County, it's an entirely lawful, licensed form of commerce. So back and forth all night on Highway 160, limos shuttle clients between the Strip and the modest-looking "ranches." For the curious, a Las Vegas cabbies' website posts a sample menu from one of these brothels, which includes something called a "Crème de Menthe French." I'll spare you the description, other than to say it ends thus: "resulting in a truly unique sensation."

Ah, Pahrump. I was here for a late lunch, looking furtively about me, trying to identify the swarms of licensed prostitutes. No place to hide in a town this size, I figured. But I was surrounded by senior citizens and cowboys. Whores must do take-out. Oh, well.

I arrived back on the Strip in midafternoon, as the streams of weekend visitors started trickling into town. I felt much better after what had turned out to be only a forty-eight-hour break from the green-felt fray. The Luxor debacle had been painful, but after spending more time gambling in the past three weeks than would have been advisable for an entire decade, I was still holding on to some 90 cents of every dollar I had brought out to Vegas. Things could—some would say, "should"—be a lot worse. I had to move on. The second half beckoned. I was still in the game.

And I was a better man, a more "highly effective" one, after my immersion in Coveyism. I wasn't sure I could keep my time-management quadrants straight, and it would be a stretch to say I'd already adopted all seven habits. It takes a week for any practice in my life to be certified a habit. But I was determined to focus, for the next few days at least, on Yoda Covey's fourth, and most casino-relevant, habit: "Think win-win." No more getting angry at lucky dealers, envying even luckier players, or muttering about local phone charges. As Covey writes: "Win-win is based on the paradigm that there is plenty for everybody, that one person's success is not achieved at the expense or exclusion of the successes of others."

In other words, both Vegas and I could thrive.

♣ ♦ ♥ ♠ When it opened in 1955, the $10 million Riviera (even back then, these places wore their prices on their sleeves) was the Strip's seventh hotel and first high-rise. It was also the town's first hotel to look like it belonged on a beach, having been built and designed by Miami hoteliers. Liberace was paid an unheard of $50,000 a week—why does that sum ring a bell?—to headline in the hotel's showroom.

Within three months, the hotel was bankrupt. Its investors had intended to build only a $6 million resort, and, well, things had gotten a little out of hand. Certain Midwestern investors took over and convinced Gus Greenbaum to come out of retirement and manage it. Greenbaum had stepped in for Ben Siegel at the Flamingo seven years earlier, walking in and announcing he was in charge the night Bugsy was shot in Los Angeles. He turned the place around in short order. Though by all accounts a mess personally, Greenbaum led the Riviera to profitability as well, which may have gotten him killed by jealous former employers. As Deke Castleman recounts in my handy Compass guidebook: "On a visit home to Phoenix for Thanksgiving in 1958, Gus and his wife Bess had their throats slashed in a hit ordered from on high." This is riveting stuff, the Vegas equivalent of going to London and learning about King Henry VIII dispatching his wives, and it's the kind of history that newer properties like the Mirage and Luxor just can't match.

Incidentally, Gus's death, much like Bugsy's, illustrated one of the cardinal rules of Mob rule in Las Vegas, the one about not pissing on the goose that lays the golden egg. You do your killing elsewhere. This rule, overlooked at times in the Mob's pathetic final days in town, depicted by Martin Scorsese in *Casino,* helps explain why most old-timers miss the wiseguys. They had their endearing qualities, they never hurt anyone outside the business, and even when they whacked one of their own, they'd try and do it elsewhere.

In the intervening years, the Riviera has been owned by a number of more reputable interests, each of which launched its own renovation and expansion. The result, much as at Caesars, is a sprawling resort that thrills architectural historians and pop archaeologists, though here the expansions were considerably less ritzy than their counterparts over at Caesars. Each layer at the Riviera feels a bit worn, a bit frayed at the edges, including the brand-new Nickel Town slots arcade designed to draw in pedestrians from the Strip.

As I waited in line to check in, a woman from Texas asked me if I was in town for the "sluht tournament." Huh? "You know, the sluht tournament," she said, this time wildly motioning back and forth with her arm as if to reel me in. She looked uncannily like former governor Ann Richards. Who else would wear as earrings the map of Texas traced in precious stones? "Governor Richards?" I ventured. Doris laughed at this, and was still laughing about it when I ran into her the next day, over at the slot tournament.

My cavernous suite had a mid-1980s Marriott décor, and was a bit too dark in the windowless sitting area. The bedroom had a nice view of the vintage Olympic-sized pool, bordered by Astroturf. I plopped down on the bed and called Joe Alston, the missionary topless-joint bathroom attendant. He needed to be at church for some service at seven and then at the Olympic Garden by nine, but he agreed to meet me in fifteen minutes for an early dinner at the Denny's down by the Stratosphere.

One of the first things Joe, a native Las Vegan, will tell anybody who listens is that he feels lucky to be alive. "From the time I was thirteen until I was thirty-seven, I was involved with drugs, and I never thought there would come a time when I wouldn't be," he said. He couldn't blame his background, he added matter-of-factly, dissuading me from making lazy assumptions about some inner-city horror show. He was brought up in a middle-class home and provided with plenty of opportunity, though filial relations were soured when his father called the cops on him. Joe was in high school at the time.

Every person Joe shot heroin with has either died of AIDS or is dying. "There was one year when I must have gone to a funeral every week for almost eight months," he said. That was in 1993, when he was released from his seventh and final stint in prison. Joe has spent some fifteen of his forty-three years behind bars, mostly for larceny, burglary, and drug possession: "I wasn't into violent crime."

Still, "the drugs do mess you up," he went on, picking at his pecan pie—"made me act in ways so wretched I can barely live with the memory." There was violence in the neighborhood; just before going off to prison for the last time, Joe was in a dope house, where he struck someone he didn't know with a bottle, right in the face. The guy had been making fun of Joe, who is not quite five ten but was fond of impressing a crowd. "That last time, I was glad to go to prison, because I saw what I had become, a frightful, hideous vision, uglier than anything you'd see in a movie," he whispered. That was when he resolved to place God, who'd always lurked at the periphery, at the center of his life. And because Joe had always been something of a leader in prison—the big dumb guy is never the go-to guy, he noted—the transition to the ministry was a natural one.

Joe is now the assistant pastor at the downtown Jesus Is the Answer Church, where "everyone is starting over." Think of it as a prison alumni ministry. Joe believes that God alone can straighten out habitual criminals; only by ceding control of his life to the Lord could he rid himself of his inner demons. No drug treatment or Twelve Step program could suffice. He speaks from experience, having been cited back in 1974 as a model graduate of a then cutting-edge state drug treatment program. "I only got more hooked in those programs; you could get better drugs in there."

Joe strives to smother with care people coming out of prison. He also likes to work with young people, to help them avoid falling as he did. These kids must have the same problem I do picturing this gentle-mannered man going off to prison seven times. Drugs are remarkable.

The fledgling church can't afford to pay Joe. He works at the Olympic Garden five nights a week, from nine to four. On two of those nights he works a shoeshine stand—"Glow by Joe," his card reads—in the club; on the other three, he mans the rest room. He used to have his shoeshine stand at the Texas Station casino, but God told him to move over to the Olympic Garden. Most nights he's lucky to clear a hundred bucks, but during a busy convention he might make enough in one night to pay all his bills for the month, and then chip in at the church.

"I see a lot of the same hurt there I used to see on the inside, guys masking their anguish with a false self-confidence, and eventually it all bursts out and I'm there to talk, to minister to them," Joe explained. The manager lets him read his Bible, so long as he doesn't approach people to spread the Gospel. But they can approach him, and often do, clients and dancers alike. Joe is so queasy about all the nudity that he has someone else retrieve his shoeshine cart from where it's stored, an area where a lot of the girls change while on break.

When Joe leaves the club at four in the morning, he goes to the church to clean up and pray. Evenings before work, depending on the day of the week, he's either holding a Bible-study session, feeding the homeless, talking to kids, or counseling people at the halfway home the church runs for men starting over.

Joe has turned his life around, of that there is no question. But he wasn't about to give me an angelic smile and tell me everything happened for the best, so that he could serve the Lord. "I have a lot of regrets, because I wasted so much talent," he said. In school, before he messed things up for good, there was talk of his getting a scholarship to play point guard at UCLA; he ranked third on a career-in-psychology test; college should have been a given.

A string of bad calls and a quarter-century later, Joe is starting over. He married last year, made peace with his parents, and is working to establish a good credit record. This raises a question in my mind. Growing up here with an addictive, tempestuous personality, had he ever been addicted to the gambling? No, Joe replied. "I was the kind of guy who always wanted something in return for my money."

♣ ♦ ♥ ♠ On my way back to the Riviera, I stopped at a bustling palm reader's. For $10 a woman read my fortune. Originally from Ohio ("There's more business over here"), she wore what looked like an old bathrobe with gold stars painted on. I worried she might die of what the Victorians called consumption, her cough was so violent. She told me not to worry about anything, it would all turn out grand, "though not necessarily in the short term." A safe reading for visitors to Las Vegas, no doubt. "But will I win at the tables?" I implored. "Not necessarily in the short run," she insisted. This was maddening; there would be no long run. But I calmed down. Think Yoda Covey. Think win-win.

♣ ♦ ♥ ♠ Of all the casinos in town, the Riviera's comes closest to what you'd expect a Las Vegas gambling hall to look like. It's gigantic and generic—no pirate crap here. *Casino, Austin Powers,* and a slew of other movies set in Vegas were filmed at the Riviera for that reason (and for the reason that, unlike some of the prissier establishments, the Riv isn't uptight about publicity or, gasp, showing people gambling on film). The crowd here is older, and the hair bigger, which also fits the mental image people my age carry of Las Vegas. Other than some marauding frat boys drawn in by the Riviera's risqué entertainment, most of the people in the casino look to be well into their fifties, or beyond.

I wouldn't want to own a casino like the Riviera or the Stardust, across the Strip. It's hard to see how they can stay alive in this increasingly competitive, quality-conscious market. Other than nostalgia for a bygone era, the Riviera has much less to offer visitors than a place like the Luxor, where room rates are comparable. Nostalgia seekers are better off staying downtown, anyway, and locals put off by the newer hotels' amusement-park feel are being siphoned off by the growing number of sophisticated off-Strip properties. The Riviera is running out of niches.

In 1997, the Riviera saw its revenue drop to $153.8 million, from $164.4 million in 1996. Earnings fell an alarming 75 percent to $2.1 million. Horse-racing magnate Allen Paulson recently backed out of a deal to acquire the hotel for $250 million. Naturally, this being Las Vegas, the company's response to its woes is to consider a massive expansion. A week earlier, the *Review-Journal* had reported that the Riviera was weighing an expansion plan, a risky double down in the form of a new tower, a domed shopping and entertainment complex, more convention space, the works.

As a Wall Street peddler of casino bonds told me back in New

York: "The next time we get a real recession in this country, coupled with high interest rates, it will be as if a nuclear bomb had gone off on the Strip, and most of the blood will flow north of Treasure Island." Until then, a struggling casino mogul can dream.

♣ ♦ ♥ ♠ I went to see the Riviera's notorious *Crazy Girls,* the "show" memorialized in bronze at the hotel entrance and on billboards everywhere. I could take only twelve minutes of it, it was so tacky. The girls weren't that crazy, or even that good-looking, though I did later read that one of them is "an accomplished real estate broker" in town. No doubt. I could have saved myself $18.95 (minus the two free drinks I carried out) by reading the *Review-Journal*'s generous review: "an absolutely dreadful jiggle show featuring silicone-enhanced topless ladies sort of dancing and doing lip-sync taped vocals as they cavort against cheap backdrops for no apparent reason."

It's puzzling that the show gets the attention it does, and has for a dozen years. After all, at a place like the Olympic Garden you get more silicone for your entertainment dollar without having to sit through the mind-numbing song-and-dance routines. Ah, but the charade's the thing. Interestingly, couples made up most of the audience at the *Crazy Girls* performance. And, as eager as some couples may be to share a little soft porn, it's a lot more respectable to take your girl to a "show" than to take her to a strip joint, even if it's to watch the same thing. It's all in the packaging, as my father-in-law mutters whenever we're trapped in a restaurant he considers a rip-off.

I'd had my fill of entertainment for the evening; it was time to get back to work. I obtained my Riviera frequent-gambler card and, as had become customary, started off by not winning Megabucks. Then I stumbled, literally, upon a baccarat table. The Riviera is so confused about what it wants to be that it has a full-fledged $10 baccarat table, something I never saw anywhere else in town, fenced off in the middle of the casino. Nobody was playing, and instead of tuxedoes the idle dealers wore T-shirts advertising the Riviera's pool tournament. It was bizarre to see a baccarat table, which casinos normally tuck away out of view, plopped down in the middle of the casino, and with such pedestrian limits. Shocking, really. Having these four people staff a $10 table is a gesture that reeks of desperation. I had to play.

I felt I was gambling in a fishbowl, with passersby stopping to watch, chat, and figure out what this baccarat thing was all about. A young couple from Wisconsin sat with me while I demystified baccarat for them. He wore a Packers shirt and viewed the game with a mixture of suspicion and disbelief. "That's it?" he finally asked, which had pretty much summed up my initial reaction back at Caesars. "Yup, it's that simple." But I still couldn't win. I lost $1,900 in over an hour, and moved on to craps and blackjack, ultimately winning the $1,900 back and getting ahead another grand or so by three in the morning. Winning that money was hard enough to beg the question: Would I ever be able to grow the nest egg back to its previous heights?

Nest egg: $45,839

Saturday, April 25

Fancying yourself a writer is inherently frustrating, because writing is one of the few endeavors humans can't seem to get much better at. If you're a doctor, an athlete, a banker, a chef, a scientist, or an engineer, even a mediocre one, and you could travel back in time to the Civil War era, you'd be the world's greatest at what you do. If I went back to the 1860s, I'd still be a hack compared to Melville, Dostoevsky, and Dickens.

I mulled this over while reading Dostoevsky's short novel *The*

Gambler and drinking a piña colada at poolside, in the early after-noon. I was determined to be the first person ever to watch *Crazy Girls* and read Dostoevsky in the same twenty-four-hour span. It wasn't as painful as you might think—at least, not the Dostoevsky part. Anyone who has spent more than an hour in a casino can ap-preciate his masterful depiction of human nature confronting fate. His crackling roulette scenes could have been written here in Vegas, yesterday. And though we often associate Dostoevsky with angst, this short novel is often hilarious.

It's nice that he could find humor in his own torment, for Dosto-evsky's insight into gambling's corrosive power was not wholly the product of a superb imagination or detached reporting. Dostoevsky was what we would today call a compulsive gambler.

Like a lot of addicts, Dostoevsky had a magical introduction to casino gambling, winning 12,000 francs in one hour at the German spa town of Wiesbaden. Hadn't Seneca written that no man is crushed by hostile Fortune who is not first deceived by her smiles? Over the next decade, no subsequent loss could erase the memory of that wondrous triumph, or the Dostoevsky's conviction that it could be replicated, many times over, if only he gambled smart.

Before Dostoevsky went on one of his gambling outings, his de-voted second wife, Anna, wrote in her diary:

> He definitely has the intention of going there; what a strange man. It would seem that fate has punished him so strongly, and showed him so many times that he cannot get rich by roulette. No, this man is incurable, he is still convinced all the same—and I am sure he will always be convinced—that he will cer-tainly become rich, will certainly win, and then will be able to help his wretches.

The "wretches" were his deceased brother's family, whom he took care of, much to Anna's distress. Dostoevsky was hounded by creditors during most of his adult life. His financial woes, gambling addiction, and prolific writing fed off one another during his most productive decade. Whenever he got his hands on a little money, he was able to rationalize his impulse to gamble. No windfall was ever enough to get him out of the deep hole he was in, but it might, he figured, be enough to finance a spectacular run at roulette that would catapult his family forevermore out of financial despair. Keep in mind there were no Internet stocks to invest in back in those years. Once he had been wiped out at the casino, typically for failing to quit while he was ahead, Dostoevsky would have to dream up some novel—*Crime and Punishment,* say—and write his publisher for an advance. He would feel terrible remorse at this point and plunge into writing some of the world's greatest literature. Then the cycle would repeat itself, making Fyodor and me kindred spirits—guys willing to stake our book advances at the tables.

What's amazing is that Fyodor's gambling forays never interfered with his writing. Gambling is such an all-consuming, exhausting pursuit. Exhibit A: my lounging by the pool, after waking up at noon, feeling raw. Keeping notes is enough of an ordeal for me. But Fyodor, during more than a month of going crazy in Baden-Baden, would retire to his rented hovel, after closing down the casino, to write the core of *The Idiot,* one of the most compassionate works you could ever read. All this without a laptop.

At several points in his frenzied gamble-despair-write cycle, Dostoevsky was forced to pawn his wife's jewelry and furniture. He was so guilt-ridden about this, it made him a more loving husband, and probably a better writer. "One thing and one thing only horrifies me," he wrote in anguish to his wife after he'd blown his return fare (he had a knack for this) on one of his gambling trips. "What will you say, what will you think about me? And what is love without respect?" Then he'd have to ask her to send more money.

Patient Anna always pardoned, never scolded, in part because she was frightened of triggering one of her husband's epileptic seizures, which she feared more than his gambling. She was ahead of her time in viewing her husband's gambling addiction as an uncontrollable disease rather than a moral deficiency. In her memoirs, she wrote: "One had to come to terms with it, to look at his gambling passion as a disease for which there was no cure."

Anna recalled a conversation with her husband in their early days together when she dismissed *The Gambler*'s protagonist, Alexey Ivanovitch, as contemptible. Alexey, a tutor to a traveling family of Russian aristocrats, is determined to alter his status forever and win the respect of his beloved by acquiring great riches at roulette. Dostoevsky, defending himself as much as Alexey, replied that "it is possible to possess a strong character, to prove that fact by your own life, and nonetheless lack the strength to conquer in yourself the passion for roulette." Anna came to believe that more than he did.

Why anyone gambles compulsively is a mystery. Dostoevsky could tell himself it was on account of his financial plight, but Sigmund Freud later speculated that the author's gambling was the result of a masochistic impulse. Maybe Fyodor just needed a buzz. The oft-repeated tale of a younger Dostoevsky escaping execution only at the last moment—when already facing the firing squad— may have left in him a lingering urge to live life on the edge. And gambling is as good a means as any to re-create such terror. "In every part of my life, I have exceeded the limit," Dostoevsky wrote in his diary after a bad night in the casino and a trip to the pawnshop. But did he write it with a trace of satisfaction, despite himself?

What prompted Dostoevsky to quit gambling in the spring of 1871 is equally mysterious. He hit the tables in Wiesbaden toward the end of a long stay in Germany, quickly crashed and burned, blew his return fare, and pledged to never gamble again. No surprises there; that was his normal gambling routine. But something must have triggered an epiphany on that trip, because in time it became clear that he meant it when he wrote his wife:

> A vile fantasy that has tormented me almost ten years has vanished. For ten years I kept dreaming of winning, I dreamed seriously, passionately. Now all that is finished. This was ABSOLUTELY the last time. Will you believe, Anya, that my

hands are untied now; I had been bound by gambling. . . . I will think about serious things now, and will not dream whole nights on end about gambling, as I used to.

Coincidentally, the *Review-Journal* reported that the Nevada Gaming Control Board would be taking a hard look at the once-neglected issue of compulsive gambling among locals. Carol O'Hare, the executive director of the Nevada Council on Problem Gambling, was among those quoted in the article. She is a reformed problem gambler raising awareness of the affliction, often training casino employees to deal with patrons who've crossed the line. When I met her later in the year, Carol mentioned that gambling, unlike alcoholism and other addictions, lacks a poster child. "We desperately need an admired celebrity or two to step forward and say they have a serious gambling addiction," she said with a bit of a laugh. I guess Dostoevsky doesn't cut it on the preventive lecture circuit these days. Still, it's a testament to gambling's power that the man who wrote *Crime and Punishment,* arguably the finest novel ever written, wasn't above this addiction. It's truly an equal-opportunity seductress.

♣ ♦ ♥ ♠ After dragging myself away from the pool, I wandered down the Strip, poking in and out of a number of amusing gift shops and casinos, ending up at Treasure Island, aesthetically my favorite resort in town. I walked over the wooden bridge into the casino and hung a right, heading straight toward the sports book. It was time to act responsibly for once and make a long-term investment.

The place was packed with guys lounging around, drinking beer, looking up at an array of screens—horse races, basketball, baseball, you name it—and studying odds sheets. Doing everything, in other words, that a healthy male ought to be doing on a Saturday afternoon. It looked like fun, but I wasn't here for instant gratification. I was here to make a wager that would outlast my entire stay in Vegas, a wager on the world's most popular sporting event, which wouldn't take place until June. If I dropped the rest of the nest egg at craps or baccarat, I could still go home with an investment socked away. I was getting goose bumps, this was so responsible, much like contributing to a 401(k).

I've always been an avid soccer fan. Growing up in Mexico, I breathed the game around the clock, from the time I was eight until it was time to go away for school. Soccer has since made some headway in the United States, but it remains an organized activity—complete with perfectly groomed fields, car pools, snazzy Umbro uniforms, and soccer moms—rather than the spontaneous craze it is elsewhere. All we needed in Mexico was a ball and a street. Here, bowling is still easier to find on the tube.

On a personal level, watching the World Cup is about more than sport. It's also about remembering the magic of childhood. We all have such things in our lives, hyperlinks to our childhood. For me, there is Christmas and, every four years, the World Cup. Mexico was never a real contender, so for as long as I can remember, I was a German fan. This was a contrarian move, like most of my other sports allegiances. One was supposed to root for Brazil once the Mexican squad was sent home in disgrace. But there was something about unpopular teams that wore black (Germany, the Pittsburgh Steelers, Mexico's ill-fated Atletico Español soccer club) that made me root for them, something we'd best not dwell on here.

The 1974 World Cup in Germany was the first I followed closely. I can still recall getting up at the crack of dawn (quite a feat for an unusually talented eight-year-old sleeper) to watch the championship game between Johann Cruyff's fierce Dutch team and the German squad. But the most shocking moment of the tournament came in the quarter-finals when I turned on the television to find Germany playing—was I going nuts?—Germany. I didn't get it. Was this some sort of gimmick—having the host nation's starters play their second team? No, the announcers were calling one team the Federal Republic and the other the Democratic Republic.

I had decided in the first round that I liked Germany, the team of Franz Beckenbauer, Gerd Müller, and Sepp Maier. But, I realized with great sadness, they were all playing for the Federal Republic. I knew enough to realize I couldn't root against the "Democratic Republic." Democratic: They had to be the good guys. And so, victimized by the treachery of Communist propagandists and the absence of truth-in-advertising norms in international law, I rooted for the imposters for half an hour. Luckily my father joined me for the second half and set me straight.

I've been loyal to Germany (at least once Mexico flies home) in every subsequent World Cup. I realize a casino is no place to act on such maudlin sentiments, as I'd learned from painful experience, but this year, I knew for a fact, Germany would win its fourth World Cup. They were the defending European champions. Plus, Germans always win on French soil.

Serious sports bettors wager on the here and now, the ball game about to start, and leave the fuzzy long-term proposition bets to what they fondly call us "square johns." But Germany was a sure thing, and it was cool to contemplate making a bet that wouldn't pay off until the tournament's final match, on July 11. How much would I win? "Germany . . . to win the World Cup . . . pays five to one," said the clerk behind the window, checking a binder. I felt I was at a bank inquiring about CD rates. Brazil, admittedly the most talented team, paid 5 to 2. Oddsmakers hadn't caught on to the fact that, at least since 1958, the "scratch du oro" always chokes on that side of the Atlantic. "Let's make it a thousand, then," I replied, counting out the bills. "A dime for Germany," he announced to a supervisor over his shoulder. How cool—"a dime." He seemed impressed, and I reckon he went home that night and told the wife: "Honey, I think we should take some of our savings and put it on those Germans to win some soccer tournament; it's where the smart money is headed."

I was given what looked like a lotto quick-pick ticket showing my wager, and was assured that I need not be present to collect. I could mail in the ticket. I also bought my father-in law a birthday present: a $25 bet that the Giants would win next year's Super Bowl. This seemed like buying someone a thirty-year Treasury Bill, it was so far off. Fortuitously, I won $1,100 at blackjack to cover the bets.

Back at the Riviera, or "The Adult Alternative" as it calls itself, I went to the Comedy Club's early show, starring Steve Kelley, a well-known political cartoonist at the *San Diego Union Tribune*. Like any great cartoonist, he has a good eye for the absurd that surrounds us and often goes undetected. He mentioned a sign he'd seen at a Burger King recently: "These doors to remain unlocked during business hours."

Relying on an old Newhart trick, Kelley asked the audience to imagine the conversation that led to its posting:

"We've been in business for six weeks now, spent a bundle on advertising, but haven't sold a whole lot of hamburgers. What do you say we try unlocking the front doors . . . just during business hours? You know, take some heat off the drive-through window. We'll even put up a sign, to remind ourselves to keep the doors unlocked . . . just during business hours."

I talked to Steve briefly after the show. He hates Las Vegas and would be taking a red-eye home to San Diego after midnight. Why bother coming? "There are no comedy clubs left in San Diego, and this is a great place to try out some new material for my corporate speaking." We all need Vegas in our own ways.

♣ ♦ ♥ ♠ Afterward, I sought out a blonde with one of those classic Vegas cone-shaped hairpieces, playing video poker at a casino bar. She was dressed to the nines, wearing chunky gold jewelry, a sequined top, and an elegant long black skirt. She was older than fifty, but beyond that I wouldn't hazard a guess, American medicine being capable of what it is. She was the only person I ever saw playing video poker—other than myself reflected in the glass—who seemed bored by it. She was undoubtedly the woman I'd been told to look for.

"Call me, let's see, Peggy," she said in a throaty voice, as if to answer my stare.

"Andrés," I mumbled. I didn't know where to begin, so we fell into an awkward silence.

"Well, for a minute there I thought you were going to ask me if I came here often." She laughed.

"Um, do you?"

"You a reporter or something?"

"Um, yeah."

"That's funny."

"I'm actually writing a book on Las Vegas."

"That's even funnier."

"Why?"

"Because, honey, you've come to the right person."

In her day, Peggy had been the ultimate comp.

Peggy first started coming out to Las Vegas from her home in Los Angeles in 1957, when she was a young secretary at an insurance company traveling with a group of girlfriends in search of some excitement. These were swank Las Vegas's glory years, when Frank, Dino, and Sammy would host Hollywood celebs, mobsters, and Kennedys at the all-night party at the Sands' Copa Room. "We'd go to the Sands, or the Tropicana, all the glamorous casinos, and turn some heads," Peggy recalled, before succumbing to a harsh cough. She was "quite a sight" in those days, if she did say so herself, and could always attract the attention of males in any room, including some "big-time politicians" whose names she says it would be "indecorous" to reveal. Women, too, would stare at her and her friends. Unaccompanied girls traveling together, in Las Vegas of all places! "Everyone assumed we were awfully fast," Peggy recalled, as I realized that her feline green eyes were indeed alluring. It was such a violation of taboo for her and her friends to go to Sin City, she routinely lied to her parents and her employer about her whereabouts.

They would have had good reason to worry. Peggy was mesmerized by the desert oasis: the gambling, the lights, the roguish casino managers with their impeccable manners, the performances featuring the biggest entertainers of the day in an intimate setting, the showgirls; it was all so intoxicating, so electrifying compared with her daily routine back home. "You cannot imagine, Andrea, what it felt like, as a beautiful woman, to walk into the Sands or Flamingo casino unattached in 1959." I certainly couldn't, even if my name had been Andrea. "It was like being queen for a night after being secretary all week, beauty being the only currency that mattered in this place."

The mutual seduction of Peggy and Las Vegas was consummated in the early 1960s. Soon she started coming to town alone. A host at one of the hotels would fly her out once a month, sometimes twice, with the "unspoken understanding" that she linger in the lounge in the evenings. The host would come by and introduce Peggy to one of his high rollers, with whom she'd sit and chat a while, enjoy a smoke, then catch the show and maybe hit the tables together afterward. *And I thought Bob Miner had given me the royal treatment.*

"Don't look at me like that, I was no hooker," Peggy snapped, pointing at my nose, just as I had resolved to freeze my features in a thoughtful, noncommittal gaze, "though I learned how to please men intensely when I desired." She met a lot of interesting, generous men, but there was never any obligation to go to bed with them. She was in control, able to pick and choose, asserting the ultimate guys' prerogative in a guys' town.

Peggy became one of Las Vegas's prized weekend warriors, known to major casino hosts and entertainment directors. One retired host remembers her as someone who was valued not only for "the length of her legs or the misty depths of her eyes," as he put it, rather poetically. No, Peggy also had a certain intelligence and social grace—the very reason the gambling oil tycoon from Texas might pause to wonder whether he was entitled to fuck her—absent in most girls who lived in town, and made themselves too available. The allure of the commuting broads is that they were still real, the ex-host explained.

I found the complexity of this commodities market in women a bit baffling. What if the sleazeball high roller just wanted some sex? "Well, we had plenty of whores for that," the ex-host told me with a sigh, disappointed by my inability to get it. A long lecture ensued. In the old days, long before it was about exploding volcanoes, geeky conventioneers, and outlet malls, back when Vegas knew how to treat people (I think he meant to say "men") decently, casinos understood that pretty broads were as indispensable to a gambling establishment as dice and cards. A good casino had an arsenal of stunning showgirls, stunning call girls, and stunning classy dames it could call on to grease the high-roller action, and it was a good host's job to match weaponry with circumstance. Would a craps player betting fistfuls of black chips on a Saturday night most appreciate an admiring showgirl by his side for an hour, blowing in his ear and making him look good? A broad to sleep with? Or someone to dine with, take to the show, maybe even see again on his next visit? Someone like Peggy?

Peggy loved the arrangement, partying in Las Vegas with rich men, high on the action. More than one of her, er, friends became convinced that she brought him good luck, so they'd let her throw the dice, make the call in baccarat, and pick her favorite numbers at the roulette wheel. They all slipped her money and presents. "A male gambler trying to win over a striking woman and impress his friends at the same time is the most generous creature out there," she said, as if reciting from a biology textbook. The most excitement and, on occasion, the most money came when she'd be given a piece of the action, say 5 or 10 percent. "I was a heavy gambler who couldn't lose, because it was never my money up front," Peggy said, echoing the premise behind my book. In fact, she'd always win, because no matter what, the host would slip her a couple hundred at the end of a weekend visit.

The money could be phenomenal when her generous "friends" were winning, but Peggy never lost sight of the fact that her mission was far more important when a friend was losing. To lose in a casino can be a very painful experience, she told me, as if this had never occurred to me. It was her job to mix compassion and fun, to help gamblers through their pain. From the casino's viewpoint, such "healing" was crucial, because, as Mario Puzo writes in *Inside Las Vegas,* discussing casinos' humane debt-collection tactics: "A degenerate gambler is regarded as a fine bit of rent-yielding property. You take care of him." Puzo also describes one of Las Vegas's legendary healers from Peggy's era, nicknamed "the nurse."

Peggy's double life became unsustainable, especially in light of one piquant detail she failed to mention to me at first. Her boss back in Los Angeles, the insurance broker, was also her boyfriend, and he was growing more and more suspicious of her frequent weekend absences. One day he confronted her about the $4,000 in cash he'd found stashed away in her desk drawer after a particularly profitable weekend jaunt. "You gotta realize, hon, in those days that was enough money to get yourself a home," she said, making clear the depth of her predicament.

Peggy came clean, sort of, telling her boss/boyfriend that she had danced a little for a Las Vegas revue and won some money gambling, but had been ashamed about the whole thing. She swore off Vegas, and within half a year, they were married. She settled down to the life of a housewife in a ranch-style home in the San Fernando Valley. That gig lasted two years, until Peggy accepted the fact that she couldn't stay away from Vegas. She's lived here ever since.

The divorcée came back with a vengeance, picking up where she'd left off, getting in deeper and deeper with more of the casino's best customers, until she was deflecting marriage proposals. In her late twenties, she retained all her beauty, magnified if anything by a cultivated grace and wisdom. But before long, she entered a period of decline, as did her adopted hometown. "One morning I woke up with more addictions than I could count, and before I knew it I was gaining weight," she said.

Peggy "retired" to one of the most enviable sinecures the old Las Vegas had to offer: a casino's gift shop. Oddly, this was a phase in her life she was less eager to discuss. She wouldn't tell me in which casino she'd launched her retailing career, whether it took a relationship with a mobster to get the shop, or what kind of money she made. "I was comfortable" was all she'd say. Indeed. In the days before a lucky gambler in Vegas could cross the Strip and shop at Neiman Marcus or at the Forum Shops, the casino's gift shops, crammed with jewelry and furs, were the only places in town a winning gambler could quench his thirst for hard goods. They were notorious gold mines.

It's been more than fifteen years since Peggy gave up the shop. She now spends most of her time doing volunteer work and, in a sign of the times, "day trading" stocks ("it's better odds than any you'll find here"). She only comes down to the Strip a few times a year, and it inevitably saddens her. It's just not what it used to be. Wall Street bean counters and fanny-pack barbarians sacked Cocktail Nation, erected roller coasters, and blew up the Sands; what're you gonna do?

♣ ◆ ♥ ♠ I lay in bed, scorned by sleep. It was a perfectly respectable bedtime, or would have been if I hadn't gotten up a mere twelve hours earlier. After trying too hard to drift off into the realm of dreams, I got up, threw on some jeans, and went back downstairs. Elsewhere I would have just flicked on the lights and picked up a magazine to pass the time, but not here, not in Vegas.

I was drawn to a craps table where everyone seemed to be having a grand time. The Moors enthralled Europeans with their dice in the eighth century, and craps has been the most exhilarating form of gambling ever since, obsessively pursued by aristocrats in Elizabethan times, GIs in World War II, and Texas high schoolers in the age of Dick Carson. Walk into any casino in Las Vegas, close your eyes, follow the noise, and you'll invariably end up at a raucous craps table. The game comes closest to being a team sport, with plenty of cheering and high-fives. Blackjack players can develop a sense of camaraderie too, particularly when the dealer busts often, but essentially each player is on his or her own. In craps, there's one shooter, on whom most people are betting. You typically win or lose as a table, and when you lose, the dice pass on, until a hot shooter is found.

It's a complicated affair. More than with other casino games, to look at the sunken craps table (from a distance, it looks as if people are playing in a bathtub) is to shake your head and wonder, *Who the hell ever thought this one up?* Craps is the most challenging game for casino employees to manage, with its layers upon layers of different bets. The basic idea is that the shooter sets the "point" with a first throw of the two dice and then seeks to throw the same "point" again before throwing a 7. Along the way, the gaggle around the table make a dizzying array of proposition bets on each throw. Typically, these are bets that a certain number will pop up before the point or the 7, when the slate is cleaned. It takes hours of study and play to get a good handle on the varying odds for these bets, but playing the basic pass/don't pass scenarios is easy enough and offers the best odds. Betting the "pass line" means you are with the shooter and will be paid if the point is rolled before a 7, or if the shooter rolls a 7 or 11 off the bat. A 2, 3, or 12 is an instant loser, or "craps." Interestingly, craps and baccarat, in contrast to blackjack, are named after the games' worst-case scenarios, "craps" being a losing throw for the shooter and "baccarat" being a hand worth zero.

There is always some antisocial element at craps, often yours truly, who persists on betting against the shooter, on the "don't pass" line. This is like shorting stocks. The bet pays when a 7 is rolled after the point has been set, to the annoyed stares of others at the table who've gambled on the pass line. I like it because I have a thing for the number 7, and the odds are marginally better.

But tonight I behaved. The nine bettors, all heavily on the pass line, were in such a splendid mood, I wasn't going to take them on. Sometimes, it's best to follow. The stickman, whose job it is to collect the dice with a curved stick and shove them to the shooter with panache, never ceased offering the dice to a stunning, suntanned woman wearing a slinky black dress, at the other end of the table. She seemed to be here for the ride, accompanying the man with the biggest chips. They were Italian, and she had the sexiest scratchy voice (too much vino?) when screaming, "Andiamo, andiamo, quattro, quattro!" Or: "Sette, perfido, sette!" By popular demand, the dice weren't rotating. She made such a show of caressing them, hiding them behind her long purple-tinted fingernails, then blowing on them before finally letting go with an elegant underhanded toss.

Her arm's motion would invariably be accompanied by a subtle grunt and just enough of a lean forward to afford the rest of us— patrons, dealers, and overhead security cameras—a splendid view of her firm (was it just me, or were they tanned as well?) breasts. Nobody would have cared if I'd bet the "don't pass" line, on second thought, but I would have started a riot if I'd asked the stickman for the dice!

In time, I fell into the most contented state, that high ground between a social buzz and awful drunkenness, until I felt we were all drifting pleasantly at sea, guided ever so gently in our green felt ship by our Italian captain, she of the frizzy hair, enticing voice, and supple, Mediterranean-hued mounds. A pretty cigarette girl in dazzling fishnet stockings came by offering smokes and lighted yo-yos, showing off her own cleavage, hazel eyes, and petulant nose. How dastardly, how powerful, this alliance of vice and beauty, which will continue to drive generations of Peggys to this corner of the desert, no matter how much corporate overlords scrub it down. I grabbed for a Macanudo, which a pit boss comped.

Things would be fine, even in the short run.

Nest egg: $46,039

Sunday, April 26

Woke up late. Ate Mexican. Took a nap. Played Megabucks at Silver City, a small, stand-alone casino next door with an Old West motif. Laughed at the sign by the entrance advertising the casino's "Scratch for Cash" paycheck-cashing promotion: "Cash your paycheck and win. You work hard all day. Isn't it time for a raise! Everyone is a winner!" Lost $60. Another day in paradise.

After dinner I entered the Riviera's smoky poker room and took a seat between a big, friendly guy from Detroit and a small, unfriendly local woman who wore one of those casino warm-up suits that give gambling a bad name among the natural-fibers crowd. "Where do they sell those cool outfits?" I asked, in an effort to win a much-needed friend off the bat, but she just grunted.

The truth is, I was terrified. It's one thing to sit down at a black-jack table and piss away my publisher's dough on a chance to beat some asshole casino mogul out of more dough, but it was quite another to sit down at a table with five total strangers—some no doubt hailing from states that have adopted concealed-weapons laws—to try and beat them out of some of their dough. The casino here is a mere onlooker, providing a dealer and some rags to clean up any blood that might flow. It takes a couple of bucks, the rake, off each pot for its trouble.

The last time I had played poker of the nonvideo variety was 1972, with my grandmother. Poor Tita tried her best to teach me the game, but I was far more interested in spilling her mesmerizing colored chips all over the living room floor to play war games, with each chip representing a battalion in some Napoleonic skirmish. If only I'd given Tita my full attention, I might have known what was going on at this game of seven-card stud.

I was befuddled by the fast-paced game's rituals, often asking my neighbor from Detroit for guidance (not about my cards, naturally, but about what the hell was going on). This let the whole table— all of whom looked to have been sitting there since sometime on Friday—know that I was, in poker lingo, a "George," someone whose role is to sweeten the pot. I won the first hand by bluffing on a pair of fours. It was exhilarating to have the unwieldy pile of chips shoved to me amidst all those resentful glares, but it was all downhill from there. I kept on trying to bluff, but Ms. "I Live Here in My Warm-up Suit" never bought it again. "Don't worry about it, man, she goes the other way, if you know what I mean," the guy from Detroit told me out of the side of his mouth when I was out of chips— "down to the felt," as they say. It took me a second to realize he was trying to tell me she was gay, and I couldn't figure out how this was supposed to console me for my $500 loss. As I walked away, though, it did strike me that I'd heard more homophobic cracks in the past few weeks than I'd heard in the previous five years.

Later, paging through John Scarne's *Guide to Modern Poker* I picked up two interesting tidbits I wished I'd read *before* launching my poker career. First, "after the fifth card, a player should fold if he does not have at least a pair of queens or a four-card straight or flush." And, second, "never attempt a bluff at stud unless you have a little something in your hand."

♣ ♦ ♥ ♠ Walked over to Treasure Island late at night and put another "dime" on Germany to win the World Cup. Then I played the reassuringly familiar game of blackjack, alone, at a two-deck $100 table. I took discreet notes on where I stood every time the dealer shuffled in order to document gambling's ferocious swings:

> 10:40: Bought in $1,200.
>
> 10:55: Shuffle. Count: $1,650.
>
> 11:04: Shuffle. Count: $1,300.
>
> 11:08: Out of money before next shuffle.
> Bought in another $1,000.
>
> 11:16: Shuffle. Count: $600.
>
> 11:22: Shuffle. Count: $3,875.

Walked away. Forty-two minutes, $1,675 profit.

Nest egg: $46,639

9

GOLDEN GATE

Ours was the first and will doubtless be the last party
of whites to visit this profitless locale.
—Lieut. Joseph Christmas Ives, U.S. Army, 1855

Monday, April 27

♣ ♦ ♥ ♠ In the early afternoon, crossing the Riviera casino in search of my rental-car keys (don't ask), I ran across a group of uniformed women. Their jackets read, "Sallie's Lounge, Evansville, Wyo." What were they, a drinking team? Close: a dart team, participating in a weeklong tournament at the hotel. Indeed. To walk back to the corridor of meeting rooms where William Bennett and Senator Lieberman had called on the world to rise against Jerry Springer what seemed like decades ago was to find an entirely self-sustaining culture. *A dart tournament?*

"If you play tennis, Wimbledon is the ultimate setting, but if soft-tip electronic darts are your thing, this is the ultimate," Michelle from Nantes, France, told me near the entrance to Banquet Room A, which the week before had hosted a pool tournament. She wore the jersey of the French national dart team—I kid you not—and was standing in line to buy a Bud from a makeshift bar. Behind her, the large banquet room had been converted into the world's largest, most antiseptic dive. Smoke wafted up to form a nasty weather pattern pressing against the ceiling. Aisle upon aisle of electronic boards, a total of 197, had been crammed into this and another ball-room, and now stood awaiting the 3,500 players who'd emerged from their darkened pubs in forty-three states and eight foreign countries to vie for the $250,000 in prize money. Unlike Michelle, most of the players represented cozy bars where everybody knows their name.

I followed around the low-key Ebony & Ivory team from Slider's Sports Bar and Grill in Fort Collins, Colorado. There were four dartists on the team. Missy, a tall, well-mannered nurse, was the most focused. "You come here after a long season back home and you want to bring your game up to a new level," she told me. I learned from her that a bull's-eye, worth 50 points, isn't the game's ultimate target. There is a small swath of board to the northwest of it, where the 20-point slice intersects with the triple-value ring, worth 60 points. Three of these make a perfect "three in a bed." Am I the only one not to know this stuff?

Her teammate Ken, a former running back with the Chicago Bears and Washington Redskins, lovingly showed me his leather dart case. This was another surprise: Dartists bring their own. A dart, like a violin or a tennis racquet, must be carefully selected. Near the entrance to the ballroom, vendors displayed the latest in dart technology. An earnest young salesman for the Great Lakes Dart Manufacturing Company told me the top of the line these days is the front-loaded "spider," made of tungsten. Tungsten? Is that like cupro?

♣ ♦ ♥ ♠ Implosion Day had finally arrived, and the excitement was palpable. I was going to do this Aladdin implosion in style, having spent $250 to attend a sumptuous fête in a tent right behind the hotel. The party was being thrown by the Aladdin to benefit the Make-A-Wish Foundation. The invitation made clear that "dust gear" would be provided. Two hours before the scheduled 7:24 P.M. big bang, the Strip was already closed to traffic, so I had to negotiate back streets to gain access to the property. Greeting me at the entrance to the Aladdin's lot was an old billboard pushing the hotel's $5.95 prime rib dinner. That's when it hit me. This "old" hotel being executed, site of Elvis and Priscilla's wedding and one of the last casinos in town from which the Mob had been dislodged, was—gulp—my age. Must be time to start changing my eating habits.

I arrived at the tent halfway through the cocktail hour, and was immediately disappointed on two counts. First, guests were assigned to tables for dinner. Second, neither Steve Wynn nor Sheldon Adelson was at mine, not that they were anywhere to be seen. Mine was the catch-all eccentric-tourist table, the one farthest from the action. "This is our third Las Vegas implosion," a couple from Seattle told me, glowing, as if on a pilgrimage to Lourdes. "How about you?" I decided to mingle.

New York investment bankers and lawyers flown in to toast their deal-making prowess seemed to make up half the crowd. The Aladdin was being imploded to make way for a new $1.3 billion resort of the same name, and these guys in pinstripes had made it all possible. So there was no reason to be mournful; this was a triumphant implosion, another seemingly cozy Teamster-financed hotel giving way to a Wall Street–fueled "megaresort." This night was all about renewal, a bright future, and fat underwriting fees. I met a few of the Merrill Lynch and Skadden Arps types milling about and we talked about what all young Manhattanites talk about when they come together over cocktails: apartments. To hell with imploding hotels. "Can you still find one-bedrooms for less than two grand a month in your neighborhood?" one lawyer asked me, after we'd dispensed with the pleasantries.

The locals present weren't exactly society's A-team. Neither were the celebs. Joan Lunden would press the button—presumably it was attached to a box marked ACME—to bring the building down. Maybe people are just imploded out, there have been so many of these things. Also, the coming Aladdin gets little buzz in town. Steve Wynn's Bellagio, Circus Circus's Mandalay Bay, Hilton's Paris, and Sheldon Adelson's Venetian are all slated to open well before it, and in a town going through one of its periodic anxiety attacks about possible overbuilding, some view the new Aladdin as an unnecessary indulgence. This might explain why at the pre-implosion auction for the Make-A-Wish Foundation, item number eight went for only $5,000. The item was two nights in a suite during the new Aladdin's grand opening celebration, two dinners, the gala opening party, and a $5,000 shopping spree at the mall that will be a part of the resort. In this tent filled with people who understood risk all too well, nobody was willing to bid a single dollar beyond the value of the shopping certificate, not even for charity. You can be sure that a similar package for the Bellagio's opening night would have fetched a premium.

The coolest thing about the whole evening was the velvet sack we each received with our blue, hooded Aladdin implosion poncho and goggles. I donned these and walked outside to catch the main event. We were all giddy—our VIP tent crowd, the media next door, the helicopters buzzing above, and the crowds on the Strip—as the hour approached and all eyes settled upon the seventeen-story structure wired with 232 pounds of explosives. People love to witness mayhem.

In this case, the mayhem had been painstakingly planned by what has to be one of the oddest family-owned enterprises, Controlled Demolition, Inc. CDI is the nation's leading "imploder," and Las Vegas has been a—here goes—booming market for the firm. In recent years CDI has brought down the Hacienda, Dunes, Landmark, and Sands hotels.

As 7:20 rolled around, a hushed silence prevailed. Wearing my ridiculous poncho and goggles, I couldn't help but think of all those pictures of scientists at the Trinity test site who witnessed the first atom-bomb tests in the desert. Joan did her thing, and we heard some pops. An eerie calm followed before the building took the plunge into itself. It was a graceful caving in, a layer cake losing its layers, leaving behind nothing but a cloud of dust and, after a couple of minutes, a breathtaking view of the previously obstructed Bellagio across the Strip. The implosion itself was so quick and so devoid of violence, leaving our ponchos so spotless, that we all felt a little cheated. "Let's blow up Bally's now, and keep heading north, taking them all down," someone to my left said, expressing the prevailing sentiment.

Later, as the dust literally settled, looking toward the rubble I marveled to no one in particular that the Aladdin's tennis courts had been spared, but the man standing next to me, Daniel Alpert of Westwood Capital LLC, one of the project's financiers, said they'd be scrapped soon, too. Oh well. "This has been a real labor of love," he continued, puffing on a cigar. Was he worried about the future? No, the going might be bumpy for a while, but the new Aladdin would ultimately thrive, he noted. "People scare themselves talking about a hundred and twenty thousand hotel rooms, but what you have to remember is that a good half of those are second-tier equity. There is plenty of room for fabulous new properties in this town." Speaking of second-tier equity, it was time for me to head downtown.

♣ ♦ ♥ ♠ Approaching downtown on I-15, I was immediately disabused of any notion that it's primarily a place where people work, as I'd once assumed. It was the massive "$1 Draft and Well Beers" sign painted onto the backside of a skyscraper that clued me in. The letters must have been two stories tall.

My destination, the Golden Gate Hotel, is Las Vegas's oldest. It opened in 1906 as the Hotel Nevada, on the corner of Fremont and Main, the spot where a year earlier railroad representatives had auctioned off land to establish the Las Vegas town site. The first three lots went for a grand total of $1,750. A year after it opened, the hotel boasted Vegas's first phone (dial 1), but its true claim to fame wouldn't arise until 1959, when the renamed Golden Gate started selling its world-famous 50-cent shrimp cocktails. The hotel's deli didn't change the price for thirty-two years, but now charges 99 cents. In 1991, hungry for any tangible historic occasion, Las Vegas threw a party to celebrate the sale of the 25 millionth Golden Gate shrimp cocktail.

The Golden Gate calls itself a bed and breakfast, which anywhere else would be a laughable claim for a hotel with 106 rooms, a diner, and a twenty-four-hour casino. But here, where most hotels appear to be on steroids, the charming Golden Gate does feel like a quaint b&b. The feeling is only enhanced by the fact that breakfast was included in my $40 room rate.

I set off to explore. The people meandering up and down Fremont and in and out of the various downtown casinos were different from those on the Strip. Here, you knew you were in a western town, not some trendy corporate marketplace. I saw more cowboy hats, string ties, boots, and shiny belt buckles in ten minutes downtown than I had in the past three weeks, and there were plenty of faces to match—craggy, weathered, sun-beaten maps that told stories, much like the earth of the Mojave Desert.

Downtown is a subsistence economy, where uniformed cocktail waitresses play video poker over at Binion's Horseshoe while on break, pawnshops hover vulturelike down every dim-lit side street, and prostitutes come cheap. You cannot spend an hour walking through downtown without coming away with a sense that gambling is a cannibalizing endeavor that will wear down and corrode those who persist at it. Here there are no swashbuckling pirates or pyramids to disguise that fact.

While I was watching old Art playing blackjack at Fitzgerald's, it occurred to me that downtown Las Vegas is what most American cities would eventually look like if casino gambling were legalized across the country. Art was either too sloshed or too blind to read his cards. His hearing wasn't too hot, either. Every time the dealer told him he'd gotten an ace he'd grumble about all these 8s, and we'd all have to yell at him before he harmed himself any more than he already had.

Most of downtown's casinos are as forlorn as their clientele. First-time visitors to Las Vegas feel little compulsion to make the trek downtown, and locals trying to steer clear of the Strip are better off going to the newer neighborhood gambling palaces. Downtown's gambling revenues in 1997 were roughly what they were a decade ago, $678.5 million, while the Strip's revenues have doubled, to $3.8 billion, in the same period. Panicked, in late 1995 downtown's casino operators opened the Fremont Street Experience, a $70 million light show that plays every night on a futuristic canopy hanging over what are now four pedestrian-only blocks. The shows are overrated, but the pedestrian walkway linking the worn casinos is rather pleasant. In 1996, downtown's revenues picked up, but then fell again in 1997 as the novelty wore off. Long-term prospects are bleak.

That isn't to say that grittiness can't be charming. I talked to many out-of-town visitors who come to Las Vegas at least twice a year and stay downtown, choosing to snub the Strip and its "pissing gold fountains," as one Texan put it. But there are too many casinos here to service that anti-pissing-fountain niche market.

At 1:30 A.M. I purchased the *Review-Journal*, fresh off the presses with a picture of the Aladdin in free fall under the banner headline of "Abracadabra," and sat down to the $3.50 steak-and-eggs grave-yard special at the Golden Gate's diner. I was shocked to read the imploders speak ill of their victim. "This is the worst construction I've ever seen," said Mark Loizeaux, president of CDI. "It's shoddy. It's a poor man's high-rise. It is extremely susceptible to collapse, it is not a building I'd want to be in during an earthquake." This guy must be real popular at funerals. The Aladdin was so poorly built, Loizeaux went on, CDI decreased the amount of explosives needed for the implosion from a projected 370 pounds to 232.75 pounds. This in stark contrast to the earlier Sands implosion, which proved more difficult than expected on account of the Mob's eager-to-please contractors having tightly packed the tower's columns with reinforcing steel.

In college, I could drift off to sleep with a half-eaten slice of pepperoni pizza in my hand; such are the wonders of youth. But not anymore, so I played blackjack in the Golden Gate's small casino before heading upstairs, while my aging digestive system grappled with the concept of steak after bedtime. The pace of the game was slower here, as novice dealers took an extra second or two after dealing to add up their cards, the way new players do. The Golden Gate and similar establishments are the McDonald's of the dealing food chain, where people take their first job and dream of making it someday to a Desert Inn or a Mirage. Most of the dealers I talked to were East Asian immigrants, and few had been doing this for more than a month or two.

One of the few who didn't pause to consider whether she had busted at the end of each hand was a Vietnamese woman who told me she'd moved to Las Vegas from Paris. I gathered her dreams involved more than dealing in a plush carpet joint. She was already playing in them. She told me she'd lost $4,000 that night at the Mirage before coming to her minimum-wage job. She mentioned it casually enough to make it sound like part of her daily routine. She was now beating me soundly at this $2 table. "Why couldn't I have this luck tonight on that side of the table?" she groaned, after pulling what felt like her tenth consecutive 20 in a row. She and her husband had been quite wealthy once, but things recently hadn't gone so well. Was the job a necessity? "It's good for me to do this now," she answered ambiguously. I never did figure out this woman who could lose $4,000 at the Mirage before rushing off to deal at the homey Golden Gate, where in eight strenuous hours she'd earn about one percent of that.

Nest egg: $46,539

Tuesday, April 28

The 1998 World Series of Poker had been going on for more than a week at Binion's Horseshoe. Past noon, I walked over to check out the scene. A pair of German onlookers near the entrance told me in broken English that today's event was the $2,000 buy-in Omaha high-low split. I wasn't sure what that meant, but it sounds like a psychedelic drug derived from hay that leaves you with a wicked migraine. There seemed to be about two hundred players battling it out at the tables strewn about; the winners of the day's event would take home a few hundred thousand dollars. Matt Damon, the math whiz from the wrong side of the tracks, was expected to drop in for the championship round, he'd gotten so into the game in filming his upcoming poker movie, *Rounders*. The Germans told me they were in town for Thursday's seven-card stud, and I nodded knowingly. That was my game.

The World Series goes on for a month each year, with different events scheduled daily, culminating in the ultimate shoot-out, the World Championship No Limit Texas Hold'em, scheduled for the week of May 11. The world champion takes home $1 million. Las Vegas being the democratic town that it is, anyone off the street can buy a shot at glory for $10,000. But poker being a game of skill, the World Series' list of champions reads like a line-up for a poker hall of fame. Most of the greats are on it: Stu Unger, Johnny Moss, Amarillo "Slim" Preston, Puggy Pearson, Doyle Brunson, and Johnny Chan, among others.

At the nearest table, as the dealer shuffled, players discussed whether reckless Stu "The Kid" Ungar would be back to defend his title and seek an unprecedented fourth. In 1997, after being written off by the game's establishment, he reappeared to reclaim the title he'd won in 1980 and 1981, back when he was hailed as the Bobby Fischer of poker. Whether he'd again interrupt his passionate dalliance with drugs long enough to win another million bucks was anyone's guess.

He wouldn't. My first week back in New York, I read that Ungar remained upstairs in his hotel room, too sick to defend his title. Six months later, he was found dead in a room at the raunchy Oasis Motel on the Strip, his weak heart vanquished by a combination of cocaine, methadone, and hydrocodone. Though he had $800 on him at the time, Ungar was so far in debt, despite his millions in poker winnings over the years, that the flamboyant casino mogul Bob Stupak had agreed to finance his tournament play. The Kid's death had been so predictable, the quotes from fellow gambling

characters in the following day's obituaries were unusually pol-
ished. Most poignantly, when the forty-five-year-old poker master
had checked into the Oasis, he gave the Mirage's phone number as
his own.

♣ ♦ ♥ ♠ As the Strip increasingly becomes the showcase of
mighty, distant corporations, downtown is still lorded over by
legendary individuals (or their descendants) trying to preserve a hint
of old Las Vegas—casino operators like Jackie Gaughan and the
Boyds. Steve Wynn, interestingly enough, can be said to have a foot
in both worlds, as he still owns the classy Golden Nugget, right
across Fremont from the Horseshoe. But it's the Binions who most
deserve to be called gambling's royal family.

Lester "Benny" Binion, one of the town's most revered gamblers,
brought the World Series of Poker to life in 1970, although many
credit Nick "The Greek" Dandolos with the idea. Dandolos was a
formidable poker player from back East who came to town in 1949
and griped about wanting to go mano a mano with a worthy adver-
sary, no limits, instead of wasting time with a bunch of hacks. Binion, the Horseshoe's enterprising Texan proprietor, had the presence
of mind to call in Johnny Moss from Dallas and let the two men face
off at a table near the entrance to his casino. They did, for about five
months, in what became Las Vegas's most legendary showdown.
Buying themselves in with a minimum stake of ten grand, the two
men started off playing five-card stud. Binion had a tough time
holding back the crowds who came to watch the two men nonchalantly vie for what soon escalated to six-figure pots. "Greek, if you
gotta jack down there, you're liable to win yourself one hell of a
pot," Moss, the younger of the two men, said at one point after stak-
ing a quarter-million dollars on a pair of 9s. The Greek turned over
a jack of diamonds, making a pair.

And so it went, week after week. They played a variety of
games—switching from five-card stud to draw and lowball—and

caught some sleep every few days. At the end, it was Moss who won the final pot, when the Greek simply stood up, smiled, and announced: "Mr. Moss, I have to let you go." He'd lost about $2 million. When Binion instituted the annual World Series twenty-one years later, it was the aura of that one showdown that he was trying to recapture.

♣ ♦ ♥ ♠ "I had to get out," Benny Binion reportedly said about his family's abrupt move to Las Vegas from Dallas in 1946. "My sheriff got beat in the election that year." Legend has it he arrived in town with $2 million stashed in a suitcase. Back in Texas, he'd been a one-man good-times conglomerate, bootlegging during Prohibition and later running a numbers game and a craps table in a Dallas hotel. Benny carried three guns to protect his business interests, and killed at least two men in what he thought was self-defense. One out of two juries agreed with him.

Once in Las Vegas, Binion had the same reaction all other immigrant gamblers have upon arrival: *Why does anyone ever bother with this shit anywhere else?* He became a partner in the Las Vegas Club on Fremont Street, then in 1951 founded the Horseshoe. Two years later he was forced to sell out and spend three and a half years in Leavenworth Penitentiary for tax evasion. Binion never got back his casino license, but in the sixties the family regained the wood-paneled casino, and he presided over it as a paid "consultant" from his booth in the cafeteria. The Horseshoe became known the world over for epitomizing the patriarch's philosophy of "good food cheap, good whiskey cheap, and a good gamble." That's right, just the basics. When someone suggested to the old man that he hire entertainers to draw in more crowds, he scoffed: "I'm not gonna let some s.o.b. blow my bankroll out the end of a horn."

The Horseshoe's table limits were the highest in town, which meant a small-stakes gambler could wring a great deal more out of a lucky streak by doubling his wager with each throw of the dice before bumping up against the ceiling. What's more, the Binions waived their already generous limits to gamblers willing to set a higher one. That's still the joint's rule: At any table game, you can set your own limit with your first bet, up to $1 million.

Acting upon this unique rule in 1980, a man named William Lee Bergstrom walked into the casino with two suitcases. One held $777,000 in cash (he couldn't quite scrape together the full million). The other was empty, in case he won. Lonnie "Ted" Binion, one of Benny's five children and the casino manager at the time, allowed Bergstrom to put it all on the "don't pass" line. Mind you, this being the Horseshoe and not some snooty Strip casino (which wouldn't even have taken such a large bet), Bergstrom's fate was played out in the middle of the main casino floor, not in some back room brimming with chandeliers. A woman rolled a 6 as her point. Then she rolled a 9, followed by the magical 7. Bergstrom had won his bet, and Ted Binion walked him out to his car with two very heavy suitcases.

I heard this well-known story from a number of people in Las Vegas. It is a popular tale, a tribute to both the Binions (true gamblers themselves, not one of these new uptight corporate players) and Bergstrom (a guy able to walk out of the casino after doubling his nest egg with one single wager!). The most common version of the story has Bergstrom never again setting foot in the casino. But that is wishful thinking. Only when I read the excellent chapter on the Binions written by A. D. Hopkins in *The Players: The Men Who Made Las Vegas* did I learn that Bergstrom did indeed come back. On one visit he won $590,000; on others, $190,000 and $90,000.

Then one day he bet a cool million on the "don't pass" line. He again rolled his beloved 7—but this time on the come-out roll, meaning he'd lost. *On one roll.* Three months later he committed suicide in a hotel room on the Strip. But he was still $400,000 ahead when he quit, Ted Binion told Hopkins, going on to speculate that the reasons for the suicide were more romantic than financial. Remember, craps doesn't kill people; guns kill people.

♣

♣ ♦ ♥ ♠ Benny Binion died on Christmas Day in 1989, and both his family and the casino he built have since suffered through some tough times. His ebullient son Ted lost his gaming license after he was linked to what libel-sensitive newspapers politely call suspected underworld figures. There had also been drug offenses. In 1993, Nevada regulators fined the casino an unprecedented $1 million for lax cash-control methods. The Horseshoe, run by the eldest son, Jack, has run up some hefty losses in recent years. In 1996, Jack's sister Becky Behnen sued him to gain control of the property, in which she had a 17 percent stake, claiming he'd mismanaged the casino. The litigation was settled after I'd left Las Vegas, in June, with an agreement by Jack, Ted (who was being forced to divest by the Gaming Control Board), and sister Brenda to sell Becky their remaining interests for as much as $40 million. Jack and Becky no longer speak.

But the *annus horribilis* of the fading Binion dynasty was far from over. In September 1998, Ted was found dead at his home, an empty bottle of Xanax prescription sedatives next to his body. Toxicology reports indicated the fifty-five-year-old bon vivant had taken not only enough Xanax to kill himself, but enough heroin as well. Ted was known to smoke heroin, but the high concentration of the drug was found in his stomach. Was it an accidental overdose or a suicide?

Neither, suspected many of Ted's closest friends and relatives, who immediately cried foul play. And indeed the plot soon thickened. You almost expected to see Lieutenant Columbo pull up in his battered Peugeot. The bumbling detective would have had to give his condolences to Ted's grieving live-in girlfriend, Sandra Murphy, whom Ted met three years earlier at a topless bar named Cheetah's. Sandra started dancing there to earn back some $20,000 she claims to have lost on a weekend gambling binge. The two fell in love, presumably at $20 a song. Two months before his death, Ted had altered his will, bequeathing Murphy $300,000, his house, and everything in it.

Things get even juicier. Two nights after Ted's death, three men were found in the middle of the night in Pahrump, near Ted's ranch, digging up some $4 million worth of silver bars and coins Ted had buried in a vault across the street from a convenience store. Gamblers are fond of hoarding jewelry, but this was a bit ridiculous; think of all the Microsoft stock he could have bought! One of the men caught that night, shovel in hand, was Rick Tabish, the contractor Ted had hired to build the vault. Tabish was charged with conspiring to steal the silver, though he claimed to have been acting on Ted's instructions that in the event of his death, he should dig up the loot and drive it over to the ranch. A preliminary hearing in the case was to take place late in 1999.

But wait, there's more. Pointing to phone records indicating a flurry of conversations between Sandra Murphy and Tabish, Ted's family and attorney claimed the two had been carrying on an affair behind Ted's back. Sandra received a phone call from Tabish a mere eight minutes before she reported Ted's death to police on the afternoon of September 17. That Ted's surveillance camera had been dismantled days before his death, and that Sandra reportedly called the maid to give her the seventeenth off also raised eyebrows. Maids carrying on about how much they enjoyed their unexpected day off were a recurring tip-off on *Columbo*.

In October an attorney stepped forward and filed a petition to amend Ted's will, claiming that the day before he died, Ted had indicated a desire to write Sandra out. A judge ordered her share of the estate held in an interest-bearing account until the whole mess was resolved. In February 1999, the police served a search warrant at Sandra's apartment early one morning seeking to gather, among other things, evidence of a relationship between her and Tabish. What they found was, well, Tabish, hanging out at seven in the morning. In June, the two were charged with murder. Both maintained their innocence.

♣ ♦ ♥ ♠ I met Dick Carson for a late lunch at the Palace Station casino, just west of the Strip on Sahara. I found him at a craps table, tossing around black chips. We got comped at the Italian restaurant, where Dick casually set his wad of $100 bills, wrapped in rubber bands, on the table.

A friend to the Binions since Benny's time, Dick has always been haunted by the notion that gamblers' kids are inevitably screwed up. Proving it wrong has been Dick's greatest accomplishment, even if it entailed raising his six children in such a way that they might ultimately deplore what he's done with his life. "I wouldn't advise anyone to follow in my footsteps," he said. The Carsons' is definitely a "Do as I say, not as I do" household. Dick counts off with relish his grown children who succeeded in college and, equally important, have moved out of town to pursue their careers. "This is not a healthy place for people to live," he will tell you. His two youngest are still in school, living at home, so it is only twenty-eight-year-old Derick who has disappointed his father by coming back to Las Vegas after college. "He should be a park ranger, that's what he studied for at Auburn," Dad grumbled. Instead, Derick works at one of the resorts.

As he spoke, Dick kept glancing at his Motorola baseball pager, which provides real-time scores, displaying a digital diamond for each ongoing game. Little blips represent runners on base. Essential, nerve-racking gaming technology. Dick had money on three daytime games, "only" a couple of grand on each. "Used to be I'd have a hundred grand at stake," he said, as if to apologize for his impoverished circumstances. "You know, I'm not doing too good," he added heavily.

"Is this at all fun to you?" I asked.

"Fun?" Blank stare.

"Yeah, do you enjoy watching games you've bet on?"

"Nah, I don't even watch them the way you would. I just sweat them now."

"Do you have certain teams you root for, you know, as a fan, regardless of the betting?"

"Nah, it's all business. That's one of the reasons I still love swimming, and can follow it as a fan—because I can't bet on it."

Late in life, Benny Binion said he would almost certainly have been a gambler again if he had it to do all over, "because there's nothing else an ignorant man can do." Of course, he was being facetious. What he really meant was that there was nothing else an "ignorant" man can do to become a millionaire. Dick told me pretty much the same thing when I asked him if he considered himself addicted to gambling.

"I'm not addicted to gambling the same way the old ladies who play video poker might be, but I suppose you could say I'm addicted to the lifestyle," he finally said, after a long pause. "Even now, in the rut I'm in, it's still easier for a guy like me to pick up the phone and borrow a hundred grand from a buddy, interest-free, than it would be to get some clerical job that, if I'm lucky, will pay three hundred bucks a week." But, he added, if someone offered him a job where he could sit in a big office all day and pull in a million a year, then he could quit gambling, no problem.

His oldest daughter, Carolyn, who shares her mother's Mediterranean skin and striking features and swam in college (as did her two other sisters), told me that growing up she didn't know her father's occupation for the longest time. The other kids would ask in school, so she finally went to her mom and asked for herself—in the seventh grade. Matilda paused before saying, "Just tell them he's a bookkeeper."

An avid painter, thirty-year-old Carolyn lives in Los Angeles, where she manages the finances of a nonprofit group. She hates Las Vegas, "a place devoid of any sense of community, where people obsess about nothing but money and status." She calls her frugal lifestyle a reaction to her father's own excessive materialism. The blue Mercedes convertible she was given as a high school graduation present, which she long ago traded in, was her first and last ostentatious possession. "If it weren't for the fact that I couldn't afford the maintenance on that car, I'd tell you I traded it in merely as an act of rebellion," she said, laughing.

While Ted Binion may have believed rules don't apply to a gambler's kids, Carolyn would beg to differ. The Carson household was highly regimented, especially once Dick got on a health kick in the late 1970s. The Cocoa Pebbles went out, and in came the Shredded Wheat. The kids had to exercise every morning before going to school, whether they wanted to or not. And, blending spiritual and physical concerns, Dick insisted the family fast on Sundays. Carolyn attended Catholic school and wasn't allowed to go on dates or watch R-rated movies while in high school. "It was certainly ironic that as a daughter of this Las Vegas gambler I could arrive at college so innocent," she told me.

His flexible schedule meant Dick was always able to make time for the children. He devoted many years, and a great deal of money, to the Las Vegas Gold swim team, and was often the only father at afternoon soccer games, recitals, and the like. More than one other big-time gambler in town pointed to Dick's exceptional time commitment to his family, a bit unkindly it struck me, in talking about his reversal of fortune. But he hasn't changed his ways. He gets up early and spends his mornings researching the week's games, but by afternoon you are likely to find him cheering on his eleven-year-old son at a golf tournament (he's something of a prodigy) or his fourteen-year-old daughter at a soccer game.

Dick has lost his millions, and then some, but clings to his pride and self-esteem. It must be a tougher struggle than he lets on. "The thing is, a man can lose his money and win it back, but you must never lose your family," he said, trotting out the same "I'm a winner in life" apologia he'd offered at our first meeting. I was starting to feel like his confessor. He mentioned a number of notorious and still-wealthy gamblers in town whose family life was a total mess. "Money doesn't buy happiness," he said in his loud, matter-of-fact monotone, though a look into his eyes suggested its absence hadn't left him altogether blissful, either.

Though it was difficult at first to pierce his façade of imperturbable provider for his family, Carolyn now frequently talks to her dad about his troubles. And whenever he goes to L.A. on one of his poker trips—which he hates doing, but the competition is weaker there—Carolyn will swing by the smoky card room and take him to lunch.

Cementing their new, adult father-daughter relationship is Carolyn's understanding of why her father chose the life he did, or rather of the fact that he had no choice. It isn't something they dwell on, but it does keep the recriminations at bay. "Gambling is the only means my father had for providing for his family the way he felt he should, that's how I look at it," Carolyn told me. She may agonize over the fact that he didn't set some money aside when he was on a roll; she may quibble with the need to fly leased Learjets to Hawaii or bemoan his persistence, but the facts remain. Her father has so far put four children through private school and college and given all six kids a strong moral code, not to mention a wonderful childhood in a big house with every luxury imaginable, from a swimming pool to an underground bowling alley and racquetball court. This is something Carolyn can't dwell on too much: She is indebted to her father for all his gambling.

♣ ♦ ♥ ♠ I went casino-hopping after dinner. I first warmed up at the Golden Gate, where I played at the $2 blackjack table nearest the raised piano. The casino is pleasant, if you don't mind the stench of shrimp, and the pictures of old San Francisco lining the walls further boost the quaintness factor. I moved on to the Golden Nugget, then the Four Queens, where I annoyed a rowdy group of cowboys by repeatedly winning on the contrarian "don't pass" line at craps. Their language got particularly salty when they learned I was from New York City, as in the old salsa commercial, and I figured that was a good time to move on. It was nice to be able to take a few steps and be in a different casino. Outside, on Fremont, the weather was pleasant, music groups serenaded the crowds, and I started feeling guilty about my initial (negative) reaction to downtown. This revisionism was encouraged by the fact that I found myself ahead $2,200 for the evening.

I sauntered over to the 24/7 Pawn Shop Plaza on one of the side streets and wandered into the store claiming to offer the lowest interest rate in town. Six percent! A month! Good thing there was a Better Business Bureau certificate on the register. The display cases were stocked with jewelry and guns. Just for kicks, I slipped off my wedding band, a custom-made one that set us back about $800, put on my most desolate face, and approached the bored salesman/creditor.

"Um, how much can I get for this?"

He put it on a scale, then toyed with it for a moment, eyeing me suspiciously. "How much did you want?"

"As much as it's worth."

"That's not how it works. How much were you thinking?"

"How about five hundred bucks?"

"Are you serious?" He seemed insulted.

"Well, it's worth more than that."

"I can give you forty bucks."

We didn't even get into the whole $5 service charge issue.

For no good reason, I then ducked into the garish Girls of Glitter Gulch strip club across from the Golden Nugget. The first room I walked into had a long, narrow runway stage on which a couple of girls lolled about, grabbing on to poles as if it were rush hour on the subway. A few men sat ringside, coughing up a dollar bill now and then. I could see a "VIP" lounge in the back, featuring what from a distance looked like an aquarium.

I took a seat ringside by the main stage, and fell into conversation with two fellow patrons, cousins in fact, who appeared bored by the spectacle. One of them lives in Las Vegas; the other, Ken, was a geologist from New Zealand spending a year teaching and doing research in the United States. He'd been in the Utah desert looking at rocks the previous week, and now his cousin was showing him a good time. Ken called Las Vegas a "glorious place," which sounded doubly complimentary on account of the accent. We talked about academic life, New Zealand, and the formation of deserts, but girls kept barging in on us, asking if we'd like a lap dance, which I thought was rather inconsiderate to the girls onstage who were pretending to dance and whom we were pretending to admire. Wasn't there some strip club etiquette about roving dancers not approaching guys sitting ringside? Not at this joint. As stripclubreview.com warns: "Hustle is still the key word here."

Ken was underwhelmed by the whole scene. "I'm a rationalist, you see, so I must weigh the money spent on an experience against the output gained, which in the case of lap dances would appear to be nonexistent," he said, all of which sounded doubly academic on account of the accent.

Just then a dark-skinned dancer named Tiara sat down next to me, introduced herself and told me we could get to know each other better in the VIP room. "What happens there?" I asked warily. I had been a bit ashamed of my prudery in the days after my visit to the Olympic Garden—if Hunter Thompson had come to one of these places he probably would have ended up partying after closing time with a bunch of the dancers—and was determined this time to partake in the experience. "The dances are a bit closer," she said, blinking. They also cost $30 instead of $20. Oh, dear. I stifled an urge to ask if my rationalist friend Ken could come along.

Time for my first Glitter Gulch confession. I didn't like Tiara's aggressive manner, her glazed eyes, or her obviously artificial breasts. But I agreed to go along with her because I was afraid she might think I was racially prejudiced if I didn't. Can you think of anything more ludicrous?

Tiara told me she was born and raised in Milan, and that she still lived there most of the year, but I doubt it. When I started talking about AC and Inter—we were waiting for a new song to start before we got down to business—all I got was a blank stare. You couldn't spend an hour in Milan without knowing that these are the city's religious cults, among the world's best soccer teams. The lap dance seemed interminable. She took off her top and started gyrating in front of my chair, mostly fondling her considerable investments and occasionally turning around to slap her taut buttocks. It was all so . . . perfunctory. I didn't know whether to look at her breasts, at the guy two seats down who was also being serviced, at the colorful fish beyond, or into Tiara's eyes. Is it a lap dancee's duty to gaze longingly at the dancer? When the song ended, she asked if I wanted her to go on, so I guess I'd adequately masked my discomfort. I thanked her, said something debonair about not wanting too much of a good thing, settled my account, and beat a hasty retreat to my ringside seat in the main room, where I told Ken that his rationalist take on the place was on target. As far as I was concerned, I'd paid $30 for the privilege of not looking like a bigot.

Glitter Gulch Confession Number 2: Andrea was amazing. She came up to us fifteen minutes later and whisked me back to the crowded VIP room, the only place being used that night, it seemed. Yes, *whisked me,* I tell you, and I put up not even a hint of resistance. A second trip to the VIP room is so much easier to contemplate than the first, and I'd be damned if I wasn't going to reward one of these girls for not giving in to peer pressure. Her smallish breasts were 100 percent organic.

A beautiful, slender redhead with radiant green eyes, Andrea told me she shuttled back and forth between Vegas and Los Angeles, where she has an agent and is trying to break into an acting career. She'd just filmed a beer commercial that would air nationwide, which made me feel I was really getting my money's worth. A girl after my own heart, Andrea said she wanted to write a book about her experiences dancing, and had read Arthur Golden's literary phenomenon, *Memoirs of a Geisha.* Wow. If ever I catch her peddling beer in a wet T-shirt on the tube, I can look over at Kat and say with some authority: "I bet she's really smart."

She approached Ken when we were done and, much to my surprise, he, too, allowed himself to be led away. There was no denying this girl her livelihood. He came back with a sheepish look on his face. "She's rather sophisticated, could play a Soviet spy in a Bond movie, don't you think?"

I nodded.

Then, ever the rationalist, Ken conceded the experience had been worth "about seven quid."

Nest egg: $48,739

Wednesday, April 29

I woke up to discover that Fremont Street—at least the pedestrian-only canopied "Fremont Street Experience" stretch—was no longer a public street. A federal judge had so ruled on Tuesday in a free-speech case brought by the American Civil Liberties Union against the city. The city, which had ceded the street to an entity controlled by the casino operators behind the Fremont Street Experience, welcomed the decision, eager as it is to curtail the distribution of tawdry handbills as part of its campaign to clean up Sin City and make it family-friendly. This is akin to the struggle on the Strip, where casino owners are trying to incorporate sidewalks into their own resorts' designs in order to ban smut or, as in the case of Sheldon Adelson, to shut out union troublemakers.

Since I was staying at Las Vegas's oldest hotel and still savoring the Aladdin's implosion, it seemed appropriate to delve into the city's past. And so I went to the town's most hallowed historical shrine: the Liberace Museum. Where other than Las Vegas could you find a museum exhibiting a Rolls-Royce clad entirely in mirror tiles, a hand-painted eighteenth-century piano on which Chopin played, the world's largest rhinestone, a desk that once belonged to Czar Nicholas II, and a collection of wild hot-pants suits?

But as is usually the case in Las Vegas, there is more than meets the eye to this over-the-top memorial. The museum's $6.95 admission fee goes to the Liberace Foundation for the Performing and Creative Arts. Created by the flamboyant musical genius himself in

1976, the foundation has given more than $3.5 million to fund scholarships at ninety-six art institutions around the world, including such esteemed places as New York's Juilliard music school.

I talked to Bruno Mezzacappa, the museum manager, who moved out to Las Vegas in 1987 from Staten Island with his wife, Josephine, after retiring from a career in the loan department at Morgan Guaranty. They bought a huge house with a swimming pool, the weather is great, same old story . . . Bruno got bored doing nothing between buffets, however, so he went to work nights at a convenience store near his home, for the hell of it, until he was robbed at gunpoint. Then he came to work at the museum, where he handles day-to-day operations.

The Mezzacappas go to the casinos every so often, the way people in other cities go to the movies. One of the highlights of their life in Las Vegas was the evening they found themselves arguing at the Gold Coast casino over whether to play their favorite Megabucks machine before or after dinner. He prevailed, so they headed straight to dinner, only to walk out afterward and find a young man standing at "their" machine, waiting for the Megabucks rapid-response team to show up with the paperwork for his $10.9 million payout. Make that "near highlight." "I was in the doghouse for a long time over that one," Bruno joked.

Bruno finds Las Vegans more private than the folks back home, where neighbors had known each other for years. On Staten Island, people were always dropping by unannounced. Here, you hardly even know your neighbors. "It's very much a backyard culture, as opposed to the front-porch culture of our old neighborhood," he said with a shrug, as if to say each has its pros and cons.

♣ ♦ ♥ ♠ From the Liberace Museum I drove over to the University of Nevada, Las Vegas, campus to meet historian Hal Rothman, for my money the foremost sage of the new Las Vegas. "All right, you want the Spiel, do you, tour included?" he asked bouncily as I entered his office. "Then let's go." Poor guy, he gets called by every carpetbagger (his word) trying to get to the bottom of the real Las Vegas. Hal is fond of saying that Las Vegas's biggest problem is too many grandstanding intellectuals and hipsters flying into town for a few days to tell the world what Sin City is all about. But he can't help himself, he meets us all, eager as he is to convert critical visitors—there's a fertile market for anti-Vegas diatribes—to his passionate belief that this is America's first postindustrial, twenty-first-century city.

We carpetbaggers call Hal because he has a way of making bombastic pronouncements and backing them up with clever reasoning. He can spurt out three catchy sound bites per minute, a rare feat for a brilliant professor. Self-respecting carpetbaggers the world over know this because we all dutifully watched the same A&E cable special on Las Vegas from a couple of years back. Hal was so good on that show, the governor called him after seeing it, just to chat. Subjected to Hal's brainy boosterism, the gov must have been doubly pumped about being a Nevadan when he got off the phone.

For all his carping about carpetbaggers, Hal is no native. He grew up in the Midwest and did his graduate work at the University of Texas. He only moved out here six years ago, and, he jokes, will leave the day the city's population surpasses the two-million mark. Hal's main academic interests are western and environmental history. He is among the nation's foremost experts on national parks. In his latest book, *Devil's Bargains: Tourism in the Twentieth-Century American West,* Hal examines how embracing tourism transformed various locales—Maui, Aspen, Santa Fe, and Las Vegas, among others.

"Tourism is the most colonial of colonial economies, not because of its sheer physical difficulty or the pain or humiliation intrinsic in its labor but because of its psychic and social impact on people and their places," he wrote in the book's introduction, which he printed out for me among other things (a carpetbagger's survival kit) from his office computer. "Tourist workers quickly learn that one of the most essential traits of their service is to mirror onto the guest what that visitor wants from them and from their place in a way that affirms that visitor's self-image."

Las Vegas was never a defined place that sold its soul to entertain outsiders, like a Santa Fe or a San Francisco. Las Vegas was invented to cater to visitors' whims, and to change with them, making it the nation's ultimate mirror, a destination Americans instinctively get. Once visitors are done taking photos of the pyramid, the Crazy Girls, the Horseshoe's million bucks, and Siegfried's endangered tigers, they realize this oasis in the desert is really about, well, them. Las Vegas is free of the hypocritical impulse not to be changed by tourism that afflicts other destinations; smart malleability is what this city is all about. "That's why we love blowing up the old hotels," Hal said, with an impish grin. "Implosions reaffirm the city's commitment to remain a mirror, depicting the nation's ever-changing sensibilities."

Hal was well into the Spiel, which he imparted with some strain over the zydeco music on his car stereo as he drove me toward Green Valley, the attractive planned community in Henderson he calls home. Hal enthusiastically drove me past new schools, parks, and the synagogue he and some other newcomers founded four years ago on Nevada Day—that's Halloween, the day, appropriately enough, the barren territory was made a state in 1864 to add anti-slavery votes in the Congress. "The downtown temple had been part of the old casino-owner establishment," Hal explained.

Las Vegas remains a place where people can move in and make their mark off the bat. This is particularly true of what Hal calls the long under-represented "grafted upper middle class," professionals who work seven-to-seven and thrive in town though they remain, like expats abroad, mostly uninvolved in local politics.

Hal joked that he chose to live in Green Valley instead of on the West Side so as to not have to cross the Strip to get to work, traffic being what it is, but he scoffs at those who claim the city has outgrown its resources. He brushed aside my feeble attempts to bring up the perennial water issue, but said he is worried about air pollution. "The fact that we use water at construction sites to wet down the dust indicates the proper hierarchy of our problems," he explained.

Nevada, in Hal's mind, is first and foremost an American colony, which developed by providing services and products—quickie divorces, a good gamble, prostitution—that the mother country eschewed but its people wanted. The identity of colonists has changed over time, from the federal government to the Mob to corporate America, but Las Vegas has always relied on outsiders to provide capital with which to exploit its resources. "The nature of our relationship to the outside world is crystallized by the sight of vehicles at Hoover Dam sporting the insignia of the Los Angeles Municipal Water District and Nevada license plates," Hal exclaimed, banging on the steering wheel. Then there's the fact that 87 percent of the state is still owned by Uncle Sam. But in time, the colony will become a colonizer (witness MGM Grand's plans to open a casino in downtown Detroit) as indigenous sources of capital continue to grow.

The natives, colonized or not, live well here, offered one of the few remaining opportunities in the United States for semiskilled workers to enter an industry and earn a middle-class income throughout their career. This makes Las Vegas, depending on how you want to look at it, a successful "postindustrial template" or "the last Detroit." And like Detroit, this is a one-industry town. That doesn't bother a bullish Hal, in part because he thinks the sole industry is no longer gambling, but entertainment writ large. And, as he puts it, "I'd rather have my future riding on entertainment these days than on the auto industry."

Amen to that.

Nest egg: $49,139

10

BALLY'S

*The gambling propensity is another
subsidiary trait of the barbarian temperament . . .
incompatible with the requirements of the modern
industrial process, and more or less of a hindrance to the
fullest efficiency of the collective life of the present.*
                                                —Thorstein Veblen

Thursday, April 30

♣ ♦ ♥ ♠ It was with a sense of nostalgia that I checked in at
Bally's, where I'd stayed with my family back in the spring of 1977,
on my first trip to Las Vegas. We were driving back to Mexico from
California then, and family lore has it that I pressed Mom to keep
driving onward to Vegas in the middle of the night, instead of stopping in Barstow. I was outvoted.

I was in awe of what was then the MGM Grand the moment we
pulled up a day later, after seeing nothing but desert for hours. It's
not just that I was an impressionable kid from Chihuahua, though I
was. Architect Martin Stern, Jr., had gone out of his way to awe even
the most sophisticated of guests with a dramatic arrival. As Alan
Hess writes in *Viva Las Vegas,* the MGM's single greatest architectural contribution to the "Strip Style" was its enormous, bustling
porte cochere, presided over by costumed doormen.

Opened by Kirk Kerkorian in 1973, the MGM vied with Caesars

to be the most prestigious address on the Strip in those days. To a ten-year-old, this was Eden. I can still recall wandering around, eyes bulging and jaw scraping the floor, enthralled by the MGM's signature lion (a real one!) posing for pictures with a showgirl (a real one!) and by the shop selling magic tricks. My brother and I played in the hotel's vast swimming pool, on its lighted tennis courts, and in its giant arcade, which featured that high-tech marvel Pong. I never stepped into the casino, but could sense that gambling had an electrifying effect on most people, making this a sort of Disney for adults.

The old MGM Grand has since been acquired by Bally's, which itself was bought by Hilton. Compared with the newer hotels in town, it is a relatively subdued, middle-aged hotel, but it enjoys a primo location, sharing the intersection of the Strip and Flamingo with Ceasars, the Flamingo Hilton, and the Bellagio. Next door Hilton is building the Paris–Las Vegas Casino Resort, one of the much-anticipated big four slated to open before the year 2000. The $760 million Paris, which a dopey corporate press release calls "the world's only resort providing the authentic feel and experience of Paris, France," will be fronted by a fifty-story replica of the Eiffel Tower, and will include replicas of the Arc de Triomphe and the Louvre (I'm guessing that'll be the high-limit slots area). Its thirty-four-story hotel tower will be fashioned after the Hôtel de Ville. In the interest of authenticity, the staff will be trained to be rude to those who don't speak the language.

♣ ♦ ♥ ♠ Roger and others had encouraged me to check out a Gamblers Anonymous meeting, though I'd only be able to report what transpired in the most general of terms. GA wouldn't be GA if it weren't zealous about protecting members' anonymity. I chose to attend a comment therapy session, where members are free to make any observations, and solicit feedback.

GA was founded in 1957, fashioned after its sister Twelve Step program, Alcoholics Anonymous. It emphasizes humility, spirituality, and camaraderie as the cornerstones of a new life free of gambling. The first step of recovery reads: "We admitted we were powerless over gambling—that our lives had become unmanageable." This is easier said than done.

Dr. Julian Taber is a psychologist who worked with addicted gamblers for many years in Cleveland and Reno and has posted an engaging account of his frontline experiences, entitled "In the Shadow of Chance," on the Internet (http://intermind.net/~pappy/). Many different types of people are attracted to gambling, Dr. Taber told me when I spoke to him later in the year, but they all seem to share one trait: immaturity.

GA preaches that the problem gambler who has hit bottom and is in meetings should abstain altogether, meaning no Final Four office pools, no coin tosses, no playing the stock market, and, certainly, no more casino action. This is an absolutist crowd that believes there are only two kinds of recovering gamblers: those who spend a great deal of time at GA meetings and those who've suffered a relapse and are back "in action," learning that they have new lows to discover.

The American Psychiatric Association didn't recognize pathological gambling as a mental disorder until 1980, when the problem was finally included in the third edition of its *Diagnostic and Statistical Manual*. Essential features of the disorder include a continuous or periodic loss of control over gambling; a progression in the frequency and amount wagered; preoccupation with gambling and with obtaining money with which to gamble; irrational thinking; and a continuation of the behavior despite adverse consequences.

To determine the prevalence of compulsive gambling is no easy task. Nor is it one that most interested parties care to undertake with objectivity. Gambling's most virulent foes would have you believe that in time we will all be addicted, while casino executives, until very recently, would have told you there was no problem. And indeed, to most people in this pioneer town with its live-and-let-live mentality, "problem gambling" is still largely understood to mean one thing, and one thing only: You've made a losing bet, and it's your problem.

But attitudes are slowly changing. The spread of gambling across the country earlier this decade led to an avalanche of stories about Iowa grandmothers getting hooked on video poker, which helped mobilize antigambling forces. Problem gambling topped the agenda of the National Gambling Impact Study Commission set up by the U.S. Congress in late 1996 to evaluate America's love affair with lady luck. Casino moguls fear this body almost as much as they fear card counters and the hordes of plaintiffs' lawyers who will be looking for a new cash cow to shake down once they are done picking the tobacco industry's pockets.

So prodded, casinos must grapple with the fact that for some, the entertainment they provide can be unhealthy. They are posting helpline numbers near their ATM machines for those who may feel in over their heads, and they are bringing in people like Carol O'Hare of the Nevada Council on Problem Gambling to help teach employees how to respond to distraught patrons who approach them for help. At a conference on problem gambling sponsored by the council over the summer, casino executives proudly showed off stacks of "collateral materials" (brochures, to you and me) they'd prepared to handle these situations.

Most programs have so far been buffet-style. Got a problem? Help yourself. Las Vegas casinos aren't ready to consider the more extreme step of approaching obviously distressed patrons to suggest they take a break. Foxwoods in Connecticut is experimenting with such a program, but interference with a degenerate gambler's right to self-destruct runs counter to Las Vegas's most cherished libertarian principles. Of course, this sort of thing does happen informally. Luxor's Bob Miner told me that when he was a casino host at the Golden Nugget some years back, he approached a client who was losing big while upset and inebriated, to suggest he call it a night. Bob says the man screamed every imaginable obscenity and looked ready to pounce on him for butting in, but did stop gambling. The next day he called Bob to thank him for being a real friend. (Bob was nowhere to be seen when *I* needed him, but that's a different matter.)

At the problem-gambling conference, I asked a Mirage Corporation vice president, Bill Bingham, if his company was considering following in Foxwoods' footsteps and instituting an intervention program. He replied: "Even if we could identify people who have a problem, which we can't because it's a silent addiction, we'd face serious privacy and liability issues if we start approaching people." Funny, these serious issues don't deter casinos from approaching card counters and asking *them* to leave. Wasn't the right to exclude anyone from a casino, no questions asked, one of the industry's most hard-earned and cherished courtroom victories?

Bingham did have a point, though. It isn't always easy to spot problem gamblers. The most visibly upset person in a casino might be a hypercompetitive billionaire down $50 at a $5 blackjack table, while a compulsive like Roger may be sitting at a video poker machine, pissing away his savings in stoic silence, masking his despair until the drive home, at which point he will fantasize about death. Still, it's not so difficult at any given time in a casino to spot patrons who could use a pat on the back and a gentle "You okay?" from a staffer. At times, all a gambler needs to snap out of it is to be shamed by another's compassion.

The most vehement antigambling zealots will tell you that casinos want a self-destructive pathological gambler's last dollar, regardless of the consequences. The industry's dirty secret, they claim, is its reliance on these poor souls for a scandalous chunk of its profits. The casinos respond that this is all nonsense, that they are in the entertainment business, and that in the long run it only hurts them to have patrons hurt themselves.

I'm willing to buy this, at least when it comes to the big names in the industry. Gambling is not smoking. It's not inherently bad for you. On the contrary, I'd venture to say that a little gambling, a taste of life on the edge, is good for the soul. Come to town, wager your budgeted $250 casino fund between pool sessions, roller-coaster rides, delectable meals, and shows and you'll feel invigorated. By contrast, use a cigarette as intended, and it's still bad for you.

But casinos do need to take further steps to prove the zealots wrong and justify my faith. They are starting to do so by self-consciously adopting the alcoholic beverage industry's approach to abuse and addiction (preach moderation, and be open about the problem), instead of the scorched-earth tobacco industry approach (deny all, and park the incriminating documents with your lawyers). The industry has set up a National Center for Responsible Gaming—does this sound like a think tank pushing conservative Stratego and Yahtzee tactics, or is it just me?—and is funding research on gambling's addictive power.

According to one such 1997 study conducted by the Harvard Medical School and financed by the American Gaming Association, 1.3 percent of Americans are pathological gamblers. While that figure may appear negligible at first glance, it represents about three million people prone to what can easily be a deadly fixation. Moreover, the study found that among America's teenagers, the incidence of compulsive gambling jumps up to 3.9 percent. And here in Las Vegas, 6 percent of Clark County residents consider themselves compulsive gamblers. A larger number of people could be termed "problem gamblers," who have a propensity to bet over their heads but who have not yet become truly addicted. The Nevada Council's Carol O'Hare believes that nationwide, roughly 5 percent of the population could be considered problem gamblers, and that many of those have had a bad experience or two and quit on their own, without much fanfare.

Gamblers Anonymous has a list of twenty questions to help people determine if they are compulsive gamblers. Among them:

- ◆ Did you ever lose time from work due to gambling?
- ◆ Have you ever felt remorse after gambling?
- ◆ After losing did you feel you must return as soon as possible and win back your losses?
- ◆ Did gambling cause a decrease in your ambition or efficiency?

◆ Have you sold anything to finance your gambling? [Does a book count?]

Answer yes to seven of the twenty questions and you're a compulsive gambler, at least according to GA. One of the group's central tenets is that compulsive gambling is a symptom and not the underlying cause of a person's despair. This can be rather unnerving to those who think they have a "gambling problem" but are otherwise fine, thank you, and just want to shake it off by popping some medication, covering a couple of bad checks and sleeping it off for twelve hours. Dr. Taber shares GA's belief: "I have never seen a pathological gambler with only that one problem."

♣ ♦ ♥ ♠ The afternoon GA meeting at a community center was more crowded than I'd expected, but then it's easy to forget how many people work nights in this town. The meeting chairman introduced me as a visitor to the thirty or so recovering gamblers sitting in a circle, some of whom hadn't made a bet in over a decade of coming to these meetings and some of whom were attending their first one. The old-timers greeted one another and got caught up as if at a church coffee hour, while the newcomers stared vacantly into space, shocked at the discovery that their misery was so widely shared.

What struck me about this group was its diversity. Sadly, you don't often see such a mix of people—Hispanic, black, white, young, poor, old, professional, rich, you name it—come together these days. Maybe in jury pool waiting rooms (before the impatient yuppies get themselves excused), at Lamaze classes, and on the New York subway. Oh, yes, and in Las Vegas casinos, which is why we were all here. Gambling attracts all kinds.

The meeting was deeply moving, the fellowship genuine. There were even some humorous moments. One of any Twelve Step program's most cherished inspirational sayings, pinned on the wall by the GA folks, says something to the effect that the worst day of your new life won't be as bad as the best day of your previous one. A member said he had a hard time buying it. "I gotta tell you, I had some damn good days when I was out there," he said, and everyone in the room burst out laughing. I thought of my own days at the Hard Rock, when Kat was in town, we couldn't lose, and all things seemed possible. These folks had all had such days, too. The meeting closed with everyone holding hands in a circle, reciting the serenity prayer.

♣ ♦ ♥ ♠ Out in the parking lot, Betsy, a young, big-boned blonde with a sweet face who hadn't said a word at the meeting, but whose eyes had remained tearful throughout, approached me, saying she'd like to ask for a favor. "I don't know who to turn to; my sponsor didn't show up today. I need to cash my paycheck to buy groceries with, and I need someone to go to the casino with me to make sure I get out of there without gambling."

Recalling this request from afar, back in New York, it seems absurd. Why would anyone, let alone an addicted gambler, cash her paycheck in a casino in the first place? But once you've been in Vegas for a while, your mind becomes far more nimble and flexible, able to transcend common sense and cope with a great deal of the surreal in everyday life. Susie Ericsson had told me that she hardly noticed the characters playing slots at her neighborhood grocery store anymore, though the sight had dumbfounded and outraged her when she and Tom first arrived.

That casinos have prevented banking from fully catching on out here is another one of those quirky realities you come to accept after a while. As we walked into the Palace Station casino, where I'd had lunch with Dick Carson, Betsy told me she didn't have a banking account because she'd just moved to town (eight months ago!), the casinos give out free stuff for cashing your paycheck, and her credit rating wasn't too hot. She had gambled away her entire previous paycheck on the spot and had felt too sick, as a result, to take the free buffet she'd been given. Betsy wasn't sure how she'd cover her rent.

"I'm really never going to gamble again," she said, this time crying with gusto as we passed a row of empty craps tables, where idle dealers discussed the odds on a ball game that night.

Betsy got her money from the cashier, who gave her a "Paycheck Bonanza" scratch-off for goodies along with her cash, and wished her a cheery "Good luck." *At least they don't charge to cash the check,* I thought dumbly. I hovered behind Betsy while she waited in line, all the while wishing I had one of those earpieces Secret Service types get to wear. "Delivery made, estimating breakout in fifty-two seconds," I'd bark into my lapel, eyeing the nearest exit. I held on to Betsy's arm and guided her to the door with an exaggerated sense of urgency that made her laugh despite herself. We emerged back out into the blinding sunlight after less than four minutes of exposure. "One more thing," I said, taking the scratch-off from her hand and tearing it up. "Cold turkey means cold turkey, right?" Easy for me to say; I was heading back to Bally's to go crazy.

♣ ♦ ♥ ♠ At a newsstand I picked up the afternoon newspaper, the *Las Vegas Sun,* intrigued by the front-page headline: "Gamblers Stunned by Robbery Victim's Lax Security." Legendary poker player Doyle Brunson had been held up as he returned to his Las Vegas home the previous weekend from finishing a lousy (for him) tenth place in one of the World Series of Poker events downtown. The sixty-four-year-old Brunson—an exiled Texan, like Dick Carson—was carrying $80,000 in Horseshoe casino chips and $4,000 in cash when he was struck on the head with a gun and handcuffed to his wife. The theory was that he'd been a marked man from the moment he left the casino without putting his money in a safe deposit box. The cool thing was, Doyle actually bluffed his assailants. They fled when he faked a heart attack.

A Horseshoe spokesman told the *Sun* that the bandits would have a hard time cashing in, given that casinos keep close track of who gets paid out high-denomination chips, as I'd discovered at the DI.

Less clear was whether the casino intended to make Doyle whole, or whether it intended to make a tidy $80,000 off the incident.

After a hurried dinner, I went to see *Jubilee,* the quintessential Las Vegas "feather show," with statuesque showgirls prancing about, both topless and in sumptuous costumes. *Jubilee* harkens back to the revues everyone used to come see in town, an endangered species threatened by the growing polarization in the entertainment market between those who want more sophistication (*Mystère*) and those who want less (*Crazy Girls*). In one scene, the *Titanic* sinks; in another, Samson destroys the temple of the Philistines. Someone ought to tell the director that she need not busy herself so; most of the guys aren't here for the history, they come to see the topless babes in the sequined thongs and feathered headdresses. Just have them read the Yellow Pages, and you can cut back on those seventy stagehands.

After the show, between 10:23 P.M. and 3:08 A.M., I lost eight grand. I should have quit at 10:27, when I was down a mere $225, and saved myself the aggravation. Those first three minutes at the blackjack table—with the dealer drawing three improbable 20s in a row, my favorite being a 2, 2, 3, 4, ace, 4, 4—should have tipped me off to the inevitability of my demise that night. I would have been far better off writing out a check to a charitable organization, or blowing the eight grand on Coca-Cola memorabilia at the corporate shrine down the Strip, or on antiquities back at Luxor, and going to bed earlier. But no, instead I kept defying fate.

Don't get me wrong; I tried mixing it up. When the going gets tough, we tough, savvy gamblers get going. I could open a bar with the number of drinks I ordered that night but couldn't afford to wait around for, the tables were so nasty. Baccarat, craps, blackjack, even Megabucks: I could do no right.

Down a couple of grand, I crossed the street and entered the Flamingo Hilton, Bugsy's old haunt, now an unremarkable skyscraper with little to commend it, other than a terrific tropical pool. I won back a few hundred and collected my twelfth frequent-gambler card, then walked back to Bally's, hoping the spell had broken. It hadn't. I kept losing at every game under the security cameras, and I was starting to take it personally, which is never a good sign. As Dr. Taber writes in his on-line treatise:

> Instead of seeing gambling as a recreational pastime, the problem-prone gambler may take up a kind of personal crusade in which entertainment is forgotten in favor of an invigorating, symbolic combat between himself, the heroic gambler, and "them," the tricky, sinister villains who own the games.

I don't know about invigorating, but I was definitely embarked on a personal crusade. I had lost the Force; I had ceased being a Covey disciple. I wasn't thinking win-win, and Bally's had definitely become, in my mind, "the tricky, sinister villains who own the game." And this meant I was "problem-prone"? Ouch. I couldn't be; I was just doing this for the book. Really. I stopped when I did only because I thought it would be too depressing to go to bed with my nest egg down in the thirties.

Upstairs, my door was blocked by two college-aged sleeping beauties wearing cocktail dresses and smudged makeup. Awesome legs—all four, I noted, in the detached manner of the happily married strip club habitué. The beauties stirred and I realized they hadn't thrown themselves at my door, but rather at the adjacent one, where they were staying with their boyfriends. "You got any dental floss I could borrow?" the brunette asked. "Um, no," I said, feeling ashamed, even though it was they who were lying in the hallway, emanating a faint scent of distilled spirits. "Flossing religiously," incidentally, had been item number six on my list of New Year's resolutions. And the boyfriends? "They left us to go gamble." Oh. Awkward pause. "Well, good night." I felt bad about it, but I closed the door behind me. They didn't seem to mind.

Lying in bed, struggling to fall asleep, all I could think of was something I'd read in Mario Puzo's *Inside Las Vegas*: "Remember, a losing streak is far more deadly than a winning streak is benevolent.

And that's all you need to know about gambling in Vegas." How comforting.

Nest egg: $41,139

Friday, May 1

May Day! To the barricades! Mulling over in the shower how much I detested Bally's, I had the bright idea of going over to the Hard Rock for a couple of hours. To hell with worrying about earning my keep and getting comped here, I needed to play in a less hostile environment.

Such was my confidence that I actually felt bad, an hour later, walking back into the Hard Rock. Hadn't I taken enough of their money the first time around? Well, it's a dog-eat-dog world, and I was in need, having lost twenty-five grand since Kat and I waltzed out of here two weeks earlier. I missed her, walking those wood floors again, listening to the blaring music. It sucks to gamble alone.

For a while, I was worried. I dipped into the thirties, which was frightening, on the roulette table of my epic victory. Out of cash, I signed over more of my traveler's checks and went to blackjack. This time I plopped down two $500 chips. "Nickels in action," the dealer called over his shoulder. It was a $5 minimum table, and the guy playing next to me made a big show of moving over a couple of seats and making all sorts of room for me, as if I were some big shot worthy of more than my allotted share of breathing room. It was all pretty ridiculous, but I couldn't worry about it. I had a lunch appointment to make and needed to win pronto. Amazingly, I got a blackjack that very first hand. We were on fire. Less than a half-hour later, I walked toward the cashier clutching $7,300 worth of chips. I loved this place, and I felt so guilty about taking more of Mr. Morton's hard-earned cash in such a callous, premeditated manner that I stopped by the gift shop on my way out and dropped $90 on a pair of plush Hard Rock beach towels. It was quite a gesture, considering we have neither need nor space for them in our cramped Manhattan apartment.

♣ ◆ ♥ ♠ I met one of the heroes of what I like calling Daiquirigate, Chuck Bennion, for lunch at a Lone Star steakhouse. Some background: In January, the Nevada Commission on Ethics had held hearings on efforts by Yvonne Atkinson Gates, the chairwoman of the Clark County Commission, to lobby casino executives to give her a lease for her proposed—you'll love this—daiquiri-stand business. Yes, Ms. Gates wanted a piece of the action, namely the concession to the movable gold mines selling exotic liquor in Big Gulp–sized souvenir glasses at the entrances of casino resorts.

Ms. Gates is the most powerful local politician, given the county's paramount position over its municipalities. Most of the Strip resorts aren't even in the city of Las Vegas proper, but in the booming unincorporated county area, and it is the county that issues their all-important building permits. So naturally, when Ms. Gates approached the casino operators, mixer in hand, she had them, er, shaken and stirred. As executives later testified before the ethics commission, they faced an unpleasant choice between antagonizing one of their principal regulators or engaging in what felt scarily like paying a bribe. Some casino moguls played ball; most brushed her off politely; Sheldon Adelson, the outspoken builder of the Venetian, had a cow.

Corruption is a lot like bad driving, in that people are perversely proud of their homegrown variety. We all want to believe that our politicians and drivers are the worst. The regret with which folks shake their heads and say, "This shit couldn't happen anywhere else," is usually feigned. When I was growing up in Mexico, a joke dripping with fond self-deprecation made the rounds: Mexico had placed fifth in a U.N. ranking of the world's most corrupt nations. The punch line: "We paid a bribe to get out of the top spot."

Chuck Bennion does not find corruption amusing. He's the young attorney directing the effort to recall the commission chairwoman, which makes him an exception to Professor Rothman's notion that the city's newly arrived yuppies don't get involved in politics.

Chuck clued me in to the fact that Gates's ethical lapses may have involved more than daiquiris. She also stands accused, along with some of the other commissioners, of inappropriately looking out for her cronies in awarding lucrative retail concessions at the new airport terminal, slated to open in June. (After I'd left town, the ethics commission concluded that Ms. Gates had broken state ethics laws in this instance but that, alas, it was too late to rescind the offending concessions. Shit happens.)

A native of Utah, Chuck is a thin man with sideburns and an intense gaze, a thirty-one-year-old throwback to the early 1960s, the time before idealism lost its manners. He'd moved to town only in the fall of 1996, after graduating from law school at George Washington University in D.C. and clerking for a Nevada Supreme Court justice. His law school friends were aghast when he told them he'd decided to move to Las Vegas. "But you're so serious," they'd invariably reply. Chuck, who practices general corporate law at a small firm, hadn't even been in town long enough to register to vote when Commissioner Gates was overwhelmingly reelected in 1996. Now he was going door-to-door seeking to collect the 4,380 verifiable signatures needed to trigger a new election and appearing on the TV news in his capacity as co-founder of the ambitiously named Citizens for Honest and Responsible Government.

But why? Why bother? Only, the implausible civic leader answered, because nobody else would. He and some like-minded friends jumped in only after the astonishing realization that notables in town were unwilling to take on this "arrogance of power." Chuck said he was also emboldened by his disgust at the nation's long "passivity" in the face of what he considers President Clinton's own arrogance and by his experience as a Mormon missionary in an impoverished province of Argentina, where he saw how people had been disenfranchised by corruption's uncontested perserverance.

"You realize there is such a thing as waiting too long before getting involved," he told me.

Then with a laugh: "Plus, once you've gone door-to-door trying to get people to talk about their relationship with God, it's pretty easy to do so when all you want is a signature on a recall petition."

♣ ◆ ♥ ♠   I spent the afternoon at Bally's pool, where I had frolicked twenty-one years earlier. I was eager to try out an ingenious contraption I'd picked up at the Body Shop: a sunscreen applicator. It is shaped like a toilet bowl cleaner, but with a spongy tip. Sometime ago it had dawned on me that this device was precisely what the world needed, that I should make it my life's work to assuage the pain of the legions of lonely, pale travelers who'd never known the joy of protected interaction with the sun, facedown. But then I saw it at the Body Shop and felt liberated to pursue less productive endeavors. *24/7* was conceived within the week.

The applicator upstaged Dostoevsky as a magnet of puzzled, pitying, and sometimes hostile looks. Carrying Dostoevsky around Las Vegas pools had earned me plenty of pointed stares—"Look at that nerd, honey"—but this was something else. Maybe all the couples arrayed around the pool took it as an act of defiance to the natural order for me, on May Day no less, to whip out this fancy gadget and satisfy my own needs, able as I was to provide PABA-free, waterproof relief to the very center of my back without a mate. In the past, solo sunbathing had always been a one-sided affair (faceup), so this was immensely satisfying, stares notwithstanding.

I finished reading *The Gambler.* After a number of other characters in the Russian entourage at Roulettenburg bust out at the tables, a wealthy granny in particular, the narrator, Alexey, rushes into the casino alone one night, encouraged by a sense of predestined glory. He doubles his bet on a series of winning spins of the wheel, riding "the astonishing regularity sometimes met in streaks," until he's accumulated 100,000 florins, presumably a tidy fortune in those days.

But Dostoevsky couldn't bring himself, all personal fantasies aside, to depict gambling as the means to a "happily ever after" ending—not that there is much pressure to end on such a note in Russian literature.

Alexey's beloved, Polina, whom he sought to conquer with his gambling winnings, rebuffs him. And when the English Mr. Astley informs Alexey, "in a tone of voice as though he had read this in a book," that "all Russians who have money go to Paris," Alexey meekly complies. He sets off with the enticing Mademoiselle Blanche, who proceeds to party away his recently acquired riches. Alexey returns to Germany, feeling continual anxiety, gambling for "the tiniest stakes," and standing for whole days at the tables, watching the action, trying to reclaim his magic touch. Mr. Astley shows up at this point and tells Alexey that Polina always loved him, but had resented the idea of being bought by anyone.

"Yes, unhappy man, she loved you, and I can tell you that, because you are—a lost man! What is more, if I were to tell you that she loves you to this day—you would stay here all the same! Yes, you have destroyed yourself."

Astley arrives at this conclusion because Alexey earlier had told him he would give up gambling as soon as he won back all that he'd lost, a sure sign someone's a goner. Astley "cross-examines" the Russian about his life and knowledge of world affairs and concludes: "You've grown rusty. You have not only given up life, all your interests, private and public, the duties of a man and a citizen, your friends—you have not only given up your objects such as they are, all but gambling—you have even given up your memories." Gambling has a way of doing that.

The book ends on an enigmatic note, with Alexey thinking to himself in the muddled manner of those who have been at the tables far too long, but somehow are still in a position to realize it:

> Oh, if only it were possible to set off tomorrow! To begin anew, to rise again. I must show them. . . . Let Polina know that I can still be a man. I have only to . . . But now it's too late—but to-

morrow . . . oh, I have a presentiment and it cannot fail to be! I have now 15 louis d'or, and I have begun with 15 gulden! If one begins carefully . . . and can I, can I be such a baby! Can I fail to understand that I am a lost man, but—can I not rise again! Yes! I have only for once in my life to be prudent and patient and—that is all! I have only for once to show will power and in one hour I can transform my destiny!

"To-morrow, to-morrow it will be all over!" reads the last line. In my case, make that "Next week, next week!"

♣ ♦ ♥ ♠ That night I stayed away from the casino as long as possible. I ate at Chinois in the Forum Shops again, this time in the more informal café, then ventured into Caesars, where I chatted with a bartender from Pittsburgh who'd been out here a couple of decades. We bonded talking about the Steelers, inclines, Homestead, and shitty winters. "A lot of guys from Pittsburgh out here; they run most of the sports books in Vegas, you know?" I nodded, suitably impressed. The Pittsburgh, Louisville, and Dallas metropolitan areas have given the nation a disproportionate number of its most talented and colorful gamblers, a geographical phenomenon crying out for doctoral dissertations in a number of academic disciplines.

"What gets to me," the bartender said, "is that you go back to visit Pittsburgh and see these guys on the South Side or on Mount Washington putting their necks on the line for pocket change, for a couple of hundred bucks, and you just want to scream at them to come to Vegas, where there's real money to be made, and it's all legal."

I went back into the Bally's casino with some trepidation, and started losing once again. Any game I tried, I got killed at. We were in reruns, and this was last night's episode. Until, that is, I stumbled upon a casino war table. At first I thought I was sitting down at an empty blackjack table, but the dealer looked me in the eye as I fumbled with my chips and asked, "You realize this is war?" "Fine, but let's try and have some fun while we're at it, dear," I quipped, being the debonair guy that I am. But no, turns out she wasn't being philosophical. This really was a gimmicky new game called war, which was nothing other than the game—and that does seem like too good a name for it—we played as kids on long trips. Highest card wins. That's it, it's so inane. War is the latest step in modern casinos' attempt to dumb down the action to the point where Trotsky my cat could come place a bet and not have to worry about making any decisions. Talk about betting on a coin toss! Dealer dealt me a 7, herself a 6. I got paid. Then it was king over 9, jack over 4. If you tie, you double down and each get another card. The action is fast; no need to wait for Aunt Sue to decide whether to hit her 16. What I couldn't figure out was where the house gets its edge. Aren't you as likely to get the higher card as the dealer is?

I was more likely, it seemed. I was on a roll, recouping my losses for the night. Then it started to turn again, and I realized that, whatever the odds, war was as streaky as anything else in a casino. That's when I decided to call it a night.

Nest egg: $46,115

Saturday, May 2

I'm sick of this place, I realized, lying in bed between wake-up calls (yes, you can request two for the price of one). What I wouldn't give to spend the day curled up with a good book back home, little Trot at my feet. Or at an art museum, a busy office, a movie theater, a mall, a post office, the dentist's chair—anywhere but at a damned casino. What had I done to deserve this fate?

I had to pull myself together and suck it up. Today was the 124th running of the Kentucky Derby, an event my editor might consider noteworthy. So I rushed back over to Caesars to check it out. I was grumbling to myself as I crossed the Strip.

Caesars' immense sports and race book looks like a movie version of NASA's flight control center, with its rows of long desks facing huge screens and digital readouts. The race book alone has sixteen ticket windows, which were doing a brisk business when I arrived, a half-hour before post time. This entire corner of the casino was crammed, standing room only, with expectant bettors awaiting what groupies call the most exciting two minutes in sports.

I certainly hadn't come all this way just to watch. A symbolic bet was in order. But on which horse? I'd only been to one horse race in all my life—a creative date, years ago—so naturally I'd never heard of any of these beasts. I scanned the list with the same bafflement with which I peruse the menu in an Indian restaurant. How's that Tikka Masala been running?

The names are what lend horse racing its cachet. Just in this race, you had Indian Charlie, National Lore, Chilito, Halory Hunter, Favorite Trick, Parade Ground, and my favorite, the unassuming but confident Real Quiet. If only the NFL could be this creative in naming franchises. How about them D.C. National Lore or the Dallas Chilitos? Names you can sink your teeth into.

My reverie was interrupted by a frazzled "Can I help you?" Shit, I was up. What to do? I went with the name. "I'll take a hundred on Real Quiet to win, please." I liked his odds, too, 8 to 1. There were four horses favored over Real Quiet, but what was the fun of going with the obvious choice? On the other hand, putting my money on National Lore, the longest shot at 99 to 1, seemed unduly quixotic. What the hell was he, anyway? A donkey?

I stood next to Kris and Linda from Minneapolis, who were pumped up for the race and by the fact that they had seen Arnold Schwarzenegger strutting (their word) through the casino with his entourage. Kris thought he looked handsome, and still seemed to be swooning. Linda called him a conceited prick who'd acted as if he owned the place. Or maybe it was the other way around. What they did agree on is that Las Vegas needs a polka-themed casino: "You know, like the polka nights Lutheran churches throw." Mr. Wynn, call your design team.

When the "riders up" call was made on the giant overhead screens, Caesars was electrified. The crowd joined in the traditional singing of "My Old Kentucky Home," and suddenly I was glad to be here instead of moping back in my room at Bally's. This was exciting. "You know, I think the Super Bowl and the Derby are more real here than they are there," a Chicago detective on his honeymoon told me, clutching a Corona. I wouldn't know.

Then I heard a man behind us, also from Chicago, tell his pals something that made my heart skip a beat. "You gotta worry a bit about this Desormeaux guy," he said with great authority, referring to Real Quiet's jockey, Kent Desormeaux. I was especially glad to hear this because Kent had struck me as a bit of a goofball when he'd first appeared on-screen, wearing a bizarre yellow and red outfit, with what looked to be a huge ad for *Melrose Place* plastered on his chest. It was the same stylized "MP" I've seen on Fox promos, but if there is a huge MP corporate sponsor in the horse-racing world that I'm unaware of, my apologies. Anyway, it was nice to know that backers of the favored Indian Charlie were worried about "my" jockey. Why hadn't I bet $1,000?

Because the horse sucks, that's why, I thought to myself a quarter-mile into the race, when the leading pack of horses included Rock and Roll, Old Trieste, Chilito, and Indian Charlie. By the half-mile point, with three-quarters of a mile to go, my buddy Kent's bright yellow speck seemed impossibly far behind. But then it started happening. By the next quarter-mile mark, Kent had maneuvered his way to the outside and was pounding on the horse, who suddenly started running as if shot out of a cannon. Have I mentioned that this horse was sired by Quiet American (title of one of my favorite Graham Greene novels) and only cost his owner $17,000?

Do you believe in miracles? I was screaming, near tears. It was mesmerizing how effortless the noble beast made it seem, blowing past the others on the outside to gain a commanding lead. In the final stretch, Victory Gallop made it a bit too interesting by having his own possessed breakaway, rapidly closing the distance with the coasting quiet one. Had we burst away a tad too soon? Nah, we still won, and Kent and I were delirious. The horse seemed smug. I collected my winnings, which I thought would be $800, but for some reason amounted to $940. I didn't ask.

In the big scheme of things, the nest egg's ultimate fate, the Derby wouldn't play a significant role. Still, I was ecstatic. I rushed to the public phone to call Kat, and ended up screaming incoherently into the answering machine something about how we'd won real quiet, some French name, and my undying love. When she heard the message, poor Kat must have thought we were suddenly millionaires and that I was sending her some froufy champagne to celebrate.

Had I picked Desormeaux and Real Quiet after following them for months and reading up on the competition, my triumph would have been more deserved, if less thrilling—more akin to work. There is nothing as exhilarating as being favored by dumb, unmitigated luck. Mario Puzo calls this a terrible truth: "I got more pure happiness winning 20 grand at the casino crap table than when I received a check for many times that amount as the result of honest hard work on my book," he wrote in *Inside Las Vegas*.

Before leaving the casino, I placed yet another "dime" on Germany to win the World Cup next July.

♣ ♦ ♥ ♠ After an invigorating squash match at the Sporting House, I went to the Desert Inn to meet my banker friend John Costa. We had planned an evening of baccarat together. Having heard all the hype, he was eager to watch the game played. What he didn't know was that I wanted us both to play on my bankroll, so that we could hedge our losses a bit if the going got rough.

We dined at the DI's Chinese restaurant as I explained to John my harebrained scheme. We'd split five grand between us and vacillate between Banker and Player, playing close attention to streaks. Whoever had the upper hand would go nuts, while the other did some slight hedging. That was the theory, at any rate. "You're the Banker guy," I told him, "so lean to the Banker, okay? I'll worry about the

Player." Then I reached into my pocket, pulled out an envelope with $2,500—John's bankroll—and told him that while it was my money, I wanted him to keep 10 percent of any profit we might make. Any losses were on me. John was understandably hesitant to take any of my money, even if only for a while. So I came clean about my doubling down my advance, about the nest egg, about how this was all, well, work. He was the first person in town I'd let in on this, and it was a relief to do so. I liked John and didn't want him thinking I usually go around passing out envelopes stuffed with C-notes.

"You're saying you talked a publisher into giving you fifty thousand dollars to come out to Vegas and gamble?" John asked, with a trace of awe in his voice. He did make it sound like a nifty talent I had there. Definitely Boondoggle Hall of Fame material. And to think that that morning I had been bemoaning my fate.

The baccarat pit at the Desert Inn is a cozy series of suites at one side of the casino, set apart by elegant drapes and a marble balustrade. There were a couple of Chinese players and an older gentleman from California at the table when we sat down. The Player started fairly strong, which rattled John's determination to hedge by leaning to the Banker. He is a driven, natural competitor, not someone who merely wants to lean the right way. So we were both betting on the Player in the early going. I gave him all sorts of urgent, meaningful looks, a little elbow even, all the while gesturing toward the Banker spot. I couldn't blurt out that he needed to get with the program, as we didn't want to advertise that we had one. Not that there's anything wrong with that.

The Banker's position firmed up, and John soon switched over to the dark side, to my immense relief. Wiped out in a little more than an hour, I sat back to observe baccarat's ebb and flow seduce my conservative banker friend. John is bright, risk-averse, methodical, and highly rational, so I'd worried a bit how he'd take to gambling. But an hour after he'd sat down at the table with some trepidation and much deference, John was The Man, eager to win and intolerant of anyone who'd stand in his way. I was so proud. Prior to that evening, ten bucks was the largest bet he had made in the few hours he'd spent in casinos with out-of-town guests. Now he was piling up those black chips on each hand, dealing from the shoe, urging our more impassive tablemates to believe that his were the hot hands.

Seasoned gamblers are easily annoyed by others who disrupt their karma in any petty way, and John developed this idiosyncrasy. After a brilliant run of six wins in a row for the Banker, orchestrated by John's hot hands, a Chinese gentleman sitting at the other end of the table switched his $5,000 bet over to the Banker from the Player. This meant he was now entitled to turn over the Banker's cards, as the highest bettor. Often in this situation you'll see the high bettor defer to the guy on a roll and let him keep taking the cards, as another Banker bettor had been doing, riding John's coattails. But this gentleman didn't, and John took it as a personal affront, particularly because the Banker lost that hand. For the rest of the night John muttered about how the guy (who I don't think realized how much he was tormenting my buddy) had it in for him. It was a testament to gambling's almost narcotic power that John could have so quickly come around to the ludicrous idea that it makes any difference who turns over the dealt cards. It's not as if that person makes any decisions. At times, when only John and Mr. Evil were betting, John would wait and see his bet, just to go the other way and make it personal. He was having a good time.

Overall, nothing too dramatic happened at our table, unless you count the moment when one of our dealers ditched his girlfriend over the phone while on break. When we decided to get up from the table, close to eleven, John had $3,100, a $600 profit, validating my hedging strategy. Had he not been there that night, I probably would have lost it all. Before leaving, I dragged John over to a blackjack table for a night cap. "This is an impossible game to win," John noted dourly, before we'd even sat down. The dealer, on an unbelievable hot streak, validated his view. In twenty minutes, we lost a grand. It was time to leave. John dropped me off at Bally's and headed back home, miles up Sahara Avenue and worlds removed from the fantastical kingdom of baccarat.

At Bally's, I walked over to the high-stakes pit and played some no-nonsense blackjack, feeling entitled to reparations for my DI loss. Wise move. I bet $500 on two spots, and, as had happened at the Hard Rock the day before, I got a blackjack on one of them. And then another. These pink chips were the way to go. The dealer was busting every which way. But alas, John had vanished, his faith in this game's futility intact. Maybe that was just as well.

Nest egg: $47,314

11

SUNSET STATION

"What are we, bedouins? Why not focus on Cuba?"
—Ben Kingsley, playing Meyer Lansky in *Bugsy*

Sunday, May 3

♣ ♦ ♥ ♠ I could sense the casino host's predicament when I called downstairs before checking out of Bally's to see what I was entitled to. He wasn't sure quite what to do with me. What he saw before him once he looked me up in the computer was not a pretty picture—a thin-skinned gambler intolerant of prolonged losses. Casinos hate such cowardice in their patrons. The pit bosses had probably even scribbled, "Hurls personal epithets at dealers when not winning," in my file. Worse, the host could see I'd fallen for that casino war game. But I clearly had a bankroll. I was a barracuda, a guy who could come in off the street and make a $500 bet. And with all the new casinos going up, a place like Bally's can't be too picky about its barracudas, even those who lose their nerve on occasion. This was like a disastrous first date that hasn't quite destroyed the relationship's long-term potential. "Did you *enjoy* your stay with us, Mr. Martinez?" the voice at the other end of the line asked in a concerned tone, as if inquiring whether I'd taken my medication. Immensely, I said, then proceeded to babble on about my warm and fuzzy memories of my prior visit, when I was ten. At that point he quickly decided to comp me for two nights, to get me off the phone if nothing else.

On my way out, I put another "dime" down on my German investment. This was becoming something of an obsession. I was taking cash off the felt and pouring it into World Cup bets—five grand in all—the way true gamblers amass jewelry. I was acting on the same impulse to turn ephemeral chips into illiquid assets.

And with that, I was off to my ninth Vegas home away from home, the Sunset Station Hotel in Henderson, near the Ericssons. Sunset is the newest of the Station casinos ("You're only minutes from a Station," their ads promise) to sprout up around the valley, strategically located to cater to locals. Back in New York when I'd chosen Sunset as one of my ten stops, I thought it would exemplify the seedy spit-and-sawdust joints to which local addicts must resort when they could not wait an additional fifteen minutes to get themselves to the Strip. I was not prepared to find in Sunset, home of the Paycheck Bonanza, such a pleasant public space.

Like the new mall across the street, the year-old Sunset Station is one of suburbia's air-conditioned answers to the fabled town square of yore. Sure, you'll find some degenerate gamblers in the house, but it's also a place for retirees to meet for a buffet, or teens for a movie. Sunset is a well-designed, clean, and welcoming environment with good restaurants, a microbrewery, row upon row of video poker machines, a Ben & Jerry's, a multiscreen cinema, and Kids Quest, where the Ericsson children celebrate their birthdays and where many a gambling parent's guilt is easily assuaged. There's even a Borders bookstore next door.

It's no wonder places like Sunset—and its sister Palace Station, where I'd helped Betsy cash her paycheck and eaten with Dick Carson—have been taking market share away from neighborhood bars' video poker action and Strip resorts. In UNLV professor Fred Preston's survey, 73 percent of local gamblers said they frequented such "locals' casinos," up from 45 percent in 1984.

I'd expected locals to be less gullible than their tourist counterparts concerning the prospect of winning in a casino, but I'd been wrong. Signs pointing to Sunset's entrance, leading lambs to their slaughter, simply read "Winning." Maybe they were tongue-in-cheek. Or maybe not: One of the first things I saw inside was a poster of a guy with a big grin telling me, "I made payday my play day," as he presided over twenty-five grand in cash.

Patricia Traveling checked me in. Only later did I learn that in this hyper-friendly joint, the "Traveling" on her name tag was a hobby. "It's meant to encourage conversation," Linda Movies explained to me the next day. As in: "What kinda movies you like, Linda?" One of foreigners' most common gripes about Americans is our fondness for superficial friendly small talk with strangers. Station Casinos was perfecting the art, providing talking points.

I splurged on a $79 suite with a separate sitting area and a wall-sized window looking back west, toward McCarran airport and the Strip. As soon as I had sprawled on the bed and revved up the TV, the phone rang. My dinner date had arrived.

♣ ♦ ♥ ♠ Al had dressed up for the occasion, looking far more dapper in a gleaming white suit, black silk shirt, and white shoes than I had remembered him. Then again, I probably hadn't even noticed what he wore the night I rode in his cab, when he'd told me in a vaguely Slavic accent to disregard "the book" when playing blackjack. Al's white outfit matched his shock of silver hair and impish grin. "We're in Vegas, no?" his natty dress seemed to state. I was just glad I had thought of throwing on my linen coat. As we shook hands, I noticed he wore a Rolex.

I'd invited Al over for dinner and some blackjack. As soon as we settled into our booth at the hotel's Costa del Sol seafood restaurant, I realized just how wise I'd been to ask Al, of all the cabdrivers I've met, for his phone number. Here was a real character.

Al was born in Bulgaria in 1925, to a highly educated Jewish family. His father was a respected judge, his mother a doctor. Al was away at school the day the Nazis rounded up his family in 1943. He never saw them again, and spent the rest of the war in hiding, caring for his baby niece. After the war, Al, a lawyer and budding playwright, was elected Bulgaria's youngest member of parliament. "See, I was shot here by the Communists while giving a speech," he said, pointing at the scar above his eyebrow. Within a year, the Communists had taken over and (along with every other opposition politician) Al was carted off to a concentration camp, where he spent a little over a year. As soon as he got out, in 1948, he fled to the new Israeli state and sought out its founding father, first prime minister, and old family friend David Ben-Gurion. Ben-Gurion had a delicate mission for the enterprising youth with a facility for languages: to lead twenty-five pilots, the nucleus of what would become the nation's fabled air force, to the United States to be trained at Nellis Air Force Base, near a desolate place called Las Vegas.

Like any passionate lover, Al vividly recalls the first date. "It was on November 25, 1948, that I first pulled up to the Flamingo Hilton, a neon beacon in the stark desert on the Los Angeles highway," he recalled. "I remember seeing Lucky Luciano pacing by the bar, grumbling about business, and a serene Meyer Lansky telling him not to worry, 've'll find a vay to fill the fifty rooms.' " Embellished or not, this is the memory you'd want to hear from someone present at the creation.

After completing his fun-filled chaperoning in Las Vegas, Al returned to Israel and worked in intelligence. He told me about some of his career's highlights, but only after getting me to promise not to mention any specifics. To a reporter, there is nothing more frustrating than listening to off-the-record nuggets you can't use. And here I was, having been transported in a matter of days from Gamblers Anonymous to Spies Anonymous.

But it was as a blackjack-playing cabdriver in Las Vegas that Al had found his "perfect moment" in life. Throughout his perilous career, he'd fantasized about a carefree retirement in Las Vegas, where he could indulge his passion for gambling night and day. "It is nice to no longer feel the need to climb into bed each night with a machine gun," Al said, in the same matter-of-fact tone with which he'd complimented the salad bar. He moved to Vegas seven years ago, and at first did little but play blackjack at all hours.

Al prefers to play alone at those rare two-deck tables. Years of experience, including thousands of practice sessions at home, have convinced him that a solo player's last card (or that of the third baseman, where more than one person plays) will approximate the dealer's hole card on the following hand, within 3 points. This is heresy to the basic strategy relied on by most players. I never got the mathematical explanation behind Al's theory, if there is one. "The thing you must keep in mind is that the so-called 'book' was written by guys who lost a lot of money, and co-authored by the casino owners," Al noted contemptuously, as we walked into the casino after dinner. Sunset's blackjack tables are arrayed around the funky circular Gaudi Bar, inspired by the haunting architecture of Barcelona's baroque-modernist genius.

Al will tell you he's won a lot of money at blackjack over the years, though he no longer plays as aggressively as he did at first. How much? All I get is a coy smile. Does he keep close records? Of course, he said, looking insulted. "Once I walked out of Caesars with seventy-six thousand dollars in cash stashed in a shopping bag," he told me. "I beat the shit out of them," he added, with a deliberate emphasis on the four-letter word, consciously mimicking American jock-speak. He's been barred from some casinos, a successful gambler's ultimate badge of honor, and is known everywhere.

"I don't need to work, you realize," Al said, anticipating my next question. He drives the cab because he enjoys people and it keeps him out of the casinos for a time. He works nights until about three or four, when he will drop in to a casino to try his luck. "Unlike in the old days, I'll quit once I've doubled my bankroll in a session," he said.

"You sound spooked," I observed.

The first and last time he tried playing a six-deck shoe, Al explained, he had a bad experience. He was at the Tropicana and he plopped down $2,000. He got two 8s; the dealer showed a 6, so he figured he was going to rake it in. He had to take a marker from the house to split the 8s. Then he got a 3, so he had to double, which meant a second marker. It all sounded vaguely familiar; I'd been there. He ended up doubling on his second hand as well. He got a third and a fourth 8, which were also followed by a 2 and a 3 for ideal double downs. Before he knew it, Al was sitting on $16,000 worth of bets, with pretty decent cards. "I think I had two nineteens, an eighteen, and a twenty, or something like that." The dealer revealed the desired face card under the 6, at which point Al practically started counting his winnings. Then the house pulled through. The dealer drew a 5, and Al had become a casino debtor, at least until he could get home and write a check. The experience—a tad less earth-shattering than I had imagined, frankly—not only confirmed Al's mistrust of the shoe but also rattled the gambler within. Maybe his time was up. That's when he decided to take it a little easier and to drive a cab to obtain a better balance in life.

Al played for a few minutes, explaining to me what he was doing as he went along. We made quite a couple, the aged foreigner who looked like a distracted physics professor dressed for a wedding, and I, his young, preppy apprentice. The pit boss rushed to our table, forehead creased with concern. Could this be a blatant card-counting tutorial on his watch? "He's my son, you know," Al told him.

Al's play seemed rather haphazard to me, despite his running commentary. He stayed on a 14 when the dealer showed a face card, and I cringed. This just isn't done. "You see, my last card in the previous hand was a 5, so that's the dealer's hole card, you'll see; she's got a fifteen and will bust," he explained. The dealer turned over a 4, followed by a 10, and seemed impressed at Al's authoritative clairvoyance. But the next time he tried the same trick, recklessly staying on a 13 despite the house's intimidating face card, the dealer unveiled another face card for a 20, as per "the book." "That shouldn't have happened," he said glumly. Then it happened again. The

casino was getting crowded, so Al suggested we go down the freeway a few miles to one of Sunset's sister properties, Boulder Station.
"I have some friends there," he said.

Boulder is a darker, older version of Sunset, known for booking
great bands. Al insisted we wait for a vacant table, and I played some
low-stakes roulette to kill time. In this game, Al coached, the ball
most often lands on one of the numbers directly opposite the last
winner on the wheel, or on one of its neighbors. We tried out this
theory for a number of spins, but with no success. Then I put down
a buck on 22 and it hit. "Wife's birthday," I explained sheepishly.

Minutes later a two-deck blackjack table opened up and we sat
down, but not before Al grilled the poor dealer. How old are these
cards? How did the last player do? We took turns playing, as he'd
been so adamant about it being best to play alone. I was playing $5
and $10 hands, with Al coaching, but I couldn't quite bring myself
to trust in the Force and sit on lousy hands when the dealer showed
a 10, on some harebrained notion that my previous hand's last card
was the clue to the dealer's unseen card. Invariably, whenever I took
a card in these situations and busted, Al would sigh deeply. Too
steeped in B.S., I was a dog unable to learn new tricks.

At one point I did profit involuntarily from Al's prescience. Out
of the blue, he thrust a pile of my chips into the gambling circle.
"You never lose after the dealer has a blackjack with an ace as his
hole card," he told me, as if reciting an immutable law of physics.
Bingo, dealer busts.

We spent a pleasant hour or so playing, especially once we
stopped talking about what we were doing. We talked politics. I
asked him what he thought about Clinton's performance in the
Middle East. "You mean Sandy Berger's performance in the Middle
East," he corrected. Actually, Al seemed fond of Clinton and, remarkably, was the only person I came across in Las Vegas who
agreed with me that the president should not be impeached, even if
it turned out he'd been lying about l'affaire Lewinsky (Sin City goes
puritanical, details at eleven).

It was readily apparent that Al is a very bright, worldly guy. All of which made me wonder what anyone who struck up a conversation with Dostoevsky at the roulette tables in Baden must have wondered. *Why is this guy here, spending so much time in these dreadful casinos, which at the end of the day, all bullshit aside, are not in the business of rewarding extraordinary talent?* Then again, maybe I should cut the man a break. Al is in his seventies.

"What do you think you are doing?" he thundered all of a sudden at the dealer, who had just shuffled the cards. Al was exercised because the man had stuck the plastic shuffle card halfway into the stack of cards, which meant we were really only playing with one deck, instead of two. "This is totally unacceptable," Al said, shaking his head in disgust. "The card should be inserted about one-fourth or one-third up from the bottom." Ken, the pit boss, walked over and backed up his dealer.

"We've been through this, Al," he said.

"This is bullshit, cheating, because you are afraid of me," Al fired back.

"This is a perfectly legitimate cut, and if you don't think it's a fair game, you can go elsewhere. Nobody is forcing you to play here," Ken said, as if reasoning with a child. If only he knew some of the shit Al had been involved in back in the Middle East.

"Take note of how they cheat here, because I've beaten the shit out of them," Al was telling me as he stormed away from the table, making me feel like a human rights observer—a very embarrassed one. The funny thing is that when we arrived at the cashier's cage, still huffing and puffing, it became apparent that we'd made $180.

Back at Sunset Station, I quickly made $500 playing blackjack by "the book."

Nest egg: $47,999

Monday, May 4

I started a wonderfully lazy day by feasting on the hotel's breakfast buffet. I sat at a table next to the very talkative Henry and Ethel, who'd moved here five years ago from Detroit. They live in a nearby retirement community. Henderson and Boulder City, mind you, are jointly rated the third best place in America to retire, according to *Retirement Places Rated.* "We come here every Monday to eat and feed twenty dollars to the machines," Henry told me, rather loudly. It was clear that many in his circle are hard of hearing, or recent immigrants with a shaky command of English. Why come on Mondays, of all days? I wondered. "Because we can play hooky now on Mondays, see, that's the beauty of it," Ethel chimed in. "What's the beauty of playing hooky on Saturdays?" She had a point.

I turned my attention to the day's *Review-Journal,* which had the ultimate everything-in-life-is-converging-into-one-database story. The MGM Grand casino announced it was linking its slot machine club to American Airlines' Advantage frequent-flier club. Imagine that. I had been comparing the casinos' frequent-gambling programs to airlines' frequent-flier clubs since my arrival in town, but in this case at least, they had become one and the same.

American and Citibank have long offered a Visa card on which you accrue a mile for every dollar you charge (the card I lost earlier on this odyssey). "Was it love? Or was it the miles?" reads one of the card's amusing print ads, depicting a dozen roses. Maybe MGM could adopt a similar campaign. Picture a man walking into a Gamblers Anonymous meeting. The tag line: "Was it the action? Or was it the miles?"

♣ ♦ ♥ ♠   There are, of course, far more insidious casino marketing ploys. Wandering about after breakfast, I was struck by the extent to which casinos serve as full-fledged financial-services firms. Station Casinos has perfected the art of paycheck-cashing ploys, in which everyone (but especially the house) is a winner. If you don't win a car or the grand prize of $25,000, you at least get a meal or a margarita. The point is, Relax, stay awhile, got some cash?

"Cash your paycheck, and you get one of these," a cashier at the cage explained when I asked about the notorious Paycheck Bonanza. She was pointing to a scratch-off ticket like the one Betsy had been given at Palace Station, and much like those instant lottery tickets you can buy in some states, but not in Nevada, where casino interests have crushed all proposals for a state lottery.

"I don't get a paycheck anymore," I said. "We also cash unemployment and welfare checks," she offered helpfully. "And do those get a scratch-off too?" I asked. "Sure do," she answered. Call it Unemployment Bonanza. That's what I love about this town; it's so democratic.

These paycheck-cashing gimmicks offer gambling critics a juicy target. I treasure convenience as much as the next guy, but there does seem to be something predatory about Paycheck Bonanza. The sensible Carol O'Hare, hardly an anticasino zealot, put it best when she told me that she counsels casinos to adopt good business practices in accord with their self-image and mission. "If I as a casino say I'm in the entertainment business," she explained, "competing with other forms of entertainment for people's discretionary income, what am I doing cashing clients' paychecks? Would a movie theater or a bowling alley do the same? Is this consistent with my avowed mission?"

I loitered, waiting for some unsuspecting paycheck-cashing soul to show up and become a vignette on these pages. But none came in the twenty minutes I stood there. That's the thing about reporting; sometimes things click and custom-tailored strangers—resilient investors in the aftermath of a market crash, eager shoppers during the holiday season, New Hampshire primary voters with something new to say—fall in your lap. Other times, you come up empty-handed.

On the edge of the casino floor, Sunset was signing people up for a Visa Las Vegas card, on which you accrue points redeemable for "casino cash." Venerable Harrah's on the Strip, known for its marketing prowess, offers a Visa card, too: "Clothes, gas, food, travel—see how quickly your credit card purchases earn Harrah's Total Gold Points redeemable toward cash or other rewards of your choice at any Harrah's nationwide," the application read. According to the accompanying chart, $5,000 in credit card purchases will get you a whopping $50 in casino cash. The card itself features two dice rolling on the heavenly green felt. The fact that image-conscious credit card companies would enter into these agreements with casinos—er, gaming companies—as they do with airlines and car manufacturers eager to build consumer loyalty via kickbacks powerfully illustrates the extent to which society has come to accept gambling as a form of mainstream entertainment.

I spent the rest of the afternoon gambling in small doses and window-shopping at the mall across the road. It was staggering to think that within a week I would no longer be in Vegas. This giddy realization robbed me of whatever focus and energy I might otherwise have mustered to pursue any of dozens of worthy stories that might shed some light on Las Vegas's elusive soul. I didn't know what do with myself.

Part of the reason was dread. Though I had tried not to dwell on it, I knew I still would have to engage in one dramatic, mano-a-mano showdown with the casinos before skipping town. After almost a month of constant high-stakes clashes, my nest egg was within a few hundred dollars of where it had begun. As any true gambler knows, this was quite a feat. Alas, my editor is no gambler, and this result—akin to a hard-fought 0–0 tie in soccer—would not amuse him.

"Dammit, Martinez," he'd bark at me back in New York, "you mean to tell me nothing happened! What the hell did you do all that time, hang out by the pool with a bunch of showgirls, counting your fifty grand?!"

No question about it, my editor would want closure, and so I would have to go crazy before boarding that plane Friday night. I'd either have to make a mint or get wiped out in one last stand. It was the least I could do. But that shoot-out would have to wait until the New York–New York hotel, my final destination. It wouldn't be right to go nuclear at mellow Sunset Station, where the featured B game is bingo, not baccarat.

♣ ♦ ♥ ♠ Doug Ericsson, Tom's brother, and his wife, Jennifer, had me over for an early dinner. They also live in Henderson, and were as warmly hospitable as Tom and Susie had been. I brought over some Ben & Jerry's I picked up at the hotel, which made me a hit with the kids. Doug is a police officer, and these days he works a night shift down in the resort town of Laughlin, almost an hour south, on the Colorado River. When it comes to law enforcement, the region wisely overcame petty city-county turf battles in 1973 and created an all-encompassing metropolitan police force. Laughlin's a cushy assignment after downtown Las Vegas, but Doug seemed to miss the action.

When I asked Doug about the department's reputation for brutality, he conceded there was room for improvement. But he also told me to keep in mind that this is a city that attracts all sorts of characters with lower moral standards. Among them, fugitives from across the country, as anyone who has seen *Con Air* knows, feel drawn here. Metro devotes a great deal of manpower, and works closely with the FBI, to track down other jurisdictions' most restless ruffians, who flock to Vegas like pilgrims to Mecca. In its 1997–1998 fiscal year alone, Metro arrested 1,731 fugitives.

♣ ♦ ♥ ♠ That night I played some craps and blackjack. The casino was packed, a shocking sight given that these were folks living their real lives (or their absence of one), unlike the tourists roaming the Strip. It seemed the only slot machines not being used were the ones advertised with the slogan "Put Your Heart into

Gaming." Get this: These are LifeCycle dual-purpose exercise bikes and slots. Oddly enough, they were the only machines in the vast casino with the legalistic "Operate at Your Own Risk" warning.

To see so many people so consumed by video poker, proudly wearing their gamblers' polyester letter jackets and baseball caps, was to wonder what people do elsewhere on Monday nights. What would this crowd be doing in Toledo? Reading Shakespeare? Watching *Ally McBeal*? Taking a pottery class?

I fell into conversation with a blackjack dealer, bearer of the most esoteric name-tag hobby: marine biology. He told me working at these local joints, even the nicer ones, could be a real drag. "We don't get all those happy-go-lucky tourists you see on the Strip who're just out to have a good time," he said. "What we get are bitter, often desperate regulars, who'll cuss you out and won't tip." I tipped him heavily, refrained from cussing, and after a while was ahead a cool grand.

Then I rushed off to do something I hadn't done in far too long. I went to see a movie. It was a good feeling to be able to simply walk across the casino and into a multiplex, buy a ticket, stock up on popcorn, and sit in the darkened theater, awaiting a slew of summer movie previews. This was life back in the real world, except that the man in front of me in line paid for his ticket with a casino comp.

Nest egg: $49,099

Tuesday, May 5

Cinco de Mayo. As a kid growing up in Mexico, I was always jealous of my brother for having his birthday fall on this national holiday. How cool was that? My June birthday, on the other hand, always seemed to fall in the middle of final exams. I now appreciate the fact that Ro's birthday falls on a date beer companies spend millions to market. It makes it hard to forget.

I called Ro at work. On the outside, you forget that people in a workplace aren't in a position to shoot the breeze for an hour. So I babbled on and on about Vegas, while Ro put me on the speakerphone and went about his business. He did groan when I told him, with considerable pride, about my World Cup investments. "The Germans are too old, everyone knows that," he said. Huh? This was disturbing. Ro was more up on these things, having recently lived in London. Then again, Brits loathe German soccer almost as much as they loathe Prussian militarism. They often confuse the two. Ro's sources were hopelessly compromised. "Wily and experienced, Ro, but not old, you'll see," I told him.

♣ ♦ ♥ ♠ I met Randy, my tennis buddy, for dinner at the trendy Gordon Biersch microbrewery, of Silicon Valley fame. The Las Vegas outpost of this yuppie heaven is on Paradise Road, at the Howard Hughes Corporate Center, where John Costa's bank has its offices. Randy seemed in a cantankerous mood—"Hardest thing for all these yuppies to understand is that it doesn't take that much money to be happy," he said, sneering toward the bar and its after-work crowd. We were the only men in the place not wearing ties.

Randy told me he'd dealt blackjack during an involuntary sabbatical from his tennis career in the early 1980s. He'd been hit by a van head-on while out jogging; his face was smashed by the windshield and he flew a hundred feet in the air. The doctors marveled that he hadn't died—at least, that's what they told him when he came out of his ten-day coma. It took him months to recover fully.

Randy made the most of his career in the gaming industry. "Blackjack dealers get laid more than all the other people in the world put together," he told me. "You get some girls from Iowa at your table and they're winning big bucks, tripling and quadrupling the twenty bucks they timidly pulled out of their purses before they started drinking, there ain't no way you won't get laid at the end of that night." Randy met his wife (on her twenty-first birthday, no less) in such a fashion in the late eighties. They have since gotten divorced.

His supervisors must have hated Randy, whose motto is "Question authority." He was fired from three different casinos (dealers are not unionized). The feelings were mutual: "Casino managers are a bunch of sixth-grade clowns, guys who came to town thinking they could make a living playing twenty-one, went broke, then got a job at the casino because it's all they know about," he said. "The funniest thing is that these jerks then go around acting like they're some big shot." Randy isn't much of a gambler, and is pretty dismissive of that whole something-for-nothing culture.

He spent most of the dinner regaling me with tales from the front. There was the dealer who'd sneak a $25 chip into his mouth every time he went on break, for decades, and the player he saw pissing in the middle of the casino because he didn't want to leave a winning streak. His bets were high enough the casino didn't care; management wanted to win the money back. Randy also clued me in on a somewhat obvious fact of the dealing life that had never occurred to me. As a purely physical matter, things are far easier for a blackjack dealer who's on a roll, beating everyone at the table. Why? Because all he has to do is scoop up all the chips on the table, instead of going around paying everyone. Only problem: "If your cards are hot, you won't get tipped, and you sure as hell won't get laid."

Randy is a big believer in fortune's streakiness, and scoffs at those who take games like blackjack too seriously, particularly casino managers who get ulcers worrying—stupidly, according to Randy—about card counters. Counters are, for the most part, "full of shit." Randy wrote an entertaining booklet on the subject entitled "Card-Counting Paranoia," in which he excoriates both the counters' claims and the casinos' fear of them.

Nest egg: $49,011

12

NEW YORK—NEW YORK

The less you bet, the more you lose when you win.

—Bonetti's law

Wednesday, May 6

♣ ♦ ♥ ♠ Nine down, one to go. Time to once again pack up my two large suitcases, heavy book bag, duffel stuffed with notes and Hard Rock beach towels, tennis and squash racquets, sunscreen applicator, shopping bag filled with dozens of bottles of hotel shampoo and a corresponding number of soaps (I ditched the conditioner at the Golden Gate to stay nimble), and laptop computer. I was heading back to the southern end of the Strip, to the New York–New York hotel, only a stone's throw away from the airport and from Luxor, where my odyssey began so long ago. I figured the Manhattan-themed resort would ease my transition back to the real New York.

New York–New York opened to rave reviews on the first day of 1997. Surprisingly, even such publications as *The New York Times* and *The Wall Street Journal* deigned to say nice things about this over-the-top masterpiece of vernacular architecture. And it is clever, these twelve Manhattan landmarks—the Empire State, Chrysler, Seagram's, and AT&T buildings among them—scrunched together, roughly at one-third scale. Someone here had fun working on the details. The hotel's parked limos were painted to look like yellow cabs; the door handles at the main entrance were little torches like the one held by the Statue of Liberty.

I was going out in style. Almost twice the size of our apartment back home, my Celebrity Tower suite was a funky, greenish (from the tinted windows) art deco stunner with a glorious view of the roller coaster's killer loop, the Strip, and McCarran airport beyond. The exterior wall, incredibly, had eight corners. Along this wall, there was a raised Jacuzzi overlooking the Strip, a curved rocking chaise lounge, a wing-tip leather armchair, and a separate dining and meeting area with a round table, wet bar, and fridge.

♣ ♦ ♥ ♠ I met Bob Faiss for lunch downtown. The *National Law Journal* named Faiss the nation's "premier gaming attorney"; he's also on its list of the "100 most influential lawyers in America," presumably thus also on the list of passengers on the first two buses to the gulag when the revolution comes. Bob, a former journalist and staff assistant to President Lyndon Johnson, represents some of the largest gaming companies on regulatory matters and is counsel to the umbrella Nevada Resort Association. He is, in short, a big shot. But he's also a refreshingly genuine and down-to-earth guy.

A native Las Vegan who now lives down the road in the casino-free tranquillity of Boulder City (the irony is not lost on him), Bob is rather proud of what Nevada has accomplished in his lifetime. He still remembers when the rest of the nation considered his home-town a Mob-infested Gomorrah. Now Las Vegas is an admired, Wall Street–financed entertainment hub whose regulatory over-sight over casino gambling is the envy of the industry's so-called emerging markets. Droves of officials from jurisdictions seeking to legalize gambling, but concerned about keeping it clean, flock to Las Vegas not only from around the nation, but also from around the world, something that once upon a time would have seemed laugh-able. When they do visit, they call on the likes of Bob Faiss—he has advised the city of Detroit and regulators in Australia, Mexico, and Turkey, to name a few places—and the chairman of the Nevada

Gaming Control Board, the implausibly if aptly named William Bible.

Bob, who doesn't gamble, is bullish on Las Vegas's prospects, despite the host of daunting short-term challenges: fewer flights into McCarran, more hotel rooms to fill, the prospect of full-fledged Indian casinos in neighboring California, Internet gambling, and a number of political threats. The spread of gambling nationwide, ironically, has made the industry much more vulnerable to political attacks. When Nevada was the only place to gamble, casinos were not on most politicians' or activists' radar screens, except for an occasional foray into the desert, such as the Kefauver Commission hearings of 1950–51. Issues of casino taxation and the like remained as esoteric to most members of Congress as, say, the Puerto Rican tax code. But the spread of casino gambling in recent years has galvanized the national antigambling movement—the same folks who brought you Prohibition and blue laws and banned classics at your local library—to oppose their neighbors' cherished right to make a stupid bet. Morality aside, the industry's growth has also created a tempting piggy bank for pragmatic politicians in need of fiscal windfalls. It's no accident that the industry's formidable lobbying group in Washington, the American Gaming Association, was founded in 1994, after President Clinton floated the idea of a new federal excise tax on casinos' profits.

Political threats abound, and not just in the form of a prying National Gambling Impact Study Commission, whose final report, issued in June 1999, recommended a national moratorium on gambling expansion. In 1998 alone, a U.S. senator floated the idea of banning all casinos nationwide within ten thousand feet of any school or other youth facility (bye-bye, Luxor and NY–NY); another was pushing to revoke the deductibility of gambling losses from winnings; and a New York congressman wanted to bar the collection of any debts "incurred in or adjacent to a gambling facility" (a provision aimed not only at casino markers, but also at credit card advances from those "NOW EXCEED YOUR ATM LIMIT" machines). By the time the Monica-obsessed 105th Congress went home at the end of the year, the gaming lobby and its friends had managed, at least for now, to bat away all these threats. In this effort, of course, the spread of gambling turned out to be a two-way street, providing Nevada casinos not only with legions of foes but also with such powerful allies as Senate Majority Leader Trent Lott, who hails from the "emerging market" of Mississippi. Hal Rothman is right: The colony is indeed becoming a colonizer.

As Bob and I ate, the five hundred millionth visitor to Las Vegas since 1960 landed at McCarran on a Southwest flight from LAX. He was kidnapped by a showgirl and an Elvis and whisked away to a lavish luncheon in his honor. Fittingly, the unsuspecting heroic traveler was an information risk manager for an accounting firm, in town to attend a conference.

I left Bob and drove to the university campus to meet Hal Rothman. I first wandered around the bookstore and student union. That stressed hush of final exams week—I remembered it so well from my own school days—cast a pall over the entire campus. How weird, though, to go to college within walking distance of a dozen casinos. Then again, many of the students finance their education by working at these resorts, and the university's acclaimed hotel management school benefits from their proximity.

Hal enjoys being at UNLV. For one thing, it's refreshing to be at a rapidly growing university at a time when most schools across the country are cutting back. He also finds it rewarding to teach a large number of older students who are already in the workforce, making the extra effort to become the first member of their family to get a college degree. That's what Las Vegas is all about, Hal is fond of saying, a cocktail waitress putting herself, or a daughter, through college.

Sitting in the student union's café, pretending to read the paper, I eavesdropped on my neighbors' conversation. After some banter about remaining finals—and the usual disclaimers about not having studied—one of the guys, apparently a swing-shift dealer at the Mirage, said he had received conflicting notices as to whether he'd been one of the employees chosen by lottery to move over to the company's new Bellagio when it opens in October. "I really hope I get it," he was saying. But how, I wondered, could anyone go to college while dealing blackjack every night for eight hours, until four in the morning? I'd gathered that being a dealer was no piece of cake, and this impression was confirmed after I'd returned to New York and read about Dennis Rodman's antics. In June a Mirage craps dealer would sue the basketball star, a notoriously high roller, for causing him "embarrassment, indignity, degradation and anger." The suit alleged that Rodman, while playing craps, rubbed the dealer's bald head and attempted to get "inside his shirt," thus interfering with his ability to conduct his job and "maintain his composure and professionalism." A female employee at the Las Vegas Hilton also sued Rodman later in the year, accusing the friendly gambler of "grabbing her sides near her breasts, causing pain, discomfort and bruising."

Over coffee at the Starbucks on Maryland Avenue, I mentioned to Hal that I was doing a "fair amount" of gambling while in town. When he picked up my book from the Borders bargain pile, in expectation of a weighty tome worthy of his collaboration, a Vegas portrait to rival David Remnick's books on Russia or Roger Cohen's on Bosnia, I didn't want him to be shocked. "Yeah, I did a fair amount of gambling, Hal, um, you know, for the book," I mumbled, fidgeting with my biscotti. "You winning?" he asked, perking up, relieved not to have go back into Spiel mode. He wanted to know every dirty detail. Hal doesn't gamble himself. "I'm better at abstinence than moderation, so I abstain," he said. He considers Las Vegas a great place to raise a family, in part because it makes parents doubly vigilant, and it's easier to inculcate values when you are constantly being prompted to do so by external factors. He believes kids can get into trouble and fall in with the wrong crowd just as easily in a small Midwestern town as they can here, the only difference being that in such supposedly wholesome places parents aren't cognizant of the danger until it's often too late.

"You're one of my favorite carpetbaggers," Hal told me as we parted. Though it may not have been the single nicest thing anyone has ever called me, it was up there, and I was suitably touched. What had I done to deserve such an accolade? I'd become as enamored as he is of the world's largest Coca-Cola bottle as the ultimate symbol of the new Las Vegas.

♣ ♦ ♥ ♠ Eager to make the most of my dwindling time in Vegas, I dashed back downtown in the evening to drop in on a Bible-study session at Jesus Is the Answer, Joe Alston's church. The makeshift church, previously a jewelry store or pawnshop, judging from its storefront, was packed. Joe, seated in one of the front benches next to the lectern facing out into the room, nodded toward me when I walked in. He wasn't conducting this session, but he was clearly an authority figure here, called upon every so often to untangle a particularly thorny passage of Scripture. Could this be the same man I'd seen handing out paper towels, stocking the mint tray, and cleaning the urinals stained by errant drunks in the rest room of a sleazy topless joint? But then, isn't humility the essence of Christianity?

Pastor Raymond McIntosh, an enormous man with a booming voice, was telling the congregation that all week he'd been preparing to preach about faith, but that early that day God had told him to focus instead on the importance of worship. He said this in a matter-of-fact tone, beads of sweat slowly forming on his forehead, as if he were apologizing for a flat tire en route. Faith was out; worship was in.

"What is the difference between praise and worship?" he asked, calling on certain parishioners, asking others to read passages from both Old and New Testaments. It was a meaty, two-hour give-and-take. At times I found myself staring down at the ragged carpeting, which looked suspiciously like Bally's carnival-themed black carpeting with a pattern of colorful confetti strewn about, and thinking about how I would approach my final gambling campaign at New York–New York. I know, I know: shame on me.

I had no excuse. This was a far more intense Bible session than I could ever attend at the bourgeois Episcopal church we sometimes go to back home. There, if Father Burns were to preach from Psalms 40:2, about God pulling man out of the "horrible pit, out of the miry clay," most of his parishioners, in trying to fathom this pit, might think of some depreciated stock in their portfolio or the truant baby-sitter who ruined their Saturday night plans. But here, in discussing how God lifted him out of his horrible pit "and set my feet upon a rock, and established my goings," as the psalm goes on to say, Pastor Raymond talked about the Lord freeing him from cocaine, prison, and hatred. I heard plenty of amens; most of his followers know how deep that pit can get. The woman sitting next to me told me later that she came to Las Vegas to be a prostitute, and exhorted me not to write some glib book about how much fun it is to come party in Vegas, but to tell "the truth."

There were about sixty people in the room—mostly African Americans, but some Hispanics and whites, too—eagerly participating and soaking up everything the pastor, and on occasion Joe, would say. The exchanges crackled, as Pastor Raymond had a knack for the Socratic method. "Sister, what does the Holy Spirit do?" Or: "Is David being real with God here?" Then: "I want to go back to the question that was raised last week about whether it's wrong for someone to be a policeman." The answer, after some discussion: No.

We were interrupted once by a man wearing little more than torn rags who wandered in and, instead of taking a seat, just stood in the middle of the room, staring at Pastor Raymond, a baffled expression on his face. Well, he tried standing; it was really a gentle swaying in place. He reeked, too. "Hey, how you doing there?" the pastor asked him. "You know, I've been seeing your brother around, over at the home, he's doing real good, we gotta get you in here, man, off the streets." "Yeah, I know, soon," the man muttered, looking as if he might cry. Then he walked away, and we carried on. Someone asked if it's OK to listen to rap and other secular music. "Me, I might go back to the old dreams and go get myself a joint, if I listen to the old tunes," Pastor Raymond said, but it was clear from his grin that he deemed this a matter of individual conscience.

"I was living the black American dream," Pastor Raymond told me after the session, when I asked him about the old tunes and life before Jesus Is the Answer. "Sometimes we just sat around and literally burned some money, we were making so much of it," he said of his glory days, the late seventies.

Raymond was always the guy who wanted the quick money— "couldn't do the minimum-wage thing," as he puts it. He admired an uncle who worked in a casino, so when he was twenty-one he went to dealing school, where—the irony still makes him chuckle— he started dealing drugs. He got jobs dealing craps at the Fremont and Stardust, while he and a partner dealt other stuff on the side. These were the glory days for "Wet Daddy," as Raymond was then known. He drove a customized Lincoln Town Car 988, wore diamonds, gambled like crazy. "On a good day we could pull in five grand, and I had no problem turning around and spending it." When his dope house got busted, it was likened in the papers to a McDonald's. Raymond wasn't caught then, but it was only a matter of time. "I was my own worst enemy," he recalled. Then he found God in prison, and swore off the drugs and the gambling.

When he came out, he moved in with his mother and, for once, did the minimum-wage thing, detailing cars at a car wash. Time was when he would have deemed that $3.35 an hour insufficient to get a decent fire going. He later took a job as a vending attendant up at the Nevada Test Site, but throughout this period his real passion was bringing God and comfort to people in prison and on the street—"everyone I knew was at one of these two places." He volunteered with a prison ministry, and one thing led to another. He's been ministering full-time since 1993.

♣ ♦ ♥ ♠ The New York–New York was rocking, hordes of fanny-packers madly trying to maximize their few dozen precious hours of vacation, so grudgingly conceded them by their miserly employer back in the cruel real world, that world where none of us would still be awake at midnight on a Wednesday night. For better or worse, I was now one of them, on a countdown. I'd be flying home in forty-eight hours.

The NY–NY is among the most entertaining hotels for nongamblers. Every nook and cranny of the property is cleverly designed and seems to click, except for the unimaginative concrete jungle of the swimming pool area. The Coney Island Emporium, where you board the roller coaster, is stuffed with video games, bumper cars, "laser tag," shooting galleries, even a Nathan's Hot Dogs. Across the casino, also on the mezzanine, is the swank Hamilton's cigar club, where I'd gone with Kat on the night of my Hard Rock roulette triumph. Most of the restaurants, off the casino on the main floor, are run by New York City's Ark Restaurants group, so instead of a generic coffee shop, you can go to a 24/7 America, similar to the company's popular eateries of the same name in Washington and New York. The powerful Culinary Union in town isn't thrilled by this arrangement, as these licensed restaurants at NY–NY are nonunion. There's also an outpost of New York's Gallagher's Steakhouse, the obligatory Chinese place, and the excellent Il Fornaio.

Instead of a drab food court with the usual suspects, the hotel has a Greenwich Village–themed series of streets with ethnic fast-food offerings. Patrons sit at "sidewalk" tables and soak up some manufactured urbanism: flowered window boxes, fire escapes, and water tanks hover above. I was particularly impressed by a manhole cover spewing steam on the pathway to the Chrysler Building and a service exit off the main casino floor made to look like a subway entrance, down to the system map on the wall and the picture of the station manager. Reviewers checking out the hotel when it first opened felt obliged to make some crack about all this being just like New York, minus the trash.

Not everyone is amused by such whimsical flourishes. The New York Stock Exchange—and this is not a joke—actually sued the casino over its "New York $lot Exchange" pillared replica of the stock exchange's famous façade on Wall Street, and the casino's use of that term for its slot club's name. The casino renamed its slot club the "New York–New York $lot Exchange." As for the demand that the façade with those words be brought down, it basically told the uptight financiers to get a life, that parody is protected free speech. In its lawsuit, the NYSE accused the casino of "mutilating and bastardizing" the appearance of its trademarks and of having "tarnished, blurred, diluted and disparaged" its reputation. An NYSE spokesman went on to say that the façade "suggests our sponsorship or licensing of the business." This mind-boggling legal scuffle can only be explained by one of three competing explanations, none of them pretty:

First, the NYSE, the most important financial marketplace on earth, is run by a bunch of morons.

Or, second, the NYSE considers average Americans visiting Vegas, the steadfast "individual investors" to whom so much lip service is paid, to be a bunch of morons capable of confusing a kitschy casino with the place where they buy their IBM stock.

Or, third, and most disturbing, the NYSE leadership knows something we don't—that there really is enough of an affinity between their business and a casino to raise brand-awareness concerns.

♣ ♦ ♥ ♠ I went up to Hamilton's balcony overlooking the casino, where I puffed on a Dunhill cigar and downed a martini while listening to the Latin group playing in the Empire Bar. Down below, fools desperately attacked the now ridiculously overdue Megabucks. The game's last jackpot, and at $12.5 million its biggest ever, was won here at the New York–New York a year earlier by a Las Vegas resident, creating an urban legend that the machines are rigged to win at new casinos. Steve Wynn must be praying that someone wins the $15-million-and-counting before October, lest local slot connoisseurs storm his upscale Bellagio's ramparts on opening night.

Sitting there with my $20 cigar, I felt like Ike (sans advisers, regrettably) at the Supreme Headquarters of the Allied Expeditionary Force in England in early 1944, pondering the grand invasion of the occupied Continent. Things were at a stalemate, hauntingly calm. I had been battling wily casinos for weeks on end, and we had acquitted ourselves with dignity and honor. We had exchanged heavy blows, yet remained standing, more or less in the positions we had held at the outset of battle. Setting aside my $5,000 World Cup investment, my nest egg was down by only $889, and I had earned far more than that in comped goodies.

The key, as it had been at El Alamein, was to gingerly probe the enemy's flanks with infantry and then pounce on any perceived weakness with armored columns, whatever that means in a casino. Knowing I had a nonrefundable ticket home Friday night, the perfidious casino wanted me to feel rushed, so that I'd launch an all-out frontal assault in haste. Instead, I had to remain cool and collected. You can win or lose a fortune in a matter of minutes, just as you can fight for a month and end in a stalemate. There was no need to panic.

I sent some light infantry down to the Central Park casino area, under cover of the trees and ornamental ironwork, to see if we could open a gap and call in the big guns. It was a slaughter. The casino showed no weaknesses whatsoever and quickly took 1,200 of my finest dollars. I ordered a retreat to my Jacuzzi upstairs. The mano a mano could await another day.

Nest egg: $47,811

Thursday, May 7

I awoke in psychedelic green splendor, the rays of sunlight streaming in transformed by the tinted glass. I looked at my watch, reluctantly. 11:39. 11:39? 11:39! Shit. I had a noon lunch appointment with the esteemed county commissioner, Bruce Woodbury, who'd graciously agreed to meet a former *Wall Street Journal* reporter writing a sober book about his city. Now I'd probably be late, on account of my lifelong desire to watch a sunrise from a Jacuzzi. I took a forty-eight-second shower, then threw on my khakis, blazer, and sole tie. I would have been late if I'd waited for the Endeavor to be fetched from valet parking, so instead I took a cab, and walked into the nearby Cozymel's restaurant at 12:05.

From my political conversations around town, I'd gathered that Mr. Woodbury, who hails from a prominent Mormon family long active in the community, serves as a sort of parent figure on the (often childish) seven-member county commission. Every so often, the soft-spoken Stanford-trained lawyer will gently try to educate his colleagues on matters of law and ethics, but to little avail. He didn't tell me this himself, of course; that would be to tell tales out of school.

I was tempted to ask my standard "Why bother?" but restrained myself, not wanting to seem disrespectful. The man has been a commissioner since I was in high school, after all. He did mention that he gets a charge out of grappling with the challenges posed by growth: The county's population has roughly tripled during his stint on the commission.

Though he seemed in no mood to discuss his colleague's yearning to sell daiquiris in casinos, Bruce did tell me he can't stand the places, on account of the machines being "so awfully noisy."

Afterward I played my final squash games in the desert, against an amiable developer. I took the first game, but then fell apart, a nervous wreck. I could hardly focus on getting to the ball. This would be the last night I slept in Las Vegas, and the realization that my time to grow the nest egg was slowly coming to an end had my stomach all tied up in knots.

Back in my suite I ordered a steak from room service and turned on the *Friends* season finale, the one in which Ross is about to marry the English chick when he mistakenly utters Rachel's name at the altar. During commercials, I chaired an angst-ridden meeting of one. What to do? First off, I resolved there would be no more war metaphors.

But the question remained: Could I simply take it easy for the rest of the night and the following day, abstaining from any further action, taking my forty-eight grand home and declaring an honorable tie? This would produce mixed results. Kat would be ecstatic, as I had prepared her for the worst. We would be able to see India, get Trot the new scratching post he so desperately needs, and, who knows, maybe even buy some stock in Amazon.com, which would surely triple in value within a year. (By year's end, the Internet bookseller's stock was worth seven times what it had been in May, which would be all the more mind-boggling if we'd actually bought some.) On the other hand, my editor would go apeshit, and would probably sue me for breach of contract. Nobody, he'd argue before a jury of my gambling peers, could be sent to Vegas with a $50,000 bankroll for a month, gamble every day and come home with forty-eight grand. The litigation, with all its fuss, would wreck whatever future I might aspire to in the clubby world of boondoggle literature. No, I had to make a dramatic move, one way or another.

I concocted my plan while watching the penultimate *Seinfeld* ever, the one in which Kramer burns the Puerto Rican flag. Instead of winging it once more, this time I decided to walk into the casino with my first fifteen plays scripted out on a card, the way former 49ers coach Bill Walsh used to approach games (with military references out, a boy must turn to football). So I jotted on a card:

I. *Blackjack.* Buy-in: $2,500.
1. Bet $500. If lose,
2. Rattle dealer by playing two separate $250 hands. If lose,
3. Groan. Repeat previous bets. If lose,
4. Bet $250, one hand. If lose,
5. Stay calm; do not refer disrespectfully to dealer's mother. Repeat previous bet. If lose,
6. Bet $500, one spot. If lose,
7. LEAVE TABLE! Go to Hamilton's for no less than 30 mins. Relax.

II. *Megabucks.* Put $100 in damned machine.
8. Go for $15 million jackpot. Refrain from pestering

novices about the need to play three coins at a time;
they may win. If lose, move on to roulette wheel.

III. *Roulette.* Buy-in: $3,500

    9. Conduct Dopey Experiment, betting $100 on
        number 22 for 35 spins. If lose,

    10. Hit gift shops, bars, wander. Relax for no less than
        30 mins. Then,

IV. *Blackjack.* Buy-in: $2,500.

    11–16. Repeat steps 1–6 above.

I can understand why Walsh would feel better walking on the
field with his laminated play card, and why some of his acolytes,
such as the Broncos' Mike Shanahan, picked up the habit. I felt se-
cure with my card in the casino, knowing I'd immunized myself
from treacherous spontaneity and raw emotion. The only problem
with my game plan was, any wins carried me off-script. In the first
blackjack sequence, I won some of my first hands, which left me
confused. I'd planned only for the worst. Now what? My stupid
card didn't tell me how to handle a win. Was I supposed to stick to
the same bet until I did lose? That's what I did, picking up the script
whenever I lost. Made sense, except that by not pressing my hands
when Big Mo was on my side, I was once again capping my wins on
the upside. Still, it was a good, tidy session, bringing me a profit of
three grand in thirty-five minutes (listen to me). This meant the nest
egg was back in the black for the first time since my Luxor debacle!
I celebrated this, per the game plan, with another cigar and a shot of
Bailey's at Hamilton's.

Then, after a wasteful stop at the Megabucks—"Lady, you have
to play three tokens at once," I yelled irritably at my neighbor, unable to hold back—I moved on to the roulette table. Number 22 hit
on the third spin, which gave me a false sense of confidence. Off the
hook, I played a bunch of other numbers on the side for the subsequent thirty-two spins, none of which hit. I drank a Singapore sling
ordered by another player who'd busted and left before its arrival,

but this was hardly an excuse to deviate. When I got up to leave, it was disturbing to realize I was down $1,500 in a session from which, had I obediently stuck to the game plan, I would have come out even.

I checked out the 24/7 gift shop, then made my way to the Empire Bar on the casino floor, featuring the best lounge act I'd heard in town. I was minding my own business when a rather attractive blonde wearing a silky green turtleneck and a tight suede skirt came up to me and asked for a light. I felt like Cary Grant in a 1940s movie, mainly because I did have a light, which in my normal life I never would. I lit her Marlboro and we chatted. When asked, the woman, who had an Ivory-girl look about her, told me she lived in Las Vegas, a Nebraskan exile.

"You must have some great stories, living here and all," I said, trying to be polite.

"Yeah, and for a price, they're all yours, up in your room."

Huh? I was stunned. This was not in the game plan. She just didn't look, well, *prostituty*. She didn't even look like someone who'd dance topless. She looked like the girls I'd gone to school with, and she was from Nebraska, for Chrissakes! I know, I know—but I was, well, really shocked. I was dazed from the gambling, stressed out and sick of the town, and this just came out of left field. One minute you're trying to have a civil conversation, and the next you're a john. Maybe I'd misheard.

"What do you do in Vegas?" I asked, giving her the benefit of the doubt. She looked startled; how dense is this guy?

"I am an en-ter-tain-er," she said, real slow, as you might speak to a Japanese tourist seeking directions.

"So, um, you, er, entertain . . . ?" I started to ask, but she'd moved on. As flushed with cash as she'd rightly surmised I was, and as charming as I am, even to a jaded pro, I wasn't worth her while. I saw her walk away from the bar with a real fat guy seven minutes later, a guy named [just kidding, buddy]. Back home, I'd rue my behavior toward this hotel lounge predator. I should have had the presence of mind to somehow get her to sit down (fully dressed) to tell me her story, but alas, my mind was totally shot from all the gambling.

It was time to go back to the top of my game plan for more black-jack, so I approached a table presided over by the kind-faced Roberta from back East. History is written by the victors, which is why the dealer Roberta is remembered as kind-faced. My first hand was a 20, followed by a blackjack. Then I split 9s against her 6 and got a 2 on the first 9 for a double down; she busted. The next half-hour was a thing of beauty. I'd let her win a hand now and then, for the sake of appearances, but I must have won 85 percent of them. Even when she showed an ace and had to peer into the little window on the felt to check for a blackjack—ordinarily a good time to panic—I feared not. *She was too cool to pull that shit.*

A pit boss hovered nervously. For a minute I thought he might ask Roberta to interrupt the game and shuffle the cards, though we had just started on the shoe. Casinos will often do this to neutralize card counters or the grotesquely fortunate. I was disappointed at not being extended the compliment.

A Filipino dealer eventually relieved Roberta, and he and I were both eager to keep it going. But we couldn't. The karma was some-how gone, and he looked genuinely pained. We both knew that for a brief shining moment, in this packed, 84,000-square-foot casino, I had had the best thing going. And you never want that to end, par-ticularly when you have spent many a previous night staring at the ceiling, wondering if you'd walked away from a profitable ride too soon. Once, at the DI, I'd grown my meager chips before me by a factor of 43. Who's to say we couldn't do that again, but here with the whole nest egg, and walk away with $2 million?

I was endeavoring to go crazy on the upside, but it's harder the higher your initial bet. It's one thing to start betting five bucks and work your way up to $100; it's a horse of a different color to move up to $10,000 a hand from an initial $500. The math's the same, but the intestines can't take the altitude; at least, mine couldn't. In retro-spect, I should have been betting even more each hand with Roberta and a lot less with this guy, but who knew? In gambling, as in life, when we hit an amazing lucky streak, we can easily feel entitled to it and lose sight of its transient nature, until it's gone.

And that's the thing about gambling: You're never fully satisfied. Unless you're painfully aware that you walked away from the table too late, you're bound to wonder whether you walked away too soon. To ride your winnings and cut your losses is an eminently sensible imperative—until there is real money on the line, as anyone who plays the stock market well knows.

Casinos everywhere should hang on the wall a saying my friend Greg is fond of—"If 'if's and 'but's were candies and nuts, we'd all have a Merry Christmas."

Enough! I was walking away from this table too late, having given back quite a few of the $1,000 chips Roberta had so kindly given me. Still, when I colored in, I had to smile. I had bought in the preordained $2,500, and now had before me $16,900. The nest egg had crept back into the sixties.

♣ ♦ ♥ ♠ My safe deposit box was a real treasure trove by this point, a variety of chips, checks and, at this stage in the game, mostly cash—six of those cool, wrapped $5,000 packets you see in movies when the bad guys open the suitcase. I grabbed one of the packets, left the rest behind, and went searching for some unscripted trouble. I hadn't gone to bed on my first night in town, and I sure wasn't going to go on my last night.

I lost a couple of thousand at a cold roulette table, then walked outside, crossing the pedestrian bridge over the Strip into the MGM Grand, where I walked the mile to the back of the casino, to one of the town's premier baccarat dens, where Australian media tycoon Kerry Packer reputedly won $25 million earlier this decade. This place, decorated à la Versailles, was white-glove treatment all the way, and I had fun at a crowded table. We were all Chinese, except myself and a classy but youngish woman at the other end of the table whom I assumed to be the casino's shill, or eye candy. She and I were the only players betting less than $1,000 a hand. It seemed ludicrous that the minimum bet at this table was only $100, given the sums being staked. The man sitting to my right, a Mr. T., had $290,000 in chips before him when I sat down. I had one percent of that amount. I wished I'd brought more dough from my box with me—say, 3 percent of his bankroll. "Do you have a credit line with us, sir?" a manager inquired. Um, no, I said, pulling out my grubby bills. He gave me my sixteenth frequent-gambler card—my favorite one, with a stylized lion on it—and treated me like the King of Spain, my paltry stakes notwithstanding.

It was soothing to return to baccarat. P–B–P–B–B . . . Soothing, at least, until the moment a couple of hours or so into the session when I was dealt the cards. How had this happened? It happened because the nine other people at the table had bet on the Banker, making mine the only, and thus the highest, Player wager. Before picking up the cards, I surveyed the table; there was $120,000 arrayed against my pathetic two hundred bucks. "God, don't let me win this one," I pleaded. He did let me. I unveiled a natural 9, winning the house a tidy $119,800 on the hand. Mr. T. clapped good-naturedly, and I decided to take a break and have a bite from the casino's spread in the back, where, at a quarter past six in the morning, I had some of the best kung pao chicken I've ever tasted. I would have enjoyed it more if a seriously wasted guy hadn't been pestering me to taste the "amazing" shrimp off his plate. "I'm so sorry I took the last ones," he kept saying, crying his heart out. I didn't go there, but I think he had graver issues than shrimp.

The sun had already risen on my final day in this oasis as I crossed back over the Strip to my hotel, $1,500 richer. It was a beautiful time of day, when only the ugliest people were still up gambling. Stupidly, I dropped $3,100 at a couple of tables before heading upstairs to bed.

Nest egg: $59,211

Friday, May 8

V-E Day. I awoke with a jolt at four in the afternoon, a good two hours after I'd acknowledged my wake-up call without bothering to get up (it's easier nowadays, when the tormentor to be fooled on the other end of the line is usually a machine). Lying in my green palace, the day's astonishing realities gradually sunk in. First: I was beating Vegas; Vegas, baby! Despite all the crap about there being no way to win in the long run, I was ahead by more than nine grand! Second, and almost as unbelievably, I was flying out of this place in a mere eight hours.

I hurriedly packed, showered, and rushed over to Gordon Biersch for a farewell beer with John Costa. I confided in him that I was ahead, but thought perhaps I should go nuts one more time. "I'm not sure this result is spectacular enough, either way . . . you know, for the book," I told him, sounding like a broken record. "You take care of yourself," he said, looking worried. Afterward I dashed over to Neiman Marcus and bought Kat the nicest piece of jewelry I ever had. It was the least I could do, and I did it with cash. The saleswoman was unfazed.

Five hours and counting. After so much agony and ecstasy, it had all come down to the one existential question that sooner or later confronts all visitors to Vegas: Dinner or gambling? I had to fight on, rise above the $67,000 peak I'd reached at the Hard Rock; it was so close. The game plan: Breeze through three casinos in a sort of farewell tour en route to the airport. At each place, I'd risk no more than $7,500, for a maximum exposure of $22,500. I'd start downstairs, then hit the DI, saving the best for last, the Hard Rock.

I walked up to an empty blackjack table in the "High Society" area, made to look like Rockefeller Center. *Come on, this time really go crazy,* I urged myself. I plopped down two $1,000 chips to play two spots. It seemed a wise decision. My first hand was a 3/3; my second, a 4/4; the dealer showed a 5. Wow. I dutifully plopped down two additional $1,000 chips to split both hands. I ended up with three crappy hands and a decent 18, but it didn't matter. The theory here is that the dealer should bust on a 5. Should, but didn't—she came up with a 19. Four grand into the drop box; that was fun. Next hand she took a 6 to a 21, and I kicked myself for giving her a second chance to show off. I then gave the other $1,500 to a roulette crew. So much for New York–New York.

Three and a half hours and counting as I pulled up to the DI. I ran into the 24/7 shop and blew $60 on a hotel sweatshirt because— don't laugh—I reckoned it would bring good luck. You know, suck up to the house. I had half put the damned thing on when I rushed into the baccarat pit, where the dapper Latin supervisor graciously welcomed me, by name. I threw a stack of bills at the dealers for some chips, but, not wanting to lose out on any of the action while they counted, I also plopped down an indeterminate pile on the Player spot. "Money plays," the dealer dramatically announced, as they are wont to do when an impetuous gambler cannot be bothered with turning his dirty paper into the more decorous plastic. It turned out to be $1,300, but I wished it had been more, as the Player won. Again and again, six times in a row. I raised my bets some here and there, of course, but never enough. Our Player streak didn't end, the shoe did, and I didn't have twenty minutes to wait around for a new one. I bade my buddies good-bye, scooped up my chips and rushed over to the main casino area, where I lost six or seven of the eleven grand I'd made at baccarat. Getting back in the Endeavor, I noticed I had a tag still dangling from my new sweatshirt. I changed into my old Hard Rock one.

An hour forty-five and counting. The Hard Rock was jamming, swarms of beautiful people—the town's IT crowd—settling in for a weekend in Gomorrah, moving about with the languorous pace of those savoring a long-awaited beginning. But I was spinning at 45 RPM, alone. *Come on, come on,* I hectored the roulette wheel. *Let's go.* I was piling on green and black chips on the whole lot of seductive numbers, but only the ugliest ones came calling—23, 29, 31, 18, 35, 00, 31. They cost me five grand. Then, at a blackjack table, I saw Teri, formerly the Coolest Dealer on Earth.

She broke my heart. I started off betting the lucky pinks. Nada. I kept having to hit on 16s and 15s. An hour and counting. *Come on; come on, Teri. Let's turn it around,* I implored inaudibly, as if praying. A pit boss kept a close eye on me, but at a distance, not wanting to interrupt my self-destruction. Teri wasn't making eye contact with me, either, opting to banter with the guys to my right who were betting $10 a hand and to whom I was providing some good stories for the folks back home: "There was this guy who kept betting $500 and getting his ass kicked—man, he was losing it." It was clear I was in a free fall that all the bulges in my jeans and coat pockets could not break. It was as if someone in the eye in the sky had pressed a button—the "This guy's headed for the airport; no more messing around" button. I'd already blown past my stipulated $7,500 maximum loss here. And there was no more time. I sheepishly wished Teri a good night and tossed her a black chip, to which she arched her eyebrows and told me to "Take care, now" with much sincerity.

Forty-two minutes and counting. Winning Megabucks was the only fitting finale for this odyssey. Inserted $20. Thirty-seven minutes to go. Inserted $20. Cherries. Diamonds. All sorts of crap, everything but the damned Megabucks eagles. Up to $140. Twenty-nine minutes to go. The line to cash in was way too long. I'd never make it. I overheard two girls who looked about fifteen wandering around, lamenting the fact that they'd lost their whole bankroll and it was, "still, like, Friday." I grabbed the brunette by the shoulder, pointed to the machine with the $140 in credits, and said, "That's yours, do good." I didn't even wait around for their reaction, but simply started sprinting out of the casino and into the parking lot. More people must miss flights out of Vegas than anywhere else, which is understandable for weekend revelers, but kind of pathetic when you've been here over a month.

I returned the Endeavor, having no time for an appropriately mushy farewell, grabbed the bus to the terminal, and ran what seemed like miles past all the ads for the shows and buffets, past the smokers' pens where addicts huddle together in a haze, and past the last row of Megabucks. I arrived at the gate ten minutes after the Kennedy red-eye's scheduled 12:15 A.M. departure time.

Thank God for delayed flights. I sat on the right side of the plane, with an awesome view of the lit-up Strip as we took off. I was numb, but not overly nostalgic. I still had Bellagio left to battle in October—calling to make the reservation for its opening weekend was the last thing I did before leaving my NY–NY suite—and I hoped that would go better than the last time I'd deviated from the script, for my ill-advised intermission.

I catapulted over the snoring guy in the aisle seat and walked back to the john, where I emptied my jumbled pockets. I had been so frazzled at the Hard Rock, desperately stripping $100 bills from six different places, that I'd lost track of the score. The nest egg, I discovered, and this not counting the deferred World Cup wager, was down to $43,264.

I didn't sleep. My mind was racing furiously, griping all the way across the country. Why hadn't I simply had dinner and seen a movie those last few hours? Why hadn't I doubled my bet on every consecutive winning baccarat hand at the DI? Why hadn't I been able to truly go crazy on the upside? For that matter, why hadn't I simply made one dramatic $50,000 bet upon first arriving in Vegas instead of going through that war of attrition? Oh yeah, because I lost that first hand at Luxor.

Over Kansas, studying the ledgers in my little black leather book, I figured that, all told, I had gambled for 137 hours and 45 minutes during my odyssey. Assuming an average bet of $100 and two bets a minute, I'd wagered a total of $1.65 MILLION. Looking at it this way, I immediately felt better about my $6,736, or .4 percent, loss. We gamblers make great spin doctors.

Nest egg: $43,264

An Ill-Advised Postlude

13

SUMMER

I have noticed an obscure melancholy in those who have given up a vice, a passion. It's the nostalgia for a dependency that reveals our weakness, our vulnerability.
—Cristina Peri Rossi, *Dostoevsky's Last Night*

♣ ♦ ♥ ♠ Kat picked me up at Kennedy Airport the next morning, but instead of going home to our apartment in Manhattan, she took me straight to her parents' tranquil place in Connecticut, the way defecting spies, returning astronauts, and rescued hostages are always spirited off to some safe house. You know, to be placed under observation and debriefed. It was my mother-in-law's birthday, and the day before Mother's Day, which may have been the real reason behind our suburban escapade. I couldn't be sure, I was so exhausted.

My in-laws' tidy colonial place is extraordinarily quiet by any measure, but after a month's sojourn in Las Vegas, it seemed mausoleum-quiet. At one point I sat on the stairs, straining to hear the chirping birds outside, and then broke into a psycho laugh at the realization that today I would not be gambling. This was exhilarating, in ways both good and bad. Judy did her best to avoid talking about the gambling, which left me straining for topics. "Boy, that Web Hubbell isn't out of the woods yet, is he?" I lamely attempted. But when Judy left the room, I whipped out a deck of cards and taught Dan, my father-in-law, the byzantine rules of baccarat. "That's all there is to it?" he asked dubiously. "Yep, nothing to it."

In the afternoon Kat and I took a drive to the local Chase branch, where we made the teller's day. I don't think she'd ever seen so much raw cash in this genteel corner of Fairfield County. The rest of the weekend was relaxing, and, I'm happy to report, not once did I go on a china-smashing rampage in Judy's living room, or shake too uncontrollably.

We returned to Manhattan to a purring Trotsky and to the discovery that I had made a lot of new friends in Las Vegas. They'd all written with the same message: Come back! Bob Miner had sent a handwritten note, and I had a stack of invitations from a bunch of the other casinos for upcoming slot tournaments, fight weekends, you name it. Come, play, we'll pay, they all screamed. Months later a host from New York–New York even called me up to ask if I'd made my New Year's plans yet.

The news out of Vegas continued to amuse. My first week home, a great deal of which I spent in my pajamas on the couch clutching my remote, Trot by my side, I watched on ESPN the last hours of the million-dollar championship hold 'em round at the World Series of Poker. The final showdown was between an old pro, Scotty Nguyen, and a remarkable rookie, Kevin McBride, who made the final two out of a field of 350 players in only his fourth month of tournament play. His was an *All's Well That Ends Well* story: He'd been fired from the Sunbeam Corporation last January by mean Chainsaw Al Dunlap himself. Instead of looking for a new job, McBride went out and bought some poker books. Trotsky and I were, naturally, rooting for him.

McBride seemed to take great pleasure in defying all poker etiquette, mainly by wearing every emotion on his sleeve. One moment he was groaning; the next he'd be bragging. Throughout, Scotty wore a pained "Who is this guy?" expression. The wily veteran ultimately won, but McBride still got to take home $687,500.

In early June, four individuals were arrested for allegedly cheating casinos out of $6 million since September 1996. What's shocking is that they cheated at slot machines, something I hadn't realized was possible. The alleged ringleader, Dennis Nikrasch, was described in news accounts as a computer expert who would program machines to win with a handheld, concealed device. Accomplices would then step forward and claim the jackpot. In October 1997, according to the federal complaint, the defendants won a Jaguar at the Luxor. I wonder if Bob Miner sent them a fruit basket.

Mr. Nikrasch had been convicted back in 1986 of participating in a similar ring that took home $10 million. He'd received a fifteen-year sentence, but was released on parole early in 1991. Incredibly, nobody thought to put the handy slot aficionado on the casinos' list of excludable persons. Duh. Mr. Nikrasch was arrested while trying to hit the Megabucks jackpot; so much for going crazy on the upside.

The Fourth of July was a bitter holiday weekend in the Martinez household. In an ugly 3–0 quarter-final loss in Lyon, France, Germany was eliminated from the 1998 World Cup. By whom, you demand, rightly devastated. Italy? Brazil? Hardly. Adding insult to injury, my nemesis was none other than Croatia! This is a country which (a) has fewer people than Germany has licensed soccer players; (b) had never been to a World Cup before; and (c) wouldn't even exist if Germany hadn't rushed to recognize it when it broke away from Yugoslavia in 1991. The ingrates. My brother called in the afternoon to crow.

He was right. The Germans *had* sucked, and for the most appalling of reasons: because they're a bunch of fat-headed, pale-skinned pigs, that's why. The English, Dutch, and French, much to the horror of their respective racists back home, all fielded multi-ethnic teams, reflecting their colonial legacies and the diversity of their contemporary societies. The champion French squad was led by the formidable Zinedine Zidane, the son of Tunisian immigrants. The dour Germans, on the other hand, could all have starred in an SS recruiting film. This reflects the continuing racial, ugly nature of that nation's immigration laws, which make it difficult for the offspring of foreign workers in Germany to acquire German citizenship unless they can lay claim to a "German bloodline." I do not rant out of some zealous political correctness, nor because I necessarily think Turks make great soccer players. The point is, a clash of different styles, a melting pot's diversity, is always a source of strength. Germany's stolid, unimaginative play stemmed from the same insular mentality that underlies its immigration laws, and cost me $5,000. Memo to self: Root for the Dutch in the next millennium.

Nest egg: $38,264

What else? Let's see . . . Have I mentioned I lost $16,915 in one weekend out at Luxor?

Long story short: I'm not proud of it, but I succumbed to an invitation from Chuck Mangione.

Having received one enticing invitation too many for every conceivable boondoggle, I accepted the Luxor's offer to spend an "exquisite evening" of wine-tasting and jazz. It was scheduled for a weekend when I'd been planning on being in Las Vegas anyway, doing some follow-up interviews with notables in town. How could I say no to Chuck Mangione?

The casino's high rollers would be treated to a six-course dinner orchestrated by the hotel's chefs and by the Robert Mondavi house, which would show off its "award-winning" Vineyard Select Wines, one for each course. After dinner, Chuck would put on a show for the intimate crowd. Wow.

Bob Miner and I really bonded that weekend. The fifty-four-year-old native of Boulder City told me his first job in the industry had been in security, over at the Las Vegas Hilton, around the time they first installed video cameras, an event that would forever shift the balance of power in the age-old cat-and-mouse game between casinos and talented cheats. "Barron Hilton used to come down in his bathrobe just to marvel at the feed from those new cameras; they were like his favorite toys," Bob recalled.

We grabbed a quick lunch together, interrupted every few minutes by his high rollers' endless beckoning, via beeper. There is no end to the show tickets, limo rides, credit lines, and kitschy suites Bob must dole out. Casinos don't bestow all this power on just anyone; a position as a host is one of the most sought-after and best-compensated in a casino. Hosts are these massive resorts' personal link to their best customers. Bob is a combination travel agent, concierge, and private banker to some of the most finicky people on earth. "My job is to attract, maintain, and retain clients," he told me earnestly. He gets a lot of odd requests, and he is usually diligent about coming through, though he draws the line at those for girls. "I'm not your pimp," he'll tell clients, referring them, if he's in a charitable mood, to the Yellow Pages.

And that's the thing about Bob; he's not the groveling type. There is a certain decency and dignity about him that I find charming, though other gamblers might dig the groveling. Some other hosts around town might hang all over you like a puppy, and, by gosh, if a prostitute is what you want, a prostitute is what you'll get. But that's not what Bob, an observant Roman Catholic with some perspective on life, will offer you. From him, you'll get a serious business relationship.

I learned from an executive in the industry that in evaluating a host's monthly performance, casinos employ the same theoretical-loss yardstick that determines a gambler's earned comps. The more business a host brings in the door, the more he or she is worth to the company. No wonder Bob had been so appreciative at having me waltz into his life that Sunday morning in April. Also, being measured by their players' theoretical, instead of actual, loss allows hosts to root for their clients sincerely. The more a player wins, the longer he plays, pumping up the host's stats.

We dined at the same table, too, along with some of his other clients. "You're my date," he quipped, alluding to the fact that our wives were home. He remembered Kathy's name, which impressed me, but thought she was a stewardess. (Kat didn't think this was as funny as I had. She wondered if I'd indeed introduced Bob to some stewardess.)

The whole evening was quite tasteful. I felt as if I were at an elegant wedding where I didn't know anybody, what with the large round tables in the flowery ballroom, strangers' awkward small talk, and the band to one side, trying to lure people onto the dance floor. The food was excellent and the little lectures with which the Mondavi vice president introduced each course were highly informative to those of us who can't keep our pinots straight. There were two young women at the table from Phoenix, a guy from Ohio (who seemed to be hitting on the Phoenix chicks with that old "Come see what $25,000 in cash looks like after dinner in my safe deposit box" line), and the Halls from Indiana. We were all of the tribe of Miner.

Mr. Hall, seated to my left, is in the insurance business, specializing in "final-expense" insurance. He told me it's a great business, what with so many baby boomers getting older. Hmm, this demographic pitch sounded strangely familiar. Ah yes, Mandalay's president, Glenn Schaeffer, is fond of making the same point in pounding the table for Vegas's future, except he also likes to say that this is a generation of *über*-consumers whose last check will bounce, which doesn't make them sound like people who'd dutifully mail in payments over a number of years to cover their "final expense."

After dinner and Mangione's stirring performance of that one song we all know, I hit the familiar casino. Scarily enough, most dealers remembered me. "Haven't seen you here in a while," one said. Geez, it had only been three months. What did they want from me, a cross-country trip every weekend?

I took three hundred bucks to seven grand, which is pretty remarkable. And with that, I abandoned any pretense that I wasn't back in the same old war. The truth is that all summer it had been gnawing at me that I had ended my month in Vegas down, when I could have walked away ahead after 133 of my 137+ hours of gambling. Maybe now, when I wasn't even supposed to be here, I'd sneak in my most spectacular breakthrough. That would make quite a story.

It didn't happen. I lost my winnings and then kept on losing, spiraling out of control, fulfilling the old adage about gambling being a lot like quicksand—the harder you try to pull yourself out of the hole, the deeper you go. After some bad breaks at baccarat and a dismal blackjack session, it was all coming back. We were picking up where we'd left off on May 8. There is no fresh start at the tables; the pain is cumulative and it's all about drinking away that nagging sense of déjà vu. Having given back the seven grand, I desperately hit the cash-advance machines with the high commissions I'd once scoffed at. The Spanish writer Cristina Peri Rossi, in her masterly novel *Dostoevsky's Last Night* (which is not about the Russian author but about a present-day bingo addict's obsession with his therapist), writes, "Inveterate losers resort to them [ATMs] like the chronically ill to emergency rooms." How true.

I lost so much so fast.

Lying in bed later, I relived the shame and pain I'd felt on my previous stay at this damned pyramid. Again, I felt a hollowness in my chest as I became unusually cognizant of my internal organs. It was an odd way to feel a gambling loss, but there it was. Heart, lungs, liver, all exposed, as if I lay on a hard metallic operating table, feeling the coolness of the surgical tongs.

The next day, Bob once again mourned my loss. This time, when he offered to cover my airfare, I took him up on the offer. We walked over to the cage, where he had the cashier hand me $441 in cash. I dropped it at a roulette table as soon as I knew he was no longer looking my way.

Nest egg: $21,349

14

BELLAGIO

*"I wanted Bellagio to represent the softer side
of the human soul."*

—Steve Wynn

Friday, October 16

♣ ♦ ♥ ♠ I'd been pumped for weeks. Kat and I were headed to the opening weekend of Steve Wynn's $1.6 billion Bellagio, the world's most ambitious hotel ever built and Las Vegas's bold statement about where it wants to go in the next century. I had set the scene masterfully, what with all those previous losses to build up dramatic tension. Though it had taken me a few weeks after the summer's indiscretion at Luxor to realize it, all had worked out for the best. A truly uplifting Hollywood ending is predicated on a passing acquaintance with adversity, as the poker flick *Rounders,* the one with Matt Damon playing the guy from the wrong side of the tracks, had recently reminded me. He ultimately won his money back, and got to drop out of law school and move to Vegas.

There could be no setting more appropriate for an epic comeback than Bellagio. Even the name hinted at pleasure, tranquillity, redemption, and stacks upon stacks of chips. Yes, I would take my nimble nest egg, raise it to spectacular heights, retire from the gambling life a winner, as so few are able to, and still have people say mine was a "poignant" odyssey. You don't get "poignant" these days unless you've suffered a bit, and if you're not poignant, well then, you're just shallow. So I'd suffered, and now I was going to win. I was itching to get back into action; it had been difficult to leave on such a sour note. Now victory seemed preordained.

I hardly needed others to add to the hype, but they did. An orchestrated drum roll in all media built up to our departure. Bellagio was getting buzz. *Vanity Fair, The New York Times, The Wall Street Journal, Newsweek, Time,* and everyone else were fawning over Steve Wynn's latest creation, particularly its $300 million art collection. As if reading all this weren't enough, the haunting pop-opera tunes of Andrea Bocelli, featured in the barrage of pre-opening Bellagio ads on national TV, had become embedded in my head; a poignant sound track for a poignant comeback. The ads' slogan: "And so it begins." And so it ends, too.

Kat was along for the finale; I wouldn't have it any other way. Not that it took much arm-twisting. She works hard, and relished the opportunity to loll in a spa and dine in heavenly restaurants all weekend. I had promised her we wouldn't gamble every waking moment. The highlights of my springtime in Vegas all involved her, and, less romantically, I was convinced she'd bring us luck at the tables. Mine seemed to have worn off, and gambling alone is unhealthy. I'd teasingly designated her my coach for the weekend, empowering her to pull the plug and demand a break in the action at any time when she could see momentum turning against us. And because she wasn't too familiar with the complexities of the game, I showed her an instructional craps video—featuring a guy with a thick Pittsburgh accent who appeared to have rented a tux and crammed a craps table into his living room—on the eve of our departure. Sad to say, I watched it in a warm-up suit.

In all this, save for the Nike suit, I was unwittingly following in Dostoevsky's footsteps. On one occasion after losing his shirt in Bad Homburg, where he'd gone to gamble alone after leaving Anna behind in Dresden, he convinced himself that his concern for her welfare was a source of "emotional disturbance" that prevented him from putting into practice his infallible method for winning. That's a good one. The solution: a romantic escape to Baden-Baden, where, together, they could get it right this time. As Anna Grigoreyevna wrote sadly in her memoirs, "He spoke so persuasively, cited so many examples in proof of his theory, that he convinced me, too."

Kat and I landed in McCarran late in the morning. A promising omen that things would be radically different this time was our arrival at the spectacular new Terminal D, all cool marble and sweeping glass, showing off at every turn the proud jets, the endless desert sky, and the very majesty of flight. I've never understood why airports built in my childhood insisted on enveloping passengers in bunkerlike environments, as if their designers feared that droves of passengers might panic if afforded a peek out the window, at the metal canisters in which they were about to propel themselves across the sky. *Let 'em think it's a subway.*

We'd upgraded our leased wheels this time around, too. For the first time in my life (and a good twenty years before my midlife crisis will drive me to the Miata dealer), I got behind the wheel of a convertible, a sprightly Chrysler Sebring. Kat and I giddily cruised the Strip, top down, toward the gleaming three-winged Bellagio tower. The valet attendant greeting us atop the hotel's driveway said, "Welcome to Bellagio," with such sonorous rapture that for a minute I imagined a chunk of the $1.6 billion had gone toward implanting chips in the employees' vocal cords, so that Steve Wynn's voice could be heard whenever any of them spoke.

The lobby was all color, dominated by the wondrous overhead chandelier, billowing trumpets and petals by the glass artist Dale Chihuly. It's the largest glass sculpture ever made (of course) and it cost $10 million, but those are trivializing stats. It's breathtaking. Behind the check-in counter, cleverly, there's what looks like the inner courtyard of a tranquil Italian villa. The impression conveyed is of being checked into someone's home. Wynn had invited his buddies to an opening bash the previous night, and the casino had already been open some twelve hours. Our room was ready, because—and this is sweet—*nobody* had ever stayed in it. The outer elevator doors didn't quite close, which must be really annoying when you've poured

$1.6 billion into a place. The resort quickly dispatched someone to become the official elevator-door-closer for the day, and he did it with such panache that later I heard an elderly woman tell her husband, "Now, that's a classy touch." You Wynn, you lucky.

It was with a sense of history that I carried my bride across the threshold into the virginal room, as the bellboy held the door open. Through all my travels, I'd never inaugurated a room, not even at the piddling Best Westerns I customarily patronize. This was special. Forevermore, as its first occupants, we'll have a special bond with those who stay in room 12054. We'll be present in spirit for all the inspiring sex, both licit and illicit, that will here ensue, as well as the jittery midnight rehearsals of countless convention speakers, the exuberant celebrating of winning gamblers, and the more frequent head-bashing of losers. Perhaps we should all get together for a 12054 reunion bash—say, in a dozen years, for the Bellagio's implosion.

We had a fantastic view of the eleven-acre lake fronting the hotel on the Strip and its astonishing choreographed fountains, which shot water as high up as our floor, the twelfth. But all hype aside, there was a problem with the room. And that's it; it was just a room. I'm not sure what I'd been expecting, exactly, what my own private nirvana should have looked like, but that was for Mr. Wynn to figure out. He's "Mr. Visionary," the one who'd been boasting for months that he was building heaven on earth. What I hadn't expected was this beige, tasteful room with insufficient closet space, the kind of room you might find at a New York hotel that caters to traveling businessmen (or at the Mirage, for that matter). The $1.6 billion had clearly not gone into the rooms. And amusingly, as much as Wynn had wanted to build a resort to appeal to the nongambler, he still couldn't shake some old Vegas dogmas. There was no mini-bar or fridge. *Let thy thirst lead you down to the casino!*

We went downstairs to join the masses shuffling around, gawking at Las Vegas's latest wonder. More than eighty thousand people wandered through the hotel in its first day. It was odd to see the fanny-pack tourists in shorts and the locals in their Sunset Station warm-up jackets in the stunning formal conservatory garden, maintained by the hotel's 115-member horticulture department, under beams of sculpted green oxidized copper set in floral patterns. The odd juxtaposition brought to mind the opening of Romanov palaces to the rabble in the aftermath of revolution, to elicit the inevitable "This was too much" reaction. But here, this was all ours—everybody's. This being Vegas, the most costly hotel ever built boasts not only the most sumptuous of baccarat rooms known to man, but also the most sumptuous of nickel slots, encased in marble.

Lunch at the beautiful café was a disaster. A mere twelve hours into its existence, the 24/7 café was out of my first two entrée choices. I struck out with my third selection, the pistachio-encrusted chicken, which I figured was a safe call, being the "signature special" and all. The place wasn't even crowded. "What do you have?" I finally asked the waitress, who for some reason persisted throughout our meal in singing to herself the old "Have it your way" Burger King tune. When I spilled my glass of water, I sat there for six minutes, desperately trying to salvage as many french fries as possible from the freezing water before our S.O.S. call—Kat's hysterical laughter—was heeded.

After lunch we checked out the rest of the hotel. Despite the stress-inducing crowds, it was hard not to be impressed. Bellagio, which Wynn likens to a symphony, is the most striking hotel I've ever seen, anywhere. This is what manufactured good taste looks like. Inside the colorful two- and three-story structures with Spanish tile roofs along the faux lake, Wynn has assembled his second great art collection, a string of restaurants to make whole cities— forget about hotels—green with envy. You've got Olives from Boston, Le Cirque from New York, Aqua from San Francisco, a new place by New York's Jean-Georges Vongerichten, and the hotel's crown jewel, Picasso, a restaurant presided over by chef Julian Serrano and decorated by Claude Picasso with works by his dad, Pablo. Our in-room propaganda even noted which famous designer designed each restaurant. All told, seven of the Bellagio chefs have won the James Beard Award, which I assume is something like a culinary Oscar because they make a big deal of that fact. Down the Via Bellagio, a space modeled after Milan's Galleria, high rollers can shop at Armani, Chanel, Hermès, Gucci, Tiffany, and other such snooty establishments. Not too shabby.

Wynn's stated goal was to build an irresistible destination to attract those holdouts across the country who haven't deigned to come to Vegas. That's you, Judy. He talks about his resort as a competitor to Paris (the city, not the hotel going up across the street), as well as a place the well-heeled nongambling vacationer might consider instead of Aspen or Palm Springs. Will Mr. Visionary succeed in this? Of course not. By definition, a hotel with three thousand rooms will never be an appealing vacation spot for those Wynn is most desperate to woo, particularly one that is a tourist attraction to tens of thousands a day. Sit out by the pool and you'll immediately see what I am talking about: someone gets paged every twenty seconds.

But Wynn doesn't really need these people; he's just getting greedy. The Bellagio will succeed by becoming the preferred Strip address of conventioneers and high rollers alike. The art gallery and restaurants and other flourishes won't draw people away from Aspen; they'll draw people away from the Desert Inn.

♣ ♦ ♥ ♠ On this opening weekend, the glitches persisted. I had brought what remained of the nest egg in the form of a certified check, faxing over a copy of it a few days earlier for the casino to verify, as they'd instructed me to do. They claimed the fax had never arrived, and we weren't the only ones with a problem. The casino's credit office was mobbed by frazzled high rollers who'd heeded the call and flocked in from around the world, eager to try their luck at the instantly most prestigious casino on earth. I closed my eyes for a second and listened to the sounds of Babylon, the clash of a dozen different tongues. Not Swedish, of course, or German, or Dutch. These were the languages of today's hot money—Spanish, Portuguese, Russian, Chinese, and some Arabic, the language of baccarat in the days of the petrodollar boom.

This fondness of emerging-market types (and their bubbly, impermanent cash) for casinos brings to mind a passage in *The Gambler* in which Dostoevsky explains his countrymen's love of roulette:

> The faculty of amassing capital has, with the progress of history, taken a place—and almost the foremost place—among the virtues and merits of the civilized man of the West. The Russian is not only incapable of amassing capital, but dissipates it in a reckless and unseemly way. Nevertheless, we Russians need money too, and consequently we are very glad and very eager to make use of such means as roulette, for instance, in which one can grow rich all at once, in two hours, without work. That's very fascinating to us; and since we play badly, recklessly, without taking trouble, we usually lose.

Obsequious hosts—there was even one specifically for Brazilians—held the foreigners' hands while they clamored for one of the hotel's finance types to help them. A Mexican gentleman wearing a warm-up suit next to me clutched a briefcase and chatted to his amiable host from Monterrey. I imagined piles of cash inside the case, wondered at their provenance, and began to feel nauseated. *What were we doing here?*

For some reason, the harried-looking man in charge, preciously named Mr. Hugs, took a liking to us, no doubt the lowest rollers in the room. He apologetically walked us over to a bar, where he asked us to wait while he dealt with our check. I asked him jokingly if the casino, now some sixteen hours into it, was winning or losing, to which he grinned. But inside, I was all turmoil. Here we were, ready to engage in one final, victorious battle, only to find ourselves with no ammo. What if Mr. Hugs couldn't get through to the bank? It was already after closing hours, the weekend, in New York, and I really didn't want to end up with the nest egg at a mere twenty-one grand because of some technical glitch. But Hugs came back to say everything was in order. He handed me a Bellagio card and told me the money was now on deposit, that I could ask any pit boss for a withdrawal from it. Cool.

Kat and I hit the art gallery. Here, as he had at the Secret Garden of Siegfried & Roy, Wynn himself walked us through the collection on an audio tour. He particularly seemed to relish saying "Van Gogh," pronouncing it the correct Dutch way, clearing the phlegm from his throat at the end, instead of ending on a fading vowel, as those who wish Vincent had been French do. But overall, his performance was subdued, and his voice sounded less smooth, a great deal raspier, than it had on Mirage TV. He sounded a little out of breath at times, too. I pictured him sitting by a fireplace, wearing his dinner jacket and taking sips of sherry as he talked to us about his collection. Wynn introduced Van Gogh's *Peasant Against a Background of Wheat* with the words "What makes this painting so valuable," but, much to my disappointment, he did not go on to mention its $47.5 million price tag. Nor did he mutter under his breath about having to sell Mirage stock to acquire the damned picture. No, the talk was very civilized.

So civilized, it's disorienting. Traditionally, Las Vegas casinos have disoriented gamblers by building gaudy sets, hiding the clocks, pushing free drinks, parading scantily clad babes, and the like. But this is more of a mind fuck. It takes two minutes to walk from craps to Cézanne, and no quantity of sleepless nights or free drinks could ever match the disorienting power of finding a sublime art gallery, the intimacy and selectivity of which bring to mind Washington's Phillips Collection, under the same roof as a casino—around the corner, just past the conservatory. Kat and I bought a box of the collection's notecards and a poster, as we might at the Met back home.

After dinner, we made our debut in the casino's crowded baccarat room, sitting down at a table with a $200 minimum bet. Incredibly, there were four busy tables to choose from—how many times had I been the sole person in the entire Luxor casino willing to play this game?—plus a second, less crowded baccarat room, where the minimum bet was $10,000 and the house had spent $250 a square yard on the plush carpeting. Were there whales gambling anywhere else in town that night?

Across the table, a Mr. E. was no longer appreciating the chandeliers or the splendid dining choices available to him. He was going through baccarat hell. We'd seen him win five consecutive $15,000 bets—an impressively bumpy ride, on which he alternated bets, not a streak—before sitting down, but now he'd lost eight in a row. His eyes betrayed the stark bewilderment of a dog grown tired from chasing his tail, which is what a bad baccarat run feels like. He asked one of the many solicitous supervisors hovering behind the table for more credit. He wanted to be Zeus again, as he'd been a mere half-hour ago. The rest of us avoided eye contact with him, lest we identify with what might become of us in a moment of weakness.

I was a bit gun-shy that night, having been away long enough to again sweat those $100 bets. This was unfortunate, because it meant—need I say it?—not increasing my stakes enough when we'd hit a lucky streak. We actually lost the first eight hands before turning it around. This happened when Kat pulled out of her purse Trot's red puppy, a Beanie Baby we'd brought along for good luck. I was willing to try anything, so I rubbed it on the green felt, and this seemed to work. The cocktail waitress looked at the pup and exclaimed, "How cute!" but nobody at the table said a word. You don't mock, or mess with, others' karma, and if a grown man brings a red dog to baccarat, there's bound to be a damned good reason for it. Who knew?

There was a seat open to Kat's left, and a Mediterranean-looking gentleman kept darting in and out of the game—very uncouth in the leisurely world of baccarat—and making huge cash bets. It would take the dealers a while to count up all the notes. Because he had a habit of storming away, the supervisor instructed one of the dealers to always collect his Banker commissions immediately after each hand. "That's how we had to do it with him back at the Mirage," she said.

He did settle down for a while, though, plopping down his foot-tall stack of C-notes, held together by overlapping industrial-strength rubber bands. During my time in Vegas, I'd acquired enough of a familiarity with money's heft—I must update the skills category on my résumé—to know that I had to be staring at something like a quarter-million dollars. Cash. "I just hope tonight's not the night this guy gets shot for whatever he's involved in," Kat whispered into my ear, and I recalled my own disgust in the credit office.

It must be hard being a thrifty Russian, Mexican, or Indonesian, eager to splurge a bit at the baccarat tables, and have people like us assume the cash in your suitcases is tainted, rogue money. We really should be more tolerant. Maybe this guy has the same aversion to complicated financial instruments my grandmother had. She put the credit card my parents pestered her to get in a safe deposit box, along with her jewelry.

If it weren't for the new-hotel smell, you'd have thought we'd been sitting at this table since the beginning of time, transfixed by the question of whether Player or Banker would next come closest to 9. Michael Jordan, flanked by guards, sauntered by our table, maneuvering through the room with feline grace. But we were unfazed; hardly anybody looked up. Only Juan from Paraguay, one of the four impeccably mannered dealers working the game, made a comment about the world's greatest athlete. "There goes the José Luís Chilavert of North America," he told me in Spanish, referring to his nation's heroic World Cup keeper. Two unrelated thoughts suddenly came to mind. First: It's odd to think of this dapper dealer, so European in his mannerisms and so at home in these surroundings, leaving this building to drive past a few Office Depots and Taco Bells to his home in the suburbs. And, second: Don't anybody bring up the '98 World Cup ever again.

Soon thereafter, Kat and I retired for the evening, ahead $1,500.

Nest egg: $22,849

Saturday, October 17

Having gone thirty-two years, somehow, without a mud wrap, I wasn't sure what the etiquette was when Mireille Alfa, the resort's head aesthetician, allegedly from Paris, began covering my body with mud. Should I strive for reverential silence or friendly chitchat? No longer able to take the pressure, I cracked: "I suppose you saved this dirt from the construction site."

This bad move—Mireille was not amused—led to a fascinating discovery. Did you know France exports mud? It's true. The purveyor of all things fine to snobs everywhere exports mud. Wow.

"All good mud for Moor wraps comes from the coast of Brittany," she said sternly. Then, once I got over the disappointment of not having my eyes covered with cucumbers—one of the motivations behind this indulgence, I must confess—I fell into that soothing limbo between wakefulness and sleep. My last vision before falling into a gentle snooze was large crates of mud on the tarmac at Charles de Gaulle, waiting to come to America, along with the Moët & Chandon.

When Mireille and I parted, she suggested I also take a Vichy shower in the spa, a suggestion that, needless to say, I found rather offensive, not to mention unpatriotic. I almost told her to go get a Pétain facial but then thought better of it.

Lingering in the spa, I read the good news in the *Review-Journal*: Pinochet had been arrested in London the night before, on a Spanish judge's warrant. It looked as if he might face trial for his atrocities after all. Things were falling into place. This had to be a good omen for all just causes, my own included.

Kat and I had lunch at the poolside café. Her day was made, because she had talked to Kevin Costner while working out. He'd said hi, or something like that, to which she'd replied hi, too, at least she thought she'd managed to. I couldn't really follow what Kat was saying; I was too starstruck myself, as our table was sandwiched between those of Michael Eisner and George Lucas. Quick, Andrés, think up a socko movie plot to pitch! Umm . . . nah, it's been done;

umm . . . nah, that's been done, too. Shit, too late. The Disney chief was gone. But how appropriate for him to be here this weekend—all the imagineers under the same roof—checking out what has become his company's main competition. Hell, Disney should just buy the Mirage Corporation, placing Mickey firmly in control of the nation's Times Square–Hollywood–Vegas entertainment axis once and for all. With casino stocks as depressed as they are, this would be the most cost-effective way for Disney to once again piss off Southern Baptists.

We spent the rest of the afternoon doing something rather prudent: Christmas shopping while we still had cash. A great deal of our motivation behind this was to spend some quality time in our cool convertible, out in the desert. So we went all the way to the outlet mall on the California border, forty-five minutes away. (Sorry, Dad, didn't pay full price for that Polo shirt.)

Back at the hotel, in Wynn's $90 million re-creation of the Paris Opera, we saw the new Cirque du Soleil show designed for the Bellagio. It was even more spectacular than the show at Treasure Island, on account of the fact that the stage was a huge swimming pool and most of the acrobats—the majority of them Olympic swimmers—exited stage, well, by going underwater.

We didn't gamble much after dinner, only enough to lose back the previous night's gain. The casino was crowded, and it didn't feel right. And when it doesn't feel right, I'd come to appreciate there is only one question you have to ask yourself: Why lose today what you can lose tomorrow?

Nest egg: $21,349

Sunday, October 18

Kat got up to go work out, no doubt in hopes of some scintillating conversation with Kevin Costner, and I dragged myself down to the sports book to watch football. It's criminal, how the games start at ten o'clock out here. How do tens of millions of Pacific Timers put up with this shit? They're like foreigners in their own country, living in a land where stock markets close at one and Monday Night Football is followed by prime-time television. Speaking of the stock market: Amusingly, the plush Bellagio sports book has a stock ticker under its scoreboard. I wonder how the touchy NYSE feels about that.

I left the Bellagio after the early games to visit Dick Carson at home. I went down to his basement, where he had a wood-paneled office next to the bowling alley, past the wine cellar, but before the racquetball court. This was like Richie Rich land, or would have been but for the layers of dust and signs of disrepair everywhere. In his office, which you entered via french doors, with a fancy C monogrammed on the glass, games were going on on three television sets lined up along the near wall. Dick, wearing a red Nike cap, studied each casino's changing line on a computer screen at his desk. Clothes were strewn about the room and there was dust everywhere, physical evidence of the burst bubble his life has become.

"There's a lot of work we need to do on the house, inside and out, but it's kind of tough right now, and we might lose it." I walked over to the trophy case crammed with swimming mementos and found one of those laminated tributes to a father you can buy at Hallmark. Carolyn had given it to him, Dick said. One of the lines read, "A father has special skills that come in handy." Dick then showed me a letter from an Israeli Olympic swimmer, whom the Carsons took under their wing when he was an exchange student in Las Vegas. Dick had paid for his travels with the swim team, and he'd become friends with the kids. After a subsequent visit a couple of years ago, the swimmer wrote Dick: "I do not know what is bothering you, but I want to encourage you and remind you to be strong and motivated, just like you taught me so much."

Dick leaned forward to tell me he was now stuck for $2 million. He owes most of that to friends, people who don't necessarily expect to get paid back. Must be nice having friends like that. "It gets harder to bounce back with age," he said, sounding like an aging athlete, "the pain stays with you longer." Still, at fifty-one, he feels he has another great comeback in him. "Unlike most rounders who've been at it as long as I have, so far all I've lost is my money." A partner has staked him $300,000 for this season, and there is talk of maybe sending Dick with a real bankroll to "the islands" next year to set up a legitimate book. Dick worries about being away from his son, but it's an opportunity he wouldn't be able to turn down. Not when his goal is to win back $5 million, pay his debts, and then live off the rest with Matilda up in Montana, where he'd get himself a little cabin and spend his days fly-fishing.

I wanted to cry at this idyllic picture . . . because he could already have been there!

"Why didn't you retire when you were sitting on seven million, or at least set aside enough for a rainy day?"

I blurted this out, rudely. It's not as if the question doesn't gnaw at Dick every night while he's lying in bed, in that last flickering moment of wakefulness. But I was annoyed with him, with the whole lot of them. Bring me a gambler who quit when he was ahead, a man who walked away with his suitcases filled with cash and really did stay away. Was that going to have to be me, assuming I could ever get my nest egg back in the black? Dick was silent, and cast a mournful glance at the TV.

Then he answered me, sort of, with a question. "If you go out and write this book and it's a huge success, and everyone is fawning all over you because you are so great at what you do, would you then call it quits?"

Huh? On its face, it seemed a nonsensical comparison. Most people do not risk everything they have by continuing to work. We're talking about gambling here! But from Dick's perspective, it was a compelling analogy. Gambling was his career, and as with any other career, you build a reputation among your peers and derive satisfaction from your successes, and yes, of course, it's going to be difficult to walk away when you're king of the hill.

A while later, as I was getting ready to leave, Dick said that gambling is not good for society and that he would be willing to make a bet—naturally—that a hundred years from now gambling will be illegal "across this great nation," as he put it. "Otherwise, gambling is going to suck up all the money that should be going to a productive use." He then made a big show of giving me one of his remaining bottles of 1945 Château Lafitte-Rothschild, though he first cautioned me that it might have gone bad during a prolonged power outage one summer. How fitting. On that sour note, I went back to the Bellagio to engage in one more night of battle and to attempt my own comeback.

Kat and I reentered the baccarat pit at seven sharp. This time we were going to go for broke. I bet a grand on the Player; Banker won. I changed over; Player won. I changed back; Banker won. Ah, I repeated the Player; Banker repeats. Down four grand. And they say it isn't personal. Where's that damned Beanie dog? We made a comeback in the next hour, eking out a few hundred here, a few hundred there. But overall, I felt oppressed by how difficult it was to get any traction and get ahead. To think that the previous weekend I'd been doodling in New York about the ramifications of quitting after growing our twenty grand by a factor of 5, versus sticking it out and trying to again see my chips grow by a factor of 43. *What drugs had I been on?* For now, all I could think of, in addition to the grime invading Dick Carson's treasured basement, was what an old man getting up to walk away from a $2 table at the Golden Gate had muttered to himself: "There's no future in this."

Such defeatism was too much. We were at Bellagio, the promised land, on the last night of my gambling life, and it was now five minutes before our 8:30 reservation at the Picasso restaurant. Things had been going better in the past few hands, and the Chinese gentleman to my left who liked to smoke his cigarettes down to his fingernails and seemed to always know which way the wind blew was turning bullish on the Player. So, what was it going to be? Another failure to suck it up and go crazy on the upside? *No, we had to break loose now.*

I put down $7,000 on the Player, $2,000 more than my Chinese neighbor had. *Seven fucking grand.* We smiled at each other. I got the cards. Kat was strangling little Trotter's dog. My hand was a mediocre 5, but the Banker had baccarat, or nothing. We were in good shape; even if we didn't improve our hand, odds were against the Banker beating a 5. Hopefully he'd get another monkey and stay at nothing. I was dealt the third Player card. In any hopeless venture, there comes a point when you see with alarming clarity that you are doomed, and right then, turning over a 5, was such a point for me. Five and 5 make 10, a big nothing in baccarat. I'd screwed myself, and all I could hope for now was not to lose, to have the Banker stay at zero, too. Adding insult to injury, he drew an ace. "Banker wins, one to nothing," the dealer announced in his annoyingly noncommittal manner.

Dazed, we went to dinner at Picasso, a fabulous restaurant of beams and arched brick ceilings. On the wall nearest to us, a set of plates and ceramics painted by Picasso were on display. Outside, fireworks were going off. We were not hungry after our roller-coaster plunge. At $75 a person—a full 1 percent of our last wager!—the prix fixe dinner seemed rather pricey. But it was good, and we did enjoy it, after our stomachs had settled down. Really.

Seeing how Bellagio hadn't turned out to be the cuddliest of casinos after all, and, still reaching for that Hollywood ending, I decided it would be most appropriate to head back to Luxor. I promised Kat—who was starting to say things like "You don't have to lose it all, you know"—that we'd cease gambling, no matter what, by four in the morning.

Luxor felt a little more plastic after the Bellagio, but I wasn't going to think negative thoughts. *We love mummies, Cleopatra, obelisks; come on, baby.* Not enough, apparently. Over the next three hours, we bounced around, as if in a pinball machine, from table to table—blackjack, craps, baccarat, you name it. We were getting killed. Nothing too dramatic, just basic math at work. I'd been here before, this land of inevitable decline. I was on full tilt, as Dick Carson would say. I cringe at the memory of dragging Kat through it. We left the pyramid, our nest egg down to $4,125.

Two hours and counting. Back at Bellagio. Won some, lost some at a blackjack table with a fun dealer; a nostalgic reminder of what gambling should be about. We moved back to baccarat. Bet a grand, lost. Again. Again. My once unfathomable bankroll was starting to scrape bottom here: $883. Incredibly, there wasn't enough to make the same bet again, unless I reached into my wallet and took out $17, but that would be no good. Who knows where that could lead. We didn't belong here anymore. We wished Juan and his cronies all the best and walked out.

Craps. Twenty-five minutes and counting. Good thing we saw the video, since this would be our last hurrah. Kat took the dice. I bet $200 on the "don't pass" line; there was nobody else playing. Point was 4. Lay odds. Six, seven! We won. And again, and again, and again. The dealers were impressed. I was a big shot, breathing normally again and all that. Kat was doing it; an epic finale was still within our reach. She was so on fire, throwing the desired 7, never on the first roll but always before the dreaded point, just the way the guy with the Pittsburgh accent had told her to on the video. Then she stopped, cold.

Her watch read 4:02 A.M.

"But, um, we can't right now, like stop, we're on a roll," I muttered, pointing at the chips. I counted them, imploringly. "Look, there's $5,120 here," I yelped. We'd multiplied our dough by five in a matter of minutes. There's no telling what we could do at this game we had foolishly neglected.

Then I made my move, stacking five grand on the "don't pass" line. "Look, we can win quickly and still get some sleep before your flight, you're on fire now," I reasoned. The stickman helped me out by again shoving the dice in her direction. Then I looked up, and realized that the last thing she was concerned about was catching some sleep before her flight. What I saw in her eyes I'd never seen before, and I will never forget.

Stark terror.

I impulsively reached for the chips, pocketed them, and guided Kat away from battle.

Nest egg: $5,120

I woke up with a start a few hours later. *The war was over.* Any chance of amassing unspeakable riches off this clever boondoggle was now foreclosed, and the finality of that realization was overwhelming. In the past months, Bellagio had tided me over, promising redemption. Now the score was immutable. Vegas, 44,880; Martinez, 5,120. The bittersweet irony, of course, was that it was my own improvising that had done me in. During my ten planned three-night hotel stays, against all odds, I had won $14,486. During my ill-advised intermission and postlude, I had lost $59,366.

Kat had taken an earlier flight out, as she was going to Washington on business. For my own trip back to New York, American had, curiously, routed me through Los Angeles. My first flight was on one of those small Saab puddle jumpers. I must confess to having a lump in my throat as the propellers lifted us off the desert floor, then grinning a bit at the sight of the sun reflecting off the black glass of the Luxor pyramid. It was another gorgeous day in the great American Southwest. "No hard feelings," I whispered, nose pressed to the window. And there weren't—I hope Vegas does better with its double down than I did.

Forty minutes later, the plane jerkily began losing altitude. I spilled my drink all over me, which seemed like a huge trauma until the captain came on to say it had become necessary to make an emergency landing ASAP, anywhere, due to a fire in the rest room. No flames were visible, but his controls indicated there was one, which could signify a short of some kind. The attendant, who'd just finished passing out drinks and now looked deadly pale, frantically reviewed with us the crash-landing position. His voice was admirably firm. But whoever had developed this position—lean forward, head between knees—had obviously not flown coach in the past quarter-century. Either that, or he was five years old. We kept dropping.

As I looked at the stark landscape below, my mind went into overdrive. My whole life didn't flash before me, though; I was too stuck in the present. I thanked God circumstances had kept Kat off this flight; I wondered if the desert below was still technically Death Valley; I decided our plane was too small for its crash to lead on the national news; and I pictured rescuers arriving on the scene to find my fifty-one C-notes fluttering in the hot breeze, not knowing how much better they could have had it. The captain interrupted my odd ruminations with an announcement that he'd spotted a military airfield we could make.

And so we landed, uneventfully, greeted by a couple of fire trucks and a ghostly line-up of six towering Cathay Pacific 747s in mothballs. "Welcome to Victorville," the base commander said enthusiastically, clearly unaccustomed to welcoming anyone. We were in the middle of nowhere. *Victor*ville—I liked that. We left the plane and headed for a shack where we would wait for American's bus to come pick us up. It was terribly hot, but a few of us opted to sit outside at a picnic table. One woman sobbed uncontrollably, and kept stammering that she didn't want to get back on that plane, not that that was an option. A group of Aussies, realizing they'd miss their connecting flight to Sydney, excitedly wondered whether we couldn't be driven back to Vegas. "It isn't over yet, mate," one told me, with a thumbs-up, producing a deck of cards for a little round of poker. We then talked the flight attendant into fetching some beers off the plane.

Maybe this was all Steve Wynn's doing, I thought with a chuckle, a nefarious ploy to get me back into his casino and take my last five grand—as in *Casino,* when Robert De Niro pretends the house's jet has engine trouble in order to keep a winning whale over another night and get his money back.

I felt raw, sitting there playing poker that Friday afternoon. Dust crept into my eyes and into my mouth; the sun ate into my unprotected nose with relish; my back ached; and the beer I was swilling had turned awfully tepid. It was a good raw, in other words, heightening one's sensation of being alive. Of being in action. Life is one long night in a casino; anything is possible. We all laughed a lot, including the once-hysterical woman.

My odyssey was over, and I felt surprisingly exuberant. Despite the scoreboard, I'd gotten my happy ending. I'd done it. I'd lost my money, true, but I'd felt the exhilaration of truly letting go, gambling with the best of them in Vegas. I'd tasted the angst of Dostoevsky, and of Dick Carson, and I suspect normalcy will never again go unappreciated. Because really, there's no such thing.

Once we finally arrived at LAX that evening, an American representative greeted me with the news that I had missed the last flight back to New York and apologized for my troubles by handing me a $100 voucher for future travel. Insulted, I talked her up to $400. I was on a roll.

Nest egg: $5,520

ACKNOWLEDGMENTS

◆

Writing a book, even a whimsical one, is an immense task, made easier in my case by a great number of people.

I should first thank my agent, the indefatigable Jane Dystel, for not throwing me out of her office when I brought her my harebrained scheme. Ditto to my wife, gambling companion, and irreplaceable editor, Kat. Thanks for not throwing me out of the apartment. *We'll always have Vegas.*

I am grateful to Brian DeFiore and my visionary editor, Bruce Tracy, for giving me this opportunity and for trusting that a man set loose in Vegas with so much cash would ever come back. This final product would be a lot less final but for the merciless yet wise pencil of Jolanta Benal. My thanks to her and to Oona Schmid and Benjamin Dreyer, also at Villard.

I benefited from the hospitality and guidance of many Las Vegans. Though they are part of my tale, I should thank the Carson family, Lisa and John Costa, Susie and Tom Ericsson, Linda and Bob Faiss, and Hal Rothman for their extraordinary generosity. Elsewhere, John Allison, Scott Feldman, Miriam Goderich, Michael McGough, Michael Newman, Julie Spellman, Greg Wiercioch, and my remarkable mother all made important contributions along the way.

As is true of any author, I am also indebted to those who have gone before me. I am particularly grateful for the works of Jack

Sheehan, Deke Castleman, Eugene Moehring, and Mike Tronnes. I commend them to anyone interested in the fascinating history and lore of Las Vegas (see the Bibliography). For an understanding of Fyodor Dostoevsky's gambling addiction, I relied heavily on Joseph Frank's magisterial biography.

In the realm of fiction, Dostoevsky's *The Gambler* remains a potent and humorous guide to the gambler's psyche. Among contemporary works, I'd single out Spanish writer Cristina Peri Rossi's wickedly funny and sensuous depiction of gambling's allure in her novel *Dostoevsky's Last Night,* which is not about the Russian author but about a Madrid bingo aficionado's relationship with his therapist.

So many wise collaborators and influences . . . It's a shame the gambling losses had to be all mine.

BIBLIOGRAPHY

Barlett, Donald L., and James B. Steele. *Empire: The Life, Legend, and Madness of Howard Hughes.* New York: W. W. Norton & Company, 1979.

Bernstein, Peter L. *Against the Gods: The Remarkable Story of Risk.* New York: John Wiley & Sons, 1996.

Castleman, Deke. *Las Vegas* (Compass American Guides). New York: Fodor's Travel Publications, 1996.

Covey, Stephen R. *The 7 Habits of Highly Effective People: Powerful Lessons in Personal Change.* New York: Fireside, 1990.

Dostoevsky, Fyodor. *The Gambler,* in *Great Short Works of Fyodor Dostoevsky.* New York: Harper & Row, 1968.

Frank, Joseph. *Dostoevsky: The Miraculous Years, 1865–1871.* Princeton: Princeton University Press, 1995.

Goodman, Robert. *The Luck Business: The Devastating Consequences and Broken Promises of America's Gambling Explosion.* New York: Free Press Paperbacks, 1995.

Greene, Graham. *Loser Takes All.* Harmondsworth, England: William Heinemann Ltd, 1955; reprint, New York: Penguin, 1989.

Griffin, Peter A. *The Theory of Blackjack: The Compleat Card Counter's Guide to the Casino Game of 21.* Las Vegas: Huntington Press, fifth edition, 1996.

Hess, Alan. *Viva Las Vegas: After-Hours Architecture.* San Francisco: Chronicle Books, 1993.

Kilby, Jim, and Jim Fox. *Casino Operations Management.* New York: John Wiley & Sons, Inc., 1998.

Kunstler, James Howard. *Home from Nowhere: Remaking Our Everyday World for the 21st Century.* New York: Touchstone, 1996.

Levy, Shawn. *Rat Pack Confidential: Frank, Dean, Sammy, Peter, Joey, and the Last Great Showbiz Party.* New York: Doubleday, 1998.

Lionel Sawyer & Collins. *Nevada Gaming Law.* Las Vegas: Lionel Sawyer & Collins, 1995.

May, Jesse. *Shut Up and Deal.* New York: Anchor Books, 1998.

Moehring, Eugene P. *Resort City in the Sunbelt: Las Vegas 1930–1970.* Reno: University of Nevada Press, 1989.

O'Brien, Timothy L. *Bad Bet: The Inside Story of the Glamour, Glitz, and Danger of America's Gambling Industry.* New York: Times Business, 1998.

Peri Rossi, Cristina. *Dostoevsky's Last Night.* New York: Picador, 1996.

Pileggi, Nicholas. *Casino: Love and Honor in Las Vegas.* New York: Simon & Schuster, 1995.

Puzo, Mario. *Inside Las Vegas.* New York: Grosset & Dunlap, 1977.

Rothman, Hal K. *Devil's Bargains: Tourism in the Twentieth-Century West.* Lawrence: University Press of Kansas, 1998.

Sawyer, Grant. *Hang Tough!* Reno: University of Nevada Oral History Program, 1993.

Scarne, John. *Scarne's Guide to Modern Poker.* New York: Fireside, 1984.

Sheehan, Jack, ed. *The Players: The Men Who Made Las Vegas.* Reno: University of Nevada Press, 1997.

Spanier, David. *Inside the Gambler's Mind.* Reno: University of Nevada Press, 1994.

Tronnes, Mike, ed. *Literary Las Vegas: The Best Writing About America's Most Fabulous City.* New York: Henry Holt, 1995.

Uston, Ken. *Million Dollar Blackjack.* Seacaucus, N.J.: Carol Publishing Group, 1998.

Venturi, Robert, Denise Scott Brown and Steven Izenour. *Learning from*

Las Vegas: The Forgotten Symbolism of Architectural Form. Cambridge: MIT University Press, 1997.

Vinson, Barney. *Casino Secrets.* Las Vegas: Huntington Press, 1997.

Wong, Stanford, and Susan Spector. *The Complete Idiot's Guide to Gambling Like a Pro.* New York: Alpha Books, 1996.

About the Author

ANDRÉS MARTINEZ was born and raised in Mexico. He attended boarding school in New Hampshire, where he experienced life-scarring cultural and meteorological shock. Then he studied history at Yale. Then he obtained a master's in Russian history from Stanford. Then a law degree from Columbia. Then, two years later, he gave up his fledgling legal career for journalism. After serving on the editorial board of the *Pittsburgh Post-Gazette* and dropping by *The Wall Street Journal* long enough to pad his résumé, he left journalism for Vegas. He's had to give that up, too.

Mr. Martinez lives in New York City with his wife, Kathy, and their cat, Trotsky. He is currently writing—what else?—a novel. Then, who knows?